Life in the Ward

Life in the Ward

by

ROSE LAUB COSER

MICHIGAN STATE UNIVERSITY PRESS
EAST LANSING, MICHIGAN

For LEW

For LCW

Acknowledgments

THE PERSONS TO WHOM I OWE THE IDEAS AND STIMULATION WITHOUT which this book could not have been written are too many to be named. A teacher who most deeply influenced my career is Professor Robert Lynd, who helped me to become a sociologist and encouraged me to pursue my goals. My debt to Professor Merton both as a teacher and as a reader and critic of this manuscript is immense. He has awakened in me whatever critical and analytical abilities I may possess. I know of no other way to thank him than to hope that I have succeeded, be it only too feebly, in applying his analytical method.

To Professor William Evans go my thanks for criticizing an earlier version of the manuscript. Whatever readability this book may have, my thanks go to my friend James McPherson.

This study could not have been done without the cooperation of the Director and Assistant Director of Mount Hermon. I am grateful for their permission, as well as for that of the chiefs-of-services, to conduct the research. The house staff and especially the chief residents not only tolerated but encouraged my endeavor. Unfortunately, they must remain unnamed.

Lewis Coser's part in my work can hardly be exaggerated. It was not simply limited to several readings of the manuscript and to indispensable critcism at every step of its growth. The book is as much his as it is mine; it is the product of thinking together—of sharing the minutest details of our concerns for many years.

Ellen, already a college sophomore, knows my debt to her. And it will not be long before Steven also will understand what I owe him.

TABLE OF CONTENTS

ix

PART II: THE SOCIALIZATION OF PATIENTS

PART III: THE ADJUSTMENT OF PATIENTS

Tables

"It is not enough for us to do what we can do; the patient and his environment, and external conditions have to contribute to achieve the cure."

Hippocrates

"The cure comes from the medicine, and the art of medicine originates in charity. Hence, to be cured is not a work of Faith, but one of sympathy."

Paracelsus

"Thus the disease, which apparently had forced on us the solidarity of a beleagured town, disrupted at the same time long-established communities and sent men out to live as individuals, in relative isolation."

Camus, *The Plague, III*

Introduction

THIS STUDY DESCRIBES AND ANALYZES THE SOCIAL ROLE OF THE patient in a ward of a general hospital, institutionalized behavior patterns and value systems that prevail in the ward, and relationships that develop among the patients and between patients and hospital staff.

Illness alters a person's social role and his social relationships; and hospitalization dramatizes this change. It "sets him down in a new medical-scientific world to which he must become acclimatized. And this transplantation is by no means an easy one to undergo. Though the hospital community in which he finds himself is supposedly geared to returning the patient to his full participation in life outside, it is nevertheless true that the distance between this newly-inherited sick world and the well world which he has temporarily left is vast indeed."[1] It is this distance between two worlds and the various ways of bridging it that are explored in this book.

How does the patient learn to take his place in the unfamiliar environment of the hospital ward? What values and attitudes must he acquire there in order to be a "good" patient in the eyes of physicians and nurses (and of other patients as well)? How does he first interpret the orders and directions of physicians and nurses? To what extent does the hospital staff help him to define and carry out his obligations? What is his relationship to other patients? And once "adjusted" to the hospital, how well prepared is he to leave it again? These are some of the questions to which this study is addressed.

Health and Disease as Social Categories

In all societies, nonliterate or literate, illness is a "social fact," if only because it arouses social concern.[2] In their efforts to restore him to his normal activities, by incantation, prayer, or medical practice, members of society demonstrate and reaffirm social solidarity.

In every society there are appropriate ways of being sick and inappropriate ways, legitimate and illegitimate types of behavior associated with illness. There is group consensus about the rights and obligations of the sick person in relation to others. Family members are expected to care for the patient; he himself is expected to cooperate to get well. He is supposed to "want" to get well, and he is a "good" patient if he "tries." If he fails to try he is a "malingerer." He has a right, however, as long as he is sick, to be relieved of previous commitments. *"Disease dispensates* . . . . It relieves us of many obligations to society . . . . Disease also releases [the patient] from the consequences of many actions. It reduces our responsibility or eliminates it entirely."[3]

Dispensation implies an exceptional condition, a "deviancy" from the normal. Established routines break down for the sick person: "Sickness throws us off our usual course, disturbs our rhythms of life . . . . The sick people live differently from well ones. *Disease isolates.*"[4]

The sick person, helpless, isolated, and exempt from his usual social duties, evokes concerted efforts from others to restore him to his "proper" place in society. The threat he poses to social solidarity leads to reaffirmation of group ties.

In complex societies health and illness become the concern of formal agencies of social control. Questions of public health and private medical practice become political questions, economic questions, social questions, transcending the technical problems of treatment that concern the medical profession particularly. It has been recognized, too, that hospitals exist not only to treat the sick but also to segregate them from the well, to relieve the healthy members of society of the burden of their care.[5] For many years social scientists have been inquiring into the social functions and social meanings of health and illness. Among the questions they have been asking are: to what extent are the definitions of illness and health *social* definitions? How do different cultures and sub-cultures handle the problem of illness and how have their methods of dealing with illness changed over time?[6] And, how are such social factors as income, age, urbanization related to frequency and type of illness?[7]

For the purpose of this study, illness, however defined, however treated, however generated within the social milieu of the patient, will not be considered in its physical aspects but as it occurs within a context of social relationships and group values.

Recent Developments in the Study of Medical Interaction

Concern with the therapeutic environment parallels closely the recent movement in biology and psychiatry known as "psychobiology," which calls for the study of "the behavior of organisms as biologic wholes and . . . the interaction of these with their environment."[8] One such study, the British *Peckham Experiment,* was built around the principle that the "laboratory of the biologist is not the isolated individual but the individual in his group: the family; what is more, a large aggregate of families . . . . It is not merely with the physiological competence of the machine that we shall be concerned in human biology. It is with the mutual synthesis of the family and its environment, including experience of every type—physical, mental and social."[9]

The environment, then, is not only a "causative" factor in health or illness but also part of the therapeutic process. What a contrast to the *Peckham Experiment* is afforded by the treatment of the "isolated case" in American hospitals! "These sick people are isolated 'specimens.' They are segregated from their environment, removed from the circumstances under which they become ill, separated from their families, stripped even of their clothes; all of which is done to create a proper atmosphere of diagnostic study and careful management on the physician's part, free from outside distractions. It may be trite to point out that these 'outside distractions' are the very things which the modern doctor, or the student interested in preventive medicine, needs to study also. For if one is to handle patients adequately, it is necessary to bring clinical judgment to bear not only on the patient, but also on the circumstances under which his illness arose."[10]

More and more, recent medical writings are reflecting a similar dissatisfaction with the "isolated case" method.[11] Iago Galdston warns that we should "first see the individual set in the matrix of his social milieu and then scrutinize the social matrix."[12] John Romano and George L. Engel report:

> It soon became clear that the difficulties in teaching—and they are many and formidable—lay less in ignorance of certain factual data of syndromes and disease entities than in the lack of a more comprehensive frame of reference or conceptual scheme of disease with which the student had heretofore been unfamiliar. This conceptual scheme is one in which psychological and social factors exist or coexist with more impersonal biological factors.[13]

And Henry Sigerist writes: "The goal of medicine is not merely to cure diseases; it is rather to keep men adjusted to their environment as useful members of society, or to readjust them when illness has taken hold of them.[14]

The development in psychosomatic medicine and the growth of psychoanalysis, have helped to pinpoint the social and emotional components of illness.[15] Investigations have been made of the socio-psychological aspects of treatment,[16] of the social factors that favor psychological regression in illness, and of the important role of the medical institution and the patient's family in assisting psychological recovery following physical illness.[17]

The increased emphasis upon the sociology of medicine in medical literature and medical education is not necessarily reflected in any radical change in medical practice. Some aspects of medical training and practice may tend to counteract and neutralize these social concerns. The process of change in medical ideology requires intensive study.

If medical educators want to produce a different kind of medical man than has characteristically been produced, if they want to incorporate into the educational process the new thinking that developed in an advanced discipline, this will require them to know a good deal about the social and psychological processes through which medical schools do in fact transform incoming aspirants into medical men, of one kind or another.[18]

Much of the theoretical sociological work that supports recent studies in medical sociology was done by Talcott Parsons and Robert K. Merton, who have followed out an earlier suggestion by L. J. Henderson that patient and physician constitute a system of interaction.[19]

Parsons analyzes role behavior in illness and therapy. The social role of the physician had been previously studied,[20] but Parsons emphasizes the social role of the sick person who enters into a system of reciprocal expectations[21] and, in return for being relieved of his normal obligations and responsibilities, is required to accept help and to make an effort to get well. The doctor is an "agent of socialization," a teacher who formulates "do's" and "don't's" and controls the process of recovery.

In the ward of a general hospital the physician is not the only agent of socialization for the sick person. It is necessary to observe the effect of other significant persons upon the behavior and expectations of patients, and to investigate the way in which the social organization of the ward affects the process of patients' adjustment. Recent phychiatric literature emphasizes the relationship between social structure and individual behavior. This is especially true of the studies made by the "Washington School of Psychiatry," which considers mental disorders to be primarily disturbances in social relations.[22] This approach is best exemplified by the journal *Psychiatry,* which bears the explanatory subtitle *Journal for the Study of Interpersonal Relations.*[23]

Application of the interpersonal theory to the treatment of schizophrenia and other psychoses in the wards of mental hospitals has produced a number of studies of reciprocal role expectations. For example, Alfred H. Stanton and Morris B. Schwartz have shown that the patient suffering from pathological excitement in a mental hospital is ordinarily the central figure in a triangle in which two members of the staff disagree about the patient but suppress their disagreement and avoid discussing it. The excitement disappears or subsides when the two staff members are induced to discuss their differences. Herbert Goldhamer, observing similar phenomena in military organizations, says: "I have the impression that the type of triadic relations discussed in the paper are most likely to occur in social structures of an authoritarian character, in which inhibited hostility to authority exists."[24]

Perhaps because bureaucratic organizations lend themselves particularly well to systematic analysis, students interested in the sociological aspects of health have turned to the structure of general and mental hospitals.[25]

The patient in the hospital who must accept the competence of doctors and nurses, must also adjust to social demands, some of which are not related to his "getting better," but to the maintenance of the social system. In the hospital ward, "there are mass standards of care, i.e., . . . a system of rules and regulations" not only aimed at maximum efficiency in therapy but at the maintenance of order and at a coming to grips with the population.[26] Hence in recent years much sociological interest has focused on the setting in which patients and hospital staff play their roles.[27] This study attempts to make a contribution to the understanding of such a setting.

Research Approach

The method pursued in this study is in the main that of "functional analysis"[28] which calls for identifying the integrating and disruptive consequences of relationships and behavior patterns in the ward for sub-groups in the ward as well as for the social system of the whole ward.

This analysis will focus on *process,* upon how the actors in the ward— physicians, nurses, patients—interpret the facts of their social life. How the situation looks to each of them determines the actions of all and has objective consequences.[29] "The individual experiences himself as such, not directly, but only indirectly, from the particular standpoints of other individual members of the same social group, or from the generalized standpoint of the social group as a whole to which he belongs."[30] The give-and-take between participants by which they guide and modify their actions is a central concern of this study.

The study was conducted at Mount Hermon Hospital, a community hospital, but also devoted to teaching and research, in a large metropolis on the Atlantic Seaboard. An outside observer can enter more unobtrusively into a teaching hospital where third- and fourth-year medical students, internes, residents, visiting doctors, resident-psychiatrists, registered nurses, student nurses, aides, volunteers, frequently laboratory and X-ray technicians and social workers throng the corridors and the wards. A "new person" or a "stranger" on the ward, as long as he wears a white coat, is readily accepted. His title of "researcher" is sufficient to explain his presence.

Like most hospitals in the United States, Mount Hermon is community supported. It has obligations to the community as well as to medical schools and to research. Unlike specialized research hospitals, it must admit to its wards a great variety of patients with a variety of illnesses.

The care of patients is excellent at Mount Hermon. Administrators, physicians and nurses are alert to recent developments in sociology and psychiatry, knowing "it's not the illness, but the patient that has to be treated." A student nurse said, "You have to look at the total personality of the patient, not just his illness." If there are difficulties in doctor-patient

xix

and nurse-patient relationships at Mount Hermon then these are hardly to be traced to failures of knowledge or competence in the staff, but rather to aspects of hospital life and organization which disturb social relationships in spite of good will, advanced knowledge, and special training.

If Mount Hermon combines some of the best features of American teaching and community hospitals, it also has certain rather atypical features, which enter into the problem of social research.

(1) It was obvious from the start that the ward patient's perception of his own role and of the hospital was complicated by his having to relate to several types of physicians—visiting doctors, residents, internes and medical students (in addition, frequently, to social workers and psychiatrists). He would encounter, certainly, a much simpler social environment in most small-town hospitals. This extreme social complexity, however, provided a basis for examining the interplay between different types of health personnel in the formation of role of patient.

(2) Mount Hermon is supported by the Jewish population of the city. Most patients and most physicians are Jewish. General sociological theory and empirical studies lead one to expect that this ethnic affiliation will affect behavior and relationships in the hospital.[31] Care must be taken therefore to distinguish those patterns of behavior that may be especially characteristic of Jewish patients. The high degree of solidarity among ward patients at Mount Hermon was at first taken to be peculiar to Jewish patients, but other studies indicate that non-Jewish patients elsewhere show similar behavior.[32] And often where ethnic differences do appear, they seem to dramatize or emphasize more general problems.[33]

The Role of the Observer[34]

I was introduced to physicians and nurses as "a sociologist who wants to study interpersonal relations in the ward." This introduction, as well as a short talk I gave to the nurses at one of their meetings, and conversations I had with chiefs of services and chief residents of the medical and surgical wards, sufficiently explained the reasons for my presence.

The behavior of the doctors and nurses in the ward was probably affected by the presence of a sociological observer. This inhibiting "observer-effect"[35] is, of course, to be expected. But also, as expected, I apparently came to be taken for granted after a while; and the medical and nursing personnel as well as the patients, behaved as they would have had I not been there; although at times, I am sure, as in the lectures of one visiting doctor about "the social needs of patients," remarks were dropped especially for my benefit. Such effects are fairly easy to spot and allow for.[36]

I attempted to emphasize to the patients my "neutrality." Patients were told that I was "a sociologist from Winslow College who is going to teach a course about hospitals and is coming here to learn about hospital work, and about conditions of patients, so as to be able to teach about it next year." This explanation came as close to stating the actual research goal as was possible, given the lack of familiarity of the patients with the meaning of sociology and social research.

The nurses advised me to wear a white coat, and the director of the hospital furnished a name plaque like those worn by doctors. The white coat served to identify me as one of the professional personnel, but since it also symbolized authority, it was not necessarily the best basis on which a sociological observer could be introduced into the ward.

Actually the patients assumed I was a member of the health team until they were expressly told I was not. And even then some patients had difficulty in revising their view of me. The patient who, at our first encounter, approached me with: "Doctor, darling, I want to go home," was still saying on the following day: "Professor, please, I don't get anything to eat. I am diabetic. I must eat. Nobody listens to me. I want milk, please, professor darling." And when she was assured again that I could do nothing for her, she pointed to my white coat and said: "But you are *somebody* here?" None of my explanations would shake her. Only when another patient in a wheelchair explained: "She can't do anything for you. She's not a doctor," did she desist from her claims and demands.

This informal channel of communication among patients proved much more effective than official channels through the hospital hierarchy,[37] and it very soon became known that "she's all right" and "she's fun to talk to."[38]

In practice, my official status, as symbolized by the white coat, created only minor problems and helped solve others which were often greater. It would hardly have been possible for me to accompany the doctors on rounds without this symbol of status. Without that coat I would not have stood at the bedside of a patient while he was being examined, or joined an interne or resident behind closed curtains during the physical examination of a newly admitted patient.[39]

The Researcher and Staff Members on the Ward

My rapport with nurses was excellent from the start and throughout my stay on the ward. Nurses readily gave me information and submitted to interviews. They kindly provided me with a desk and stationery, placed phone calls for me and kept me informed about patients to be discharged (whom I wanted to interview).

Among other personnel, my reception varied. The senior surgeons tolerated me in the ward and on rounds, but they implied that they considered my study of little importance. Their defensiveness was revealed by those visiting doctors who came to the surgical ward already briefed, greeting me in the manner of, "Oh, yes, I've heard about your being here." However, relations with the house staff became very friendly after a short time. On the medical floor, thanks to the cordial cooperation of the chief resident, I was invited to attend all rounds and conferences; I was given explanations about procedures; I was introduced to every visiting doctor and given the opportunity to talk with all of them. The junior staff on the medical floor did show some resistance which became evident during formal interviews. These interviews, however, provided an occasion for a better and closer understanding once I became aware of the resistance among them.[40]

Social service workers felt that I was interested in the very problems that concerned them and that I could help them greatly in pointing out situations that had escaped their notice. (This expectation, of course, was incorrect.) The fact is that social service has only an auxiliary function in a hospital; social workers believe that doctors look upon them as second-class citizens.[41] I was greeted by them as an ally.[42] Some of the bloom rubbed off this relationship later as they discovered my complete impartiality.

Those who welcomed me most at first were the psychiatrists. Their interest in the psychological and environmental aspects of illness made them accept a sociologist as an intellectual partner. Unlike the social workers, the psychiatrists never had special rounds with the house staff. They came to the ward only when invited to deal with a particular patient (so that in effect non-psychiatrists determined which patients needed psychiatric help), or to follow-up on a patient whom they had previously seen. Some psychiatrists informally indicated to me that they wanted me to point out cases in the ward needing their attention. They pointed out that although the house staff members usually learned over the months to make sounder judgments about the mental condition of patients, the turnover of medical staff and their lack of psychiatric training resulted often in hit-or-miss referral.

The discharge of a patient was wholly at the discretion of the non-psychiatric house staff. Though physicians were expected to look at the psychiatrist's notes on the patient's chart and to notify the psychiatrist upon the discharge so the patient could be given an appointment in the outpatient department, the lack of explicit procedures meant that the psychiatrists worked in an atmosphere of some unpredictability. Some psychiatrists saw in me an ally, some others thought my work trespassed on their terrain. We were both strangers on the ward, (although to a different degree), and so in the eyes of some junior psychiatrists, in competition.

On the surgical floor rapport was most easily maintained with the house staff throughout the period of research in spite of the initial "cold" reception. Internes and residents took the initiative in letting me know, as far as their time permitted, about ward problems. They were the first to invite me to one of their house parties. The difference between the staffs on medical and surgical appears to reflect a difference in the social structure of the two wards (see Chapter IX). The strong informal relations among the surgical staff, from which they derived a large measure of security, seemed to make them more willing to admit a stranger.[43]

My changing relationships with medical, social work, and psychiatric workers suggest that rapport is not necessarily facilitated by preoccupations with similar problem areas. Status in the hospital, and the ambiguous and shifting social position of the researcher might affect the development of relationships more than does the sharing of intellectual insights.[44]

Collecting Data

I spent a summer and fall at Mount Hermon. For the first three months (July through September) I was in the wards eight hours a day. For the rest of the year I visited the ward periodically to follow up earlier leads and to fill up gaps in information. During my first month there I became acquainted with ward routine and organization; and closely observed medical procedures and social interaction among patients. After the first month I began to give special attention to specific situations; the physician-patient relationship at the time of admission, the behavior of patients in the ward and in the television room, and the expressive behavior of physicians during rounds. No notes were taken during observations, as this would have made the people observed self-conscious. Several times a day I returned to my desk and recorded observations made during the preceding hour or two. After such a short interval there was little loss of detail. Moreover this arrangement gave me time to reflect about what I had seen; on occasion what had seemed unimportant at the time would take on significance in conjunction with other observations, and I would be alerted to watch out for other behavioral clues that might appear. In the evening I reviewed and ordered the notes made during the day.[45]

After the first month I began attending physical examinations at admission. Some resistance to my doing this on the part of the junior physicians tended to be alleviated by the opportunity afforded them to tell me about the patient who had been examined, and to show me their competence and understanding. My formal interviews with physicians were begun at the same time, providing further occasion for them to talk with me.

After the first month of orientation, I began to interview patients on discharge. I did not give standard interviews in the ward for fear that the grapevine would affect what patients had to say, but a private interview in a private room just before they left the hospital had no feedback.[46] Furthermore, on this occasion I could learn how patients felt about returning home. Street clothes were symbolic of the role of nonpatient, and the immediate anticipation of leaving the hospital made home rather than hospital the frame of reference. Patients' anticipations of home are examined in Chapter VII.

A total of fifty-three intensive interviews were conducted with patients from the female and male medical and surgical wards. The composition of this group of interviewees by age, sex and type of ward is given in Appendix I. The interviews were taken in shorthand and were typed on the same day they were given. My impressions of the attitudes of patients during the interview were included in the record.

There were difficulties at each stage of observation and the usual probable biases in favor of outgoing and responsive patients. Some patients were too sick to be talked to in the ward. Patients who are completely withdrawn can hardly be reached; a patient who pulls the sheet over his head makes communication impossible. Long persistence might have yielded some good results, but this seemed too exorbitant a price to pay; time would be better spent observing other patients while I accompanied physicians on their rounds.

Patients with whom I had previously often talked in the wards were likely to talk at greater length during the formal interview than patients who knew me only slightly.[47] Yet even when answers were brief and elliptical, the interviews generally were fruitful. Of fifty-three interviews, only two had to be omitted from the analysis because the patients were excessively disturbed and insisted on talking about matters other than those under review. (Much of this extraneous material could, however, be used for other purposes.)[48]

NOTES

1. Talcott Parsons and Renée Fox, "Illness, Therapy and the Modern Urban Family," *Journal of Social Issues,* VIII (No. 4, 1952), 31-44.

2. Cf. for example, Aubrey Lewis, "Health as a Social Concept," *British Journal of Sociology,* IV (June 1953), 109-124; Henry E. Sigerist, *Man and Medicine,* New York: W. W. Norton and Co., 1932.

3. *Ibid.,* pp. 84-85 (emphasis in the original).

4. *Ibid.,* p. 76. On the special position of the sick, see also, by the same author, *On the Sociology of Medicine,* Milton I. Roemer and James M. Mackintosh, (eds.), New York: M. D. Publications, 1960, pp. 9-22.

5. Cf. "Less apparent than . . . technological determinants [of hospitalization] but fully as significant are the . . . brick walls between the sick and the healthy: the special appropriateness of illness as a deviant expression in our society and the unique defenselessness of the American urban family when faced with the illness of one of its members" (Parsons and Fox, *op. cit.,* p. 39).

6. Cf. Henry E. Sigerist, *Civilization and Disease,* Ithaca, New York: Cornell University Press, 1943; by the same author, *A History of Medicine,* Vol. I, New York: Oxford University Press, 1951. See also the work of Erwin H. Ackerknecht, "Problems of Primitive Medicine" and "Primitive Medicine and Culture Pattern" in *Bulletin of the History of Medicine,* XI (1942), pp. 503-21 and 545-74, respectively; "Natural Diseases and Rational Treatment in Primitive Medicine," *ibid.,* XIX (1946), 467-97. See also Lyle Saunders, *Cultural Differences and Medical Care,* New York: Russell Sage Foundation, 1954.

Related to the problem of differential cultural definitions of illness is Mark Zborowski's "Cultural Components in Responses to Pain," *Journal of Social Issues,* VIII (No. 4, 1952), 16-30.

Among the existing studies of environment and illness, see Jurgen Ruesch, A. Jacobson and M. B. Loeb, "Acculturation and Illness," *Psychological Monographs: General and Applied,* LXII (1948), 1-40; Jurgen Ruesch, "Social Technique, Social Status and Social Change in Illness," in Clyde Kluckhohn and Henry A. Murray, (eds.), *Personality in Nature, Society and Culture,* New York: Alfred A. Knopf, 1948, pp. 117-130. Marian Radke Yarrow, John A. Clausen, Paul R. Robbins, "The Social Meaning of Mental Illness," *Journal of Social Issues,* XI (No. 4, 1955), 33-48.

7. See, e.g., Jean Lownes, "Social and Environmental Factors in Illness," *Milbank Memorial Fund Quarterly,* XXVI (October 1948), 336-381. For bibliography of studies on morbidity and mortality relating to one or several social factors, see Odin W. Anderson, "The Sociologist and Medicine," *Social Forces,* XXXI (October 1952), 38-42. With regard to mental illness, see August B. Hollingshead, R. Ellis and E. Kirby, "Social Mobility and Mental Illness," *American Sociological Review,* XIX (October 1954), 577-584; August B. Hollingshead and Fredrick C. Redlich, "Social Stratification and Psychiatric Disorder," *ibid.,* XVIII (April 1953), 163-169; by the same authors, "Social Stratification and Schizophrenia," *ibid.,* XIX (June 1954), 302-306. By the same authors, *Social Class and Mental Illness,* New York: John Wiley and Sons, 1958. See also Jerome K. Myers and Bertram H. Roberts, *Family and Class Dynamics in Mental Illness,* New York: John Wiley and Sons, 1959; a pioneering work was that by Robert E. L. Faris and H. Warren Dunham, *Mental Disorders in Urban Areas,* Chicago: University of Chicago Press, 1939.

For a more complete bibliography, see William Caudill, "Applied Anthropology in Medicine," in A. L. Kroeber, (ed.), *Anthropology Today,* Chicago: University of Chicago Press, 1953, pp. 771-806.

8. Elmer Klein, "Psychologic Trends in Psychiatry Since 1900," *American Journal of Psychiatry,* VIII (July 1928), 273-283.

9. Innes H. Pearse and Lucy H. Crocker, *The Peckham Experiment,* London: George Allen & Unwin, 1943, p. 45. About the need for considering the family, rather than the individual, as a unit for treatment, see Henry B. Richardson, *Patients Have Families,* New York: The Commonwealth Fund, 1945.

Increasing attention is being paid recently to the relation between family structure and mental illness. See, e.g., the papers on "The Intrafamilial Environment of the Schizophrenic Patient," by Theodore Lidz *et al.,* and by Stephen Fleck *et al.,* in *Psychiatry,* XX (November 1957), 329-350, and Rhona Rapoport, "The Family and Psychiatric Treatment," *Psychiatry,* XXIII (February 1960), 53-62. Diagnosis and treatment of family relationships has been dealt with by Nathan W. Ackerman, *The Psychodynamics of Family Life,* New York: Basic Books, 1959.

10. John R. Paul, "Preventive Medicine at Yale University School of Medicine, 1940-49," *Yale Journal of Biology and Medicine,* XXII (January 1950), 199, quoted by Leo W. Simmons and Harold G. Wolff, *Social Science in Medicine,* New York: Russell Sage Foundation, 1954, p. 177.

11. See, among others, George Canby Robinson, *The Patient as a Person,* New York: The Commonwealth Fund, 1939.

12. *Social Medicine: Its Derivations and Objectives,* New York: The Commonwealth Fund, 1949, p. 25.

13. "Teaching Experience in General Hospitals," *American Journal of Orthopsychiatry,* XVII (October 1947), 602-604.

14. *Civilization and Disease, op. cit.,* p. 66.

As early as 1848 Rudolph Virchow stated that "Medicine is a social science." This and other early references are quoted by William Caudill in his bibliographical article "Applied Anthropology in Medicine," *op. cit.,* p. 790. See also Harold G. Wolff, *Stress and Disease,* Springfield, Ill.: Charles C. Thomas, 1953, p. 20.

15. See especially Harold G. Wolff, Steward G. Wolf and Clarence C. Hare, (eds.), *Life Stress and Bodily Disease: Proceedings of the Association for Research in Nervous and Mental Diseases,* Baltimore: Williams and Wilkins, 1950.

Of the numerous studies of the psychological aspects of illness only a few can be noted here: David A. Hamburg, Beatrix Hamburg and Sydney deGoza, "Adaptive Problems and Mechanisms in Severely Burned Patients," *Psychiatry,* XVI (Feb. 1953), 1-20; Helene Deutsch, "Some Psychoanalytic Observations in Surgery," *Psychosomatic Medicine,* IV (1942), 105-115; Florence Clothier, "Some Thoughts on the Psychology of Post-Operative Convalescence," *Diseases of the Nervous System,* II (1941), 266-270; E. Kahn, "Some Aspects of Normal Personality Experiencing Disease," *Yale Journal of Biology and Medicine,* XIII (1941), 397-408; Lawrence K. Lunt, "Attitudes in Relation to Illness," *New England Journal of Medicine,* (1938), 557-561; John Romano, "Emotional Components of Illness," *Connecticut State Medical Journal,* VII (1943), 22-25; Morton A. Seidenfeld, *Psychological Aspects of Medical Care,* Springfield, Ill.: Charles C. Thomas, 1949.

16. See Lawrence K. Frank, "Psycho-Cultural Approaches to Medical Care," *Journal of Social Issues,* VIII (No. 4, 1952), 45-54.

17. Roger G. Barker, Beatrice A. Wright and Mollie R. Gonick, *Adjustment to Physical Handicap and Illness: A Survey of the Social Psychology of Physique and Disability,* New York: Social Science Research Council, 1946. Most relevant for this study is Chapter VI, "Social Psychology of Acute Illness," pp. 228-264. For a comprehensive bibliography on the subject, see *ibid.,* pp. 325-332.

18. Robert K. Merton, *A Proposal for the Sociological Study of Medical Schools,* New York: Bureau of Applied Social Research, Columbia University, 1952 (mimeo.), pp. 10-11.

For a first report of some of the results of this study, see Robert K. Merton, George G. Reader and Patricia Kendall, *The Student Physician,* Cambridge, Mass.: Harvard University Press, 1957.

19. L. J. Henderson, "Physician and Patient as a Social System," *New England Journal of Medicine,* 212 (May 1935), 819-823.

20. Oswald Hall, "The Stages of a Medical Career," *American Journal of Sociology,* LIII (March 1948), 327-336. By the same author, "Types of Medical Careers," *ibid.,* LV (Nov. 1949), 243-253. See also Alfred McClung Lee, "The Social Dynamics of the Physician's Status," *Psychiatry,* VII (Nov. 1944), 371-377. For a more comprehensive bibliography, see E. Gartley Jaco,

(ed.), *Patients, Physicians and Illness*, Glencoe, Ill.: The Free Press, 1958.

21. Talcott Parsons, *The Social System*, Glencoe, Ill.: The Free Press, 1951, Chapter X; and "Illness and the Role of the Physician," *The American Journal of Orthopsychiatry*, XXI (July 1951), 542-558.

22. Harry Stack Sullivan, "Conceptions of Modern Psychiatry," *Psychiatry*, III (1940), 1-117.

23. In such papers as: Howard Rowland, "Interaction Processes in the State Mental Hospital," *Psychiatry*, I (Aug. 1938), 323-337; by the same author, "Friendship Patterns in a State Mental Hospital," *ibid.*, II (Aug. 1939), 363-373; Charlotte Green Schwartz, Morris S. Schwartz and Alfred H. Stanton, "A Study of Need-Fulfillment on a Mental Hospital Ward," *ibid.*, XIV (May 1951), 223-242; William Caudill and Edward Stainbrook, "Some Covert Effects of Communication Difficulties in a Psychiatric Hospital," *ibid.*, XVII (Feb. 1954), 27-40.

In August 1957, *Psychiatry*, (Vol. XX), published a special issue on the convergence between sociology and psychiatry, with contributions by Robert A. Cohen, Erving Goffman, Paul D. Swadon, Maxwell Jones, Stewart E. Perry, and Gertrude M. Shea, Morris S. Schwartz, Kai T. Erikson, Charlotte Green Schwartz.

Needless to say, while *Psychiatry* has pioneered in this type of publication, other psychiatric journals followed suit—testifying to the challenge that the new trend in psychiatry and sociology has provided for research. See, among others, William Caudill, F. C. Redlich, H. K. Gilmore and E. B. Brody, "Social Structure and Interaction Processes on a Psychiatric Ward," *American Journal of Orthopsychiatry*, XXII (1952), 314-334.

24. "The Management of a Type of Institutional Participation in Mental Illness," *Psychiatry*, XII (Feb. 1949), 13-22; discussants: Herbert Goldhamer, Jerome D. Frank, Harry Stack Sullivan, Alfred H. Stanton. See also a second article, "Observations on Dissociation as Social Participation," by these authors bearing on the same problem, *ibid.*, (Nov. 1949), 339-354.

25. See Harvey Smith, *The Sociological Study of Hospitals*, unpublished dissertation, University of Chicago, 1949; A. F. Wessen, *The Social Structure of a Modern Hospital*, unpublished dissertation, Yale University, 1950; Paul Barrabee, *A Study of a Mental Hospital: The Effect of Its Social Structure on Its Functions*, unpublished dissertation, Harvard University, 1951; Jules Henry, "The Formal Social Structure of a Psychiatric Hospital," *Psychiatry*, XVII (May 1954), 139-152; Elaine Cumming, I. L. W. Clancey and John Cumming, "Improving Patient Care Through Organizational Changes in the Mental Hospital," *Psychiatry*, XIX (August 1956), 249-261; Elaine Cumming and John Cumming, "The Locus of Power in a Large Mental Hospital," *ibid.*, (Nov. 1956), 361-369; Merton J. Kahne, "Bureaucratic Structure and Impersonal Experience in Mental Hospitals," *Psychiatry*, XXII (Nov. 1959), 363-375. On some complexities of the bureaucratic system of the hospital, see Oswald Hall, "Sociological Research in the Field of Medicine: Progress and Prospects," *American Sociological Review*, XVI (Oct. 1951), 639-644. See also Rose Laub Coser, "Authority and Decision-Making in a Hospital," *American Sociological Review*, XXIII (Feb. 1958), 56-63.

26.   Howard Rowland, "Interaction Processes in the State Mental Hospital," *Psychiatry,* I (Aug. 1938), 323-337.

27.   Maxwell Jones, *The Therapeutic Community,* New York: Basic Books, 1953; Alfred H. Stanton and Morris S. Schwartz, *The Mental Hospital,* New York: Basic Books, 1954; William Caudill, *The Psychiatric Hospital As a Small Society,* Cambridge, Mass.: Harvard University Press, 1958; Ivan Belknap, *Human Problems of a State Mental Hospital,* New York: McGraw-Hill Book Co., 1956; Warren H. Dunham and K. Weinberg, *The Culture of the State Mental Hospital,* Detroit: Wayne State University Press, 1960; Erving Goffman, "The Characteristics of Total Institutions," in *Symposium on Preventive and Social Psychiatry,* Washington, D.C.: Walter Reed Army Institute of Research, 1957, pp. 43-84; by the same author, "The Moral Career of the Mental Patient," *Psychiatry,* XXII (May 1959), 123-142; Milton Greenblatt, Daniel J. Levinson and Richard H. Williams, (eds.), *The Mental Hospital,* Glencoe, Ill.: The Free Press, 1957.

28.   For a comprehensive treatment of this approach, see Robert K. Merton, *Social Theory and Social Structure,* Glencoe, Ill.: The Free Press, 1957, pp. 21-81.

29.   Cf. W. I. Thomas' dictum: "If men define situations as real, they are real in their consequences." On the further development of this idea, see "The Self-Fulfilling Prophecy," in Robert K. Merton, *Social Theory and Social Structure, op. cit.,* pp. 421-436.

30.   George Herbert Mead, *Mind, Self and Society,* Chicago: University of Chicago Press, 1934, p. 138.

31.   On cultural differences among patients, see, e.g., Mark Zborowski, "Cultural Components in Responses to Pain," *op. cit.*

32.   Cf., e.g., Temple Burling, Edith M. Lentz and Robert N. Wilson, *The Give and Take in Hospitals,* New York: G. P. Putnam's Sons, 1956, pp. 30 ff. Renée Fox, *Experiment Perilous,* Glencoe, Ill.: The Free Press, 1959, Chs. IV, V and VI, *passim.*

33.   The use of the "abnormal" for the purpose of learning about what is "normal" has long been a justified method, at least since Freud. Recently, Erving Goffman in a study on "The Nature of Deference and Demeanor" in American society, uses data obtained in a mental hospital, i.e., in a milieu where rules of deference and demeanor are being violated, to throw some light on socially expected behavior, [*American Anthropologist,* LVIII (June 1956), 473-502].

34.   On the general point of field work procedure, see the detailed account in F. J. Roethlisberger and W. J. Dickson, *Management and the Worker,* Cambridge, Mass.: Harvard University Press, 1934, Chapter XIII; see also William Foote Whyte, "Observational Field-Work Methods," in Marie Jahoda, Morton Deutsch and Stuart W. Cook, (eds.), *Research Methods in the Social Sciences,* New York: The Dryden Press, 1951, Vol. II, pp. 493-514; Marie Jahoda, Morton Deutsch and Stuart W. Cook, "Data Collection; Observational Methods" in *ibid.,* pp. 129-150; Benjamin D. Paul, "Interview Techniques and Field Relations," in A. L. Kroeber *et al.,* (eds.), *Anthropology Today, op. cit.,* pp. 430-451.

35.   See, among others, Peter Kong-Ming New, "The Personal Identifi-

cation of the Interviewer," *American Journal of Sociology*, LXII (Sept. 1956), 213-214; Morris S. Schwartz and Charlotte Green Schwartz, "Problems in Participant Observation," *American Journal of Sociology*, LX (Jan. 1955), 343-353; Melville Dalton, *Men Who Manage*, New York: Wiley & Sons, 1960, pp. 78 ff.

36. In one instance the presence of the observer had an apparent and pronounced effect upon hospital routine. A patient asked the observer to get in touch with Dr. X for her. The observer declined, explaining that the patient would have to ask her nurse. The patient thereupon went to the nurses' station and demanded that the head nurse call Dr. X. The head nurse did not do this but called Social Service instead.

This incident created some turmoil. Interrupted in her routine, the nurse had to assert her authority over the patient and ignore her demands; the social worker, who was engaged in other work at the time, was called onto the scene. This did not improve the already tense relationship between this patient and the nurse or social worker. It is possible that the patient would not have had the temerity to go to the nurses' station had she not felt encouraged by the observer's remark that she would have to talk to the nurse; the observer carried enough authority in her eyes to perceive a mere piece of information as an authoritative suggestion.

This was perhaps the only clear example of modification of social relationships as a result of the observer's behavior which occurred during the field work at the hospital. On the whole, the lack of a make-believe role for the observer put her in a relatively passive position, with little occasion for interference. But even deliberate attempts at noninterference may have unanticipated consequences for the relationships between patients and their environment.

37. See Chapter VI.

38. It might seem preferable to have the observer introduced to patients as a volunteer aide rather than as a sociologist. Volunteer aides are familiar to patients and have definite and accepted functions. A pseudo-role, however, raises the ethical problem of trying to obtain information from people without their knowledge. It also has the disadvantage of tying the observer to one work-obligation when it might be more significant for the researcher to be observing elsewhere, or interviewing patients in quite different situations.

39. About problems faced by the unidentified researcher, see Henry W. Riecken, "The Unidentified Interviewer," *American Journal of Sociology*, LXII (Sept. 1956), 210-212. See also Fox, *Experiment Perilous, op. cit.*, p. 141.

40. It was found that the formal interview did much to "break the ice"; where informal relationships were difficult at one point, they were easily established once I had occasion to talk with a physician for an hour in the structured interviewer-respondent relationship. Relationships with nurses, which never suffered from resistance on their part, became still closer after the interview. It seemed that the interview made clear to the staff member what "the sociologist was after," and subsequently nurses as well as physicians several times approached me with additional information concerning questions asked in the interview.

The field experience gained in this research suggests that it might be better to conduct formal interviews with hospital personnel before patients are interviewed, both for the purpose of gauging the early extent of rapport and as a basis for effecting improved working relations with the staff at this early stage.

41. For the problems facing the social service in a general hospital, see the excellent formulation by Burling, Lentz and Wilson, *op. cit.*, Chapter 9, "Social Service Workers."

42. All medical and surgical rounds are very punctual. Physicians are not absent or late. But social workers have some difficulty in impressing on them the need for similar discipline on social service rounds. The following observation may be indicative: in the beginning of the summer, a social worker was seen waiting on the female floor ready for rounds, but the house staff was absent. They drifted in slowly later, one by one. The same thing happened on the male ward. The social worker explained: "That's because there is a new staff. They have to be trained to get here on time." That same afternoon the same thing happened in the surgical ward. Another social worker was sitting there, waiting for the doctors; nobody came for quite a while. The social worker explained: "It's always the same; they're never there although they know they should be." This typifies the difference between the two wards: on medical, the social worker felt that the difficulties were due to the newness of the staff, while on surgical the social worker pointed out that "they're *never* there." This difference between the two wards was corroborated by further observations. The surgical house staff continued to be unpunctual; the medical staff, after another week or so, were ready for social service rounds when scheduled. On medical all physicians participated in the rounds, but this was not so on the surgical ward. There, although reports were given efficiently, they were given quickly, and physicians were moving in and out while some other physician was making a report. They gave the impression of being too busy to spend much time on social service rounds.

Two weeks after these above episodes, the social worker again was waiting on the surgical floor. There was nobody there; physicians had to be paged. Suddenly an interne showed his head out of a room; seeing the social worker, he said kiddingly, "You here again?" The nurse, overhearing this, turned to the social worker: "Aren't they glad to see the social worker!" Social worker: "Isn't it nice to know you're welcome!" (On the difference between the medical and the surgical ward, see Chapter IX.)

43. For some of the problems inherent in the relations between different medical groups in a hospital and in the provision of social services, see Oswald Hall, "Some Problems in the Provision of Medical Services," *The Canadian Journal of Economics and Political Science,* XX (Nov. 1954), 456-466.

44. On the problem of the change of the social position of the researcher during the period of research, see Arthur J. Vidich, "Participant Observation and the Collection and Interpretation of Data," *American Journal of Sociology,* LX (Jan. 1955), 354-360.

On the general problem of the relation between the social researcher and the physician, see Mary E. W. Goss, "Collaboration between Sociologist and Physician," *Social Problems,* IV (July 1956), 82-89.

45. On the role of the participant observer and the recording of observations, see Schwartz and Schwartz, "Problems in Participant Observation," *op. cit.*

46. Several factors made it possible for me, although not invested with authority, to keep a patient after his discharge (and to keep his relatives waiting): (1) My white coat was in itself usually sufficient as a symbol of authority to procure acquiescence when I said, "would you mind stepping out with me and answering some questions?" (2) I had the cooperation of the head nurse, who must be informed at all times about the whereabouts of a patient until the moment the nurse's aide wheels him into the elevator. The nurse often acted as an intermediary, telling the patient that I wanted to talk to him before he left. Her authority was, of course, not questioned. (3) Many patients are in no hurry to go home. Indeed some of them spent the first five minutes of the interview trying to convince me that they shouldn't have been discharged.

No patient refused to accompany me into the interview room. Only one patient made it very clear that she didn't like the idea, refused to sit down, answered the questions quickly, and said that she didn't have time because her daughter was waiting for her. A few other patients who seemed a little resistant at first soon "warmed up" when they were given a chance to talk. Most patients responded readily, perhaps in large part because of previous acquaintance with me on the ward.

47. This kind of bias in field work has been systematically identified in other studies. For example, one inquiry into this matter found that group differentials in rapport with the investigators greatly affected the amount of material made available to them and that the qualitative analysis was consequently based on evidence drawn from the more cooperative informants. See Robert K. Merton, "Selected Problems of Field Work in the Planned Community," *American Sociological Review,* XII (1947), 304-312.

48. The schedules for interviews with patients, doctors, and nurses are reproduced in Appendix I.

PART I

WHERE PATIENTS MEET DOCTORS

"They went on, but K. did not know
whither, he could discern nothing. . . . The
effort that it cost him merely to keep going
made him lose control of his thoughts. Instead of remaining fixed on their goal,
they strayed. Memories of his home kept
recurring and filled his mind. . . ."

Franz Kafka, *The Castle*

CHAPTER I

Life on the Ward

MOUNT HERMON HOSPITAL EXISTS TO TREAT THE SICK, TO TEACH medical students and young doctors, to train nurses, and to carry on medical research. It thus serves the community, the university medical schools, and the nursing and medical professions.

The hospital is more than a physical plant, and an organization of technical facilities. It is also a social and symbolic system. To the sick person and

> to the family of the sick patient, the hospital is a battlefield between life and death, the focus of intense anxieties and hopes. To the physician, the hospital is an institution for the practice of medicine and a central agency through which the study of disease is pursued, the boundaries of medical knowledge widened, and medical skill increased. From the standpoint of the businessman and taxpayer, the hospital represents a financial enterprise.[1]

Tight Little Island

"The hospital is like a ship," one patient explained. Like a ship or fortress the hospital is a world unto itself. Illness has placed the patient into the hands of doctors and nurses who command his destiny and control the levers of life and death. And all are bound together within the hospital walls.

In the hospital ward, perhaps more than on the private floors, most nurses and doctors are part of the hospital, if not always on duty, for twenty-four hours a day. All student nurses, and many registered nurses also, live in special quarters in the hospital. All internes, and many residents, live in the hospital. Many of the staff do not leave the hospital premises even when they are off duty. An administrator summarized this isolation when he replied to someone who asked his way in the neighborhood: "I've been here for more than a year now, but I don't know what's going on outside of these buildings."[2]

Here is a description of life on an armed-guard ship: "Function, prescribed organization, physical restriction and the unavoidable, continuous face-to-face contacts constitute the framework within which experiences are shared and informal organization develops—within which the land-lubber becomes a sailor. . . ."[3] Just so does the hospital separate a man or woman from family life and erect around him a new social framework within which he learns to be a patient.

On the fourth and fifth floors of one building—Mount Hermon extends in all over an area of four city blocks—there are ninety-two beds for men and women, twenty-three each in the male surgical, male medical, female surgical, and female medical wards.[4]

While the patient lies in his bed in the ward, the outside world recedes from view. Through the windows, if any appear within his range of vision, he can see only the roofs of surrounding buildings, all part of the same hospital. A little piece of sky, with sunshine or rain, is the main reality from the outside world directly visible to him. Even his relatives drifting in at 1 p.m., may come to seem "strangers," divorced from the main problem that faces him now: the problem of cure. Family and friends belong to past or future; and wear an air of unreality.

Why is he here? He is here, of course, because he needs sustained nursing care and medical attention, because he faced a problem so serious that it could not be solved in his normal every-day environment. Now he has been relieved of the routines of daily life and torn from the contexts of home. His attention is focused upon himself. And just as his physical condition has gained critical importance in his own eyes he enters an environment where emergency is routine.

In many occupations, according to Everett C. Hughes, "the workers or practitioners deal routinely with what are emergencies to the people who receive the services."[5] Nowhere, perhaps, do such "routinized emergencies" occur so regularly as in a hospital. The *organizational* commitment to deal with emergencies elevates the functional importance of discipline in an organization. For emergency means that remedial decision and action can brook no delay. Success depends upon the coordination of the actions of many people and the reliability of all of them.

> The content of discipline is nothing but the consistently rationalized, methodically trained and exact execution of the received order, in which all personal criticism is unconditionally suspended and the actor is unswervingly and exclusively set for carrying out the command. In addition, this conduct under orders is uniform.[6]

The interne in the hospital, like the sergeant in the army, must obey orders punctually and in turn rely on the punctual performance of people serving under him. Hospital schedules and duties, as well as uniforms and insignia, call to mind a military organization. A fatalistic recognition of the necessity for quasi-military organization in a hospital was grudgingly

4

granted by a middle-aged man who fetched his mother from the ward at Mount Hermon:

> A hospital is like a defense plant: they're the boss and you're being kicked around. Doctor's orders they call it, or the rules. I'm not blaming anybody; they got their work to do and they're doing a grand job out here. I'm telling you. And if they let the patient do what he wants, they couldn't do a grand job, see what I mean? Just the same it's better to be out than in.

Like a defense plant, a military outpost, an armed-guard ship, the hospital is a place to "ward off danger," and discipline must be particularly compelling in organizations devoted to warding off and fighting danger. So, like the army, the hospital is a "command society, rigidly stratified, self-contained," socializing or atomizing its members and in which "procedures are uniform and ordered."[7]

Mount Hermon Hospital

To whom does Mount Hermon belong? In most hospitals the trustees or patrons tend to be drawn from the upper class, the hospital functionaries from the professional levels of society, and the clients most often from a lower stratum.[8] But at Mount Hermon, for special historical reasons, quite a number of ward patients once were patrons, or at least associated with patrons or with patronizing organizations.

The admission of the first patient to Mount Hermon Hospital on February 4, 1917, marked the victory of a campaign by the Jewish community to establish its own hospital, a hospital to take care of the needs of Jewish patients, and to provide learning opportunities for Jewish doctors.

This victory had symbolic as well as practical significance. Through this philanthropic effort a minority group, which felt itself to be an "out-group" in society at large, reaffirmed and reinforced its solidarity. The campaign for the hospital more nearly resembled a social movement than a charity drive. At the dedication exercises on October 22, 1916, "a column of marchers 5,000 strong, headed by a military band of 45 men and featured by floats, paraded from the synagogue on Marble Head Avenue to the hospital."[9]

This was to be "their" hospital, where religious and cultural needs would be respected, where Jewish doctors would treat Jewish patients, and where dietary rules and a distinctive language would not be looked down on as alien customs. In the beginning most of the support came from Jews of Eastern European origin rather than from those of higher status who had earlier emigrated from Germany. The poorer more recent arrivals conducted the drive and contributed most of the dimes and quarters, as well as some of the larger gifts, that went toward the establishment of this hospital of their own. We are told that "at the outset there were few prominent or well-to-do men identified with the project."

The hospital grew. In the beginning, at its original location in a predominantly Jewish section of the city, it held forty-five beds. In 1923 it moved to the vicinity of the Holyoke Medical School with which it since became affiliated. Today it has a capacity of 366 beds. It is strongly supported by the Jewish population and is a rallying point of community spirit and a proud symbol of achievement.

Mount Hermon, with its high standards and excellent reputation, has special cultural significance to the Jewish community. Medical study has appealed to the strong tradition of learning among the Jews and has also satisfied the desire, strong among all immigrant groups, of winning prestige in the eyes of native Americans. Often the pride of "my son, the doctor" came to replace the pride of "my son, the rabbi." To many elderly Jews the doctor, like the rabbi, seems endowed with almost magic powers. Furthermore he has been accepted in the "hostile, discriminating" world and is thereby the man who has "arrived" and can help lead his people out of the ghetto. Mount Hermon over the years has trained in its wards many young Jewish doctors who might otherwise have had difficulty finding interneships.[10]

In the eyes of the older people, who had worked hard to build the hospital, it has all manner of collateral meanings, then. Many of today's ward patients are proud to report, "I gave money for this hospital when you weren't even born." They concentrated their efforts on making the future for Jews in general and for their own sons in particular brighter than their own lives had been.

Today Mount Hermon still draws a large part of its ward population from the generations of Jewish immigrants from Eastern Europe, but outside the ward great changes have come. If it were not for the Hebrew name of the hospital and for the patient population on those few floors that constitute the wards, this hospital would be indistinguishable from the many others in the same area affiliated with Holyoke Medical School.

Upward mobility within the Jewish community has brought in its wake some striking family divisions, as the following comments by doctors indicate:

> You know, we often have a father in the ward and at the same time his son is on the private floor. I've seen this happen. You wouldn't think that these sons would let their parents go to the ward when they can pay for private medical service, would you?

Or:

> Once there was a man in the ward, and he told me his brother was upstairs in a private room. He said his brother was ten years

6

younger and didn't have to help his parents in the shop and could go to school. But he didn't complain. He said all of Holyoke Medical School was taking care of him. . . .

The patients in the ward are poor; they are old; and they "do not belong." Some of these men and women, so proud of their creation, are strangers in "their" hospital. Their children, as well as the doctors in the hospital, can say to them today in Mephisto's words: *"Du gleichst dem Geist, den Du begreifst, nicht mir."* After pushing their sons to become assimilated in the alien culture and concentrating their efforts on building a symbol of emancipation, they were left behind. Their estrangement is well illustrated in the experience of Mrs. Wolsky, the indomitable.

Mrs. Wolsky,[11] 87 years old, cannot speak English. However, she would not meekly submit to being excluded and ignored on the ward. She insisted on speaking Yiddish, and on trying to maintain some measure of control over her situation as a patient. For several days, she would detain any house doctor who happened to pass by her bed and demand in Yiddish to be told about her situation and the prospects of surgery. Her efforts were all in vain. The doctors would only nod and tell her in English, which she could not understand, to relax and wait, she would be taken care of.

One afernoon, when the physicians were making rounds with the visiting doctor, she called out in Yiddish: "You speak Yiddish?" The visiting doctor ignored her. Finally, she raised herself in bed, pointed with her finger to her bedside and shouted: "Come here." The visiting doctor was taken aback, but went compliantly to her bedside, while the house doctors remained standing at the foot of her bed. For five minutes she spoke excitedly in Yiddish, while the visiting doctor listened but said nothing. When she finally paused, he stroked her hand, turned away, and motioned the house doctors to follow him into the hallway.

"You know," he said, "it's astonishing. This woman gave me an excellent history of her stay in this hospital. . . ." He might have been speaking of a bright child. Then he explained apologetically, "The reason I could understand her is that I heard Yiddish spoken by my grandparents when I was a kid. My parents never spoke Yiddish, neither did I." The discussion about Mrs. Wolsky was then dropped.[12]

Patients and Physicians[13]

Unusual as this story of Mrs. Wolsky is, it illustrates a problem faced by patients in all hospitals.

Although at Mount Hermon emphasis on "the needs of the patients" and on their emotional and social problems permeates the teaching of both medical students and student nurses, a persistent tension exists between staff and patients. Why should this be?

Even in his own home, and with his own doctor, the patient may find some measure of incompatibility between the rapport that he craves and the social distance that is required for the maintenance of professional authority. In the ward where physicians form a professional group, distance is increased. Doctors must maintain their solidarity not only in relation to the patients in the ward, but also in relation to the nurses. Albert Wessen observed in another hospital that "there was general agreement among both doctors and nurses that their professional status tended to build a wall separating them from close contacts with laymen."[14]

The physician is armed with the double authority of his technical training as a professional and his official identification with the hospital; and so the patient is expected to accept without question the physician's definition of the situation. A "bad" patient is one who, like Mrs. Wolsky, refuses to conform. In the presence of the medical team, the patient is expected to remain relatively passive. He is not expected to enter actively into a relationship with members of the team.

The ward then has many of the characteristics of the "total institution": "Social mobility between the two strata is grossly restricted; social distance is typically great and often formally prescribed; even talk across the boundaries may be conducted in a special tone of voice."[15]

A rising tension is often felt in the ward during rounds, perhaps because the patients cannot completely accept the "separating wall." There may be sudden eruptions of nonconformist behavior, as in the case of Mrs. Wolsky; or there may be excessively demanding behavior after rounds are over, or attempts by patients during rounds to seduce the doctor into informal and supportive conversation.[16]

Many efforts appear to be directed toward identifying oneself as a "person" among the many anonymous "cases" lined up in the beds of the ward. The ward patient's need for recognition is probably greater than that of the private patient, who at least has his own doctor. The ward patient is one among many and he faces a large number of doctors he has never seen before. Naturally, he feels he must first establish his identity, particularly since he is quickly made aware of the fact that "from the point of view of ward personnel, the patient is considered as a member of an out-group."[17]

The patient cannot cheerfully accept the unspoken demand that he efface himself before the group of house doctors. The authority of the physician allegedly to expect passivity is only partially legitimized by the patient's helplessness. It is felt to harbor also some measure of arbitrariness like the authority, for example, of master over servant or of parents over children.[18]

An analogy to the relationship between master and servant is not amiss. In eighteenth-century England, according to J. Jean Hecht, "The servant was viewed as a person who had temporarily relinquished his freedom."[19] The master was under the necessity of "rendering servants tractable,"[20]

8

or of keeping them sometimes "at greatest distance."[21] The servant was reminded in contemporary tracts, of such desirable qualities "as 'humility and lowliness,' 'meekness and gentleness, good temper and fearfulness, respectfulness and submissiveness.' "[22] Similar behavior is demanded of the ward patient, especially during doctors' rounds.

However, the servant, or the ward patient, cannot help but take account of what is happening. The servant, Hecht says, sees and hears but is himself not "seen" or "heard." "For whilst I unregarded stand, with ready Salver in my Hand . . . I hear, and mark. . . ."[23]

Hecht goes on to say: "To a certain extent the probing eyes and attentive ears of the servant even imposed on his master an onerous constraint. It seemed to the Scotsman Alexander Carlyle that the average English employer was so aware of being observed and had such deference for the opinion of his servant that he regulated his conduct with him constantly in mind. . . ."[24]

Although patients, too, seem to be ignored (except as "cases") doctors are keenly aware of them as a "passive audience." Some medical conversation, even when the patient is being ignored, is being phrased with the patient's presence in mind. Yet, physicians who feel that their technical language will not be understood by the patient act the way adults often do when they use esoteric language in the presence of children believing that matters not designed for children's ears will thus be safeguarded.[25]

Doctors, like most parents, also sometimes "let things slip" or "talk out of turn." The best educated and most self-controlled parents sometimes have trouble suppressing remarks that should not be made before children; and almost every doctor at some time or other will violate the rule that he should not talk in front of the patient, in spite of all the complaints by patients and nurses, and in spite of the admonitions prevailing in medical circles.

So persistent a pattern in the face of counterpressure and directive suggests that talk in front of the patient must serve a definite function.[26] By ignoring the presence of the patient the doctor reminds him of his hospital role, and of the expectation that the patient shall accommodate himself without murmur to the established routine. The patient is reminded that he is not in a position to have any say or to make important decisions, and the authority of the physicians (and their students) is emphasized. Doctors feel responsible *for* the patient, to be sure, but not, to the same degree, responsible *to* the patient.

Since rounds are not only designed for diagnosis and follow-up of treatment but also for teaching, some discussion of a patient's condition must take place simultaneously with demonstration. The supervising physician cannot always control the types of questions addressed to him, nor is he always quick enough to refuse to give certain answers. "Ignoring the patient" at such times often means that the physician is engulfed in thoughts

9

about "the case." The effect upon the patient may be the same, however, as if he were deliberately being ignored.

NOTES

1. C. Rufus Rorem, *The Public's Investment in Hospitals,* Chicago: University of Chicago Press, 1930. This quote from the introduction by Michael M. Davis, p. vii.

2. Such isolation from outside society is one of "The Characteristics of Total Institutions," (Erving Goffman, *op. cit.*). On a discussion about the difference between "inmates" and staff in regard to total time spent on the premises, as well as regarding other aspects of institutional life, see Goffman's discussion on "Interpersonal Relations," in *Group Processes; Transactions of the Third Conference of the Josiah Macy, Jr., Foundation,* Bertram Schaffner, (ed.), New York: The Foundation, 1957, pp. 117-93.

3. Paul Berkman, "Life Aboard an Armed-Guard Ship," *American Journal of Sociology,* LI (March 1946), 380-387.

4. In actual fact, the medical ward was often overpopulated so that a number of patients from that ward were often "boarded out" to the surgical ward.

5. *Men and Their Work,* Glencoe, Ill., 1958, pp. 54-58. A good example of the paradox inherent in the "routinized emergency" is the coronary patient in a medical ward: he lives in the fear of death, while his treatment consists in procedures that have by now become fairly well routinized.

6. H. H. Gerth and C. W. Mills, (eds.), *From Max Weber,* New York: Oxford University Press, 1946, p. 253.

7. Howard Brotz and Everett Wilson, "Characteristics of Military Society," *American Journal of Sociology,* LI (March 1946), 371-375.

8. Cf. Oswald Hall, "Sociological Research in the Field of Medicine: Progress and Prospects," *op. cit.*

9. Accounts of the early history of Mount Hermon are drawn from official history.

10. Today, a patient in the ward, the owner of a candy store in a lower-class section of the city, can proudly say: "My son, he was an interne here; he went to Holyoke Medical School, *cum laude.* He left for California, he's in the army, on a beautiful ship. . . . I have a candy store, my son helps me; this one isn't so bright, he's different. It's the other one I'm talking about. He's the one I lived for, he has a beautiful ship. You know, he was an interne here. . . ."

11. All proper names used in this book are fictitious. They were selected in such a way as to indicate the ethnic origin of the subjects.

12. House doctors were occasionally heard talking Yiddish to patients when they thought they were alone with them, but refused to use this means of communication and rapport in the presence of others.

13. A more detailed consideration of doctor-patient relationships follows in Chapter IV. The present account is designed only to establish some of the atmosphere of life in the ward at Mount Hermon.

14. Wessen, *op. cit.,* p. 207. For an analysis of "Teams," see Erving Goff-

man, *The Presentation of Self in Everyday Life,* New York: Doubleday Anchor Books, 1959, Chapter II.

15. Goffman, "The Characteristics of Total Institutions," *op. cit.*

16. Some patients—there was always at least one such patient in the female ward—seem always to have a box of candy on the table, a device set "accidentally" to elicit some responsive expression from the physicians on rounds. With a flirtatious smile and a suggesion, "Have some, doctor," she could generally evoke some jocular remark: "You must be the most popular patient in the ward," or "Good thing we have you around here to cheer us all up."

17. Wessen, *op. cit.,* p. 199.

18. Erving Goffman has called attention to the role of the "non-person." He says: "Perhaps the classic type of non-person in our society is the servant. This person is expected to be present in the front region while the host is presenting a performance of hospitality to the guests of the establishment. . . . In certain ways he is defined . . . as someone who isn't there. . . . In addition to . . . servant-like roles, there are other standard categories of persons who are sometimes treated in their presence as if they were not there: the very young, the very old, and the sick are common examples." (*The Presentation of Self in Everyday Life, op. cit.,* pp. 151-152.)

19. J. Jean Hecht, *The Domestic Servant Class in Eighteenth Century England,* London: Routledge and Kegan Paul, 1956, p. 179.

20. *Ibid.,* p. 96.

21. *Ibid.,* p. 87.

22. *Ibid.,* p. 73.

23. *Ibid.,* p. 207.

24. *Ibid.,* pp. 207-208.

25. However, both the child and the patient sometimes do understand, and sometimes misunderstand; in either case with unanticipated consequences. For an insightful comparison of the doctor-patient relationship with the parent-child relationship see Barker, Wright and Gonick, *op. cit.,* p. 231.

26. The function of such conversation for relationships within the medical hierarchy will be discussed in the next chapter.

CHAPTER II

The Social Structure of the Ward

Lines of Authority

A CLOSE-UP

On an average morning between 10:30 and 11:30 a.m. there may be as many as fifteen people milling about the ward among the twenty or twenty-five patients. Physicians are making rounds, medical students are attending patients, nurses are taking temperatures, giving medication and answering calls. Out in the corridor a group of doctors are talking to a head nurse, attendants may be wheeling patients on stretchers. Student nurses and nurses' aides go in and out of the ward with bedpans, medical appliances, orange juice or water, and from time to time a volunteer may be seen wheeling a patient to the TV room or to the elevator. The first impression is one of utter confusion, but nevertheless there is an underlying order in this chaos and there prevails here a well-defined division of labor with a rigid role differentiation and a firm status hierarchy.

As soon as we begin to observe closely the behavior of a single group on a single occasion, we see which people most often initiate action and which ones defer to others:

> Three medical students, two internes, the assistant resident, the resident, and the visiting doctor, after making rounds in the ward move out into the hall and continue their discussion near the nurses' station. These eight men block the hallway from wall to wall. A student nurse who wants to go by with a bedpan stands waiting but without giving a sign until after almost a minute when one of the medical students moves without looking at her, and she passes. A nurse tries to wheel a patient out of the ward and finds her way blocked. She looks at the preoccupied group of doctors, then leaves the stretcher to attend some business at her desk. Several minutes later when she returns to the stretcher she is still unable to wheel it on. In the ensuing moments some of the students and internes glance at her occasionally but give no sign of recognition. Finally, the chief

12

resident says, "Let's move away from here. It seems we're in the way." They all proceed to the door marked "Exit." The nurse gives them an angry look as they are going out, but not a word is exchanged between doctors and nurses.

I am invited to join this same group in conference on the steps. The visiting doctor and I are offered chairs; the others sit on the steps. Visiting doctor: "I'm utterly confused." Everyone laughs. "Now let's see how we will proceed. Do you have any hunches on this case? Let's have everybody's opinion. Let's go up the totem pole." With a smile he points to a medical student. Everyone laughs.

While they are conferring on the steps a nurse approaches. Unable to pass she stands there waiting. Nobody looks at her. Slowly, and still without looking at her, an interne clears a passage for her, but there is no interruption of the discussion. Later a Negro orderly carrying a tray with a dozen bottles up the steps comes to a stop below the group. Nobody looks at him; nobody moves. After a moment or so he turns about and goes back down the stairs.

In these brief scenes, several details stand out. The physicians, as they block the hallway immediately outside the ward and cause a "traffic jam" appear to be insensitive to the nurses' tasks. Both in the hallway and later on the steps, it was the lowly medical student, or the interne, who finally made some move to let the subordinate, i.e., the nurse, go by. It was the chief resident, however, who initiated the action at last to move the entire group away from the nurses' station. And it was the visiting doctor, highest of all in prestige who introduced some jocular remark to "clear the air," and dissipate some of the tension built up in the group.[1] As for the Negro orderly, he was so low in the hierarchy of the hospital that he was ignored altogether.

Generally, physicians like to consider themselves "the bosses." "It's all right to smoke here," an interne reassured me when I was about to put out my cigarette in front of a "No Smoking" sign. He pointed to his own lit cigarette and to the ashtrays on the desk. *"We* are the boss around here; they—" (with a movement of the head toward the nurses' desk) "—can't tell *us* what to do." [They can, though.]

Although the head nurse is responsible for the ward and for the efficiency of work and medical procedure, she finds it hard, because of her inferior status, to use her well-specified authority. The head nurse of one of the medical wards, on the eve of leaving the ward for a teaching position in the hospital's school of nursing, said: "I have the right to interfere because I'm responsible for the ward, but I generally don't." Another nurse who complained of doctors clustering in the halls and congregating around the desk, interfering with nurses' rounds, said:

You have to cater to the students as well as the doctors; you have to set the blood up, set the medication up. Naturally, if they're here as students, they feel they're doctors and that they deserve the honor of being waited on.

Asked whether she couldn't tell them to move, she said: "You *can't tell them all the time*. They may explode. That's very embarrassing. . . . It's not for us to say: it's just for us to do."

The nurse-doctor relationship is only one aspect of the authority structure. When the same nurse says of a medical student, "Wait till he's an interne, someone will snap him down to size," she is recognizing additional controls that operate within the hierarchy of the hospital.

"LET'S GO UP THE TOTEM POLE"

The medical staff on each male and female ward consists of three medical students, two internes, one assistant resident. The chief resident is in charge of both medical wards. In each ward, responsibility for the patients is divided between the two internes. They treat "their" patients, under the supervision of, and in agreement with the assistant resident, who is responsible to the chief resident for medical procedures in the ward.[2] The chief resident, although he is in turn responsible to the chief-of-service, has full delegated authority over both wards. "I have complete say in the ward," said a chief resident. "I may accept the suggestion of a visiting doctor or of the chief-of-service, but I don't have to. I have the last word." In practice, however, the chief resident usually accepts the word of a visiting doctor or the chief-of-service. (For a diagram of the ward structures, see Charts I and II.)

On the two surgical wards, the formal authority structure is roughly the same as in the medical wards and the division of labor among the medical students and doctors differs only slightly. There are between three and six medical students, two internes, a junior assistant resident, a senior assistant resident and a chief resident—all of whom work in both the female and the male wards. The assistant residents oversee the work of the internes and the chief resident is responsible for both wards. As in the medical ward, the internes are in direct contact with the patients, but the authority of the surgical interne is much diminished. As one of them said, "On surgery the interne does not have as much responsibility as on the medical ward. . . . He is responsible for the routine care. . . . Internes do not operate, and it is those who operate who are responsible for their patients."

On the surgical ward, lines of communication are quite flexible, which gives the impression of informality. Someone observing the house staff in the absence of the chief resident might easily draw the conclusion that on the surgical ward there are no strict lines of authority. All doctors write orders for patients in the nurses' order book; and joking and banter between physicians and nurses in the hallway and at the nurses' station is frequent. On the medical wards, in very sharp contrast, the chain of command is strictly respected. Only the internes write orders in the order book, and the head nurse usually refers information on patients to the internes, who later pass it on to the senior staff.

But while the line of communication on the medical floor is clear-cut and follows a scalar system, decision-making there generally proceeds through consensus.[3] On the surgical floor, however, where the line of communication is not strictly adhered to, authority is not, as might be expected, diffused and shared, but tends to be concentrated and *arbitrary*,[4] with decisions proceeding by fiat from the visiting doctor or the chief resident.[5]

THE VISITING DOCTOR

A "visiting doctor" is present on the ward at least once a day for an hour or two. He finds himself in the ambiguous situation of possessing personal and professional authority and at the same time lacking organizational authority in the ward. This equivocal situation merits some detailed analysis.

At Mount Hermon, the visiting physician was a private physician of some prominence who had hospital privileges, i.e., the right to send his patients to the private services of the hospital. In return for this privilege, he was required to devote several hours a day for three months a year to teaching and counseling.

Much of this teaching takes place in the ward. The visiting doctor, making rounds with the hospital staff and medical students, must do two jobs at once: advise the house staff on diagnosis and therapy, and teach the internes and the medical students. Both of these tasks, by their very nature, carry authority and prestige.

The visiting doctor's authority in the ward, then, is derived from professional seniority and prestige[6] rather than from his official position in the organization, of which he is only a casual member.[7]

The visiting doctor is an expert, like those experts in industrial organizations who are "called in to help in giving a decision with as much prescience and caution as possible."[8] In this capacity he writes (or dictates) his recommendations, which are filed in the patient's record. These carry all the weight of decisions even though he has no *formal* authority to make decisions; and he is responsible for his suggestion—as attested by his signature under his recommendations.

The ambiguity in the staff-role of the visiting doctor does not stem from an "error" in hospital organization but rather from the insistence of medical practitioners in this country that medicine is a "free" profession. The

Chart I

SOCIAL STRUCTURE OF THE MEDICAL WARD

Formal Line of Authority and Decision-Making

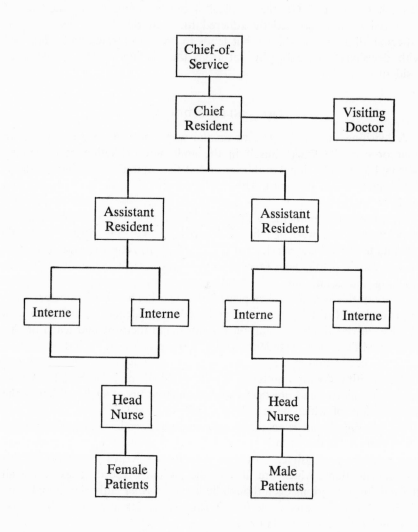

Chart II

SOCIAL STRUCTURE OF THE SURGICAL WARD

Formal Line of Authority and Decision-Making

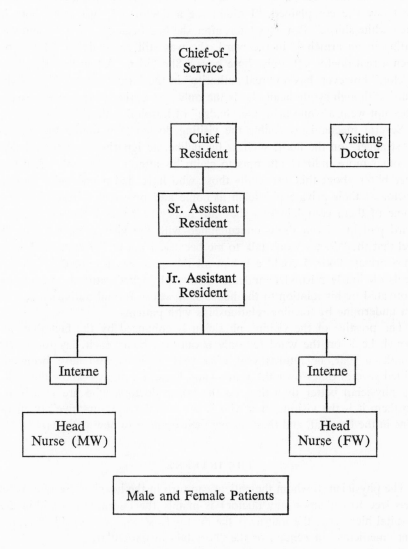

doctor is not "employed"; he offers his "services" in return for "privileges."[9]
This leads to the peculiar situation that, although the visiting doctor sets
up a course of therapy for the patient, the patient has no way of appealing
to him. This situation generates considerable frustration among the patients,
who tend to consider the visiting doctor as the "real doctor." The more
daring patients made their claims clear, as did Mrs. Macdonald, who
breached the rules of etiquette to yell across the ward during the visiting
doctor's rounds: "Well, what about me? I came here to see a doctor." The
next day she complained, "I didn't see a doctor yet, just those boys in
their white shirts." Ten days later, after she had been operated on and was
sitting in an armchair in the ward, she was still complaining, "I haven't
seen a real doctor yet, only those boys." She did not know that this "real
doctor," however, has no "real authority" in the formal organization of the
ward, although symbolically he is the only one during rounds who usually
does not wear a white coat, the "badge" of hospital authority.

Several mechanisms enable the visiting doctor to maintain his role as
a "stranger" on the floor, such as his deliberate ignoring of patients' calls
or other more indirect attempts to claim his attention. Patients often feel
very bitter about this, especially those who have had a particular visiting
doctor as their private physician at home and now feel rejected by him.
Some of them complain that they are neglected because they are "only"
ward patients. Even those unacquainted with the visiting doctor tend to
feel that the "doctor won't talk to me because I am in the ward. If I were
on a private floor, I could ask him all the questions I wanted." Yet, patients obviously misunderstand the visiting physician's attitudes which are
motivated by his relation to the house staff whose formal authority he will
not undermine by forming relationships with patients.

The prestige of the visiting physician is enhanced by the fact that, although he is on the ward for only about two hours each day for a few
months a year, he returns year after year. Patients who have been admitted several times over the years—and there are many—know the visiting physician better than they do the house doctors, who are transients.
To them it is the visiting man who is the actual "representative" of medicine in the hospital, and they convey their opinion to new patients.

THE INTERNE

The physician to whom the patient can turn in the hospital (insofar as he
feels free to call upon any doctor) is mainly the interne. And within the
hospital hierarchy, the interne is the doctor least equipped of all to repre-
sent "medicine" in general or the "hospital" in particular.

For all practical purposes, the interne may be considered an employee
of the hospital: he is given a yearly salary in exchange for his working a

specified number of hours. He does not see himself as an employee, however. He feels that in relation to the patient he is a "doctor," and in relation to the hospital he is a student on his way to becoming a free professional. His anticipatory role makes it possible for him to accept the terms of interneship, in spite of the gross inadequacy of monetary compensation. The fact that his working conditions are not comparable to working conditions in industrial society, and hence cannot be measured against them, helps to emphasize the fact that he is not an employee but a trainee.

The interne is at the bottom of the hierarchy of the house staff.[10] He works eighteen hours a day for $300 a year with room and board.[11] He is on the ward at 7:30 in the morning, and several times a week he is kept busy until 11 or 12 o'clock at night. He is off duty every other night and every other weekend, but when he is off for the weekend, he has to give one more night a week to the ward. He is on call all during the night, every night. Frequently he is called during the night after two or three hours' sleep and cannot go back to sleep at all since he has to be present at the morning rounds at 7:30. Working all through the night is not a rare experience for an interne.[12]

The interne would be the "proletarian" in the hospital were it not for the fact that he does not think of employer-employee relations but of the medical "fraternity." He tends to perceive his internship as a rite of passage.

CONTRADICTORY STATUS RELATIONSHIPS

Many members of the hospital staff are caught up in a network of contradictory relationships, some of which closely parallel certain status difficulties that have been remarked in other organizations. In any modern large-scale organization status is generally, and on principle, based upon competence and knowledge on the job (achieved status). A person with much training and experience is supposed to hold a higher position than a person with less training and experience.

But large organizations, especially line-staff organizations, are complex, and this principle cannot always be maintained. As tasks become ever more specialized, comparisons of knowledge and competence become more difficult, and rival claims to superiority more common. Specialists tend to vaunt their own field of knowledge and to downgrade someone else's. The young staff engineer may claim to have greater knowledge and competence than the old-time foreman, who, in turn, boasts of superior experience and skill in matters of line-production.[13]

A complex organization consists of several hierarchies, each with its own criteria for competence; and each hierarchy is jealous of its own rights to judge and reward its own members. In a university, professors resent what they take to be interference by the administration, and maintain faculty committees to decide upon appointments and promotion within their own ranks. The recent tendency to make an academic person president of a college, or make a physician the director of a hospital, may be a compromise attempt to bridge the gap under the conviction (often erroneous) that administrators drawn from the profession will be guided by criteria of competence laid down by the profession rather than by those of the administrative hierarchy.[14]

In the hospital, the existence of several separate lines of authority creates acute problems. While in an industrial organization, a staff man cannot give orders to a line man—the research engineer cannot give orders to the foreman—in the hospital:

> doctors *may* and *do* give orders to nurses. On the other hand they are not called upon to discipline a nurse for failure to carry out an order. Nor are doctors held accountable for the failure of a nurse to carry out an order which they as doctors have formulated. Such divergencies from the normal pattern of institutional function place heavy demands on the personnel.[15]

It is obvious that many of the physicians will be younger, and have fewer years of experience than the nurses to whom they give orders. Some of the physicians, especially among the visiting doctors, are but tenuously associated with the permanent staff organization. Moreover, most of the house staff, are "transients" who will soon move on from the ward, and then from the hospital altogether; hence, most of the physicians in the hospital are oriented to the outside, i.e., to private practice. They do not want to be an integral part of the hospital organization and yet they feel that they should have the main say in the hospital regarding medical procedures. The more permanent and more hospital-oriented nurse is obliged to acquiesce.

A PARADIGM OF AUTHORITY AND EXPERIENCE

There are, in the hospital as elsewhere, people with much training and experience, who hold a great deal of authority, such as, for example, the chief-of-service or the director-of-nursing; there are those with little training and experience, as for example the internes, who yet have some authority since they give orders to nurses; there are those with much training and experience but relatively little authority, such as the registered nurse; finally there are those with little training and experience and no authority, such as orderlies, aides, etc. Problems are bound to arise where training and experience are not rewarded by an adequate authority position.[16]

Assuming for purposes of simplification that competence and experience can be measured in a single scale, we can distinguish four theoretical combinations of authority and experience:

| | | Training and Experience | |
		More	Less
Authority	More	I	II
	Less	III	IV

and the following theoretically possible relationships (aside from relationships between equals):

I - II	II - III
I - III	II - IV
I - IV	III - IV

In the relationship I-II both persons have much authority, but one of them has more training and experience than the other; the relationship between the chief resident and the visiting doctor can be offered as an example. The latter has *de facto* authority based on experience, the former has *de jure* authority in the ward based on his official position. Tension and overlapping authority might be expected here but in this case the chief resident is likely to defer to the visiting doctor. Friendly relations with an experienced professional colleague are more important to his future career than the exercise of his formal authority in the ward.[17]

The relationship I-III might also give rise to tension insofar as one person has to submit to another without, however, finding his lack of authority legitimized by less training and experience. The relationship between visiting doctor and chief-of-service comes to mind: both have a high reputation and many years of medical practice behind them, but the chief-of-service has authority over the ward both *de jure* and *de facto,* while the visiting doctor has no *de jure* authority. However, the relationship between these two physicians is usually devoid of tension (1) because they interact very little with each other[18] and (2) because the visiting doctor, as an outsider, is not competing for formal authority in the hospital and enjoys high prestige anyway.

In the relationship I-IV a person with more training and experience, as well as with more authority, encounters someone with less training and experience and less authority; such are the relationships between chief resident and interne, or between interne and student nurse, or between the head nurse and the medical student. In all these cases, authority is legitimized by longer training and experience and the relationship is likely to be acceptable to both parties.

In relationship II-IV two persons with equally little training and experience stand in a superordinate-subordinate relationship. We observed no relationship of this type, although it occurred in another hospital when two volunteers were placed in positions where one initiated action for the other. In such cases there exists a source of tension which is mitigated if (1) the amount of interaction between them is minimized, and (2) the subordinate is more outside- than organization-oriented.

In the relationship III-IV neither has authority over the other, but one has more training and experience. An older and a young registered nurse on the same floor would be a case in point. The more competent person might be dissatisfied because she had not been given a higher status than her less able colleague, but since no exercise of authority over the other person is involved, there is little occasion for tension in the relationship.

The relationship II-III, where a person with little experience and training has authority over a person with more experience and training, applies to the nurse and the interne. Of all possible status relationships this one, clearly, is potentially the most explosive.

EXCURSUS ON THE INTERNE-NURSE RELATIONSHIP

The formal definition of the relationship is quite simple. The interne gives orders to the nurse, and the nurse carries out the interne's orders. However, the actual authority relations between these two persons are much more complex.

> . . . I remember my interne days," says one physician. . . . "The interne who first comes on the floor better watch out for the nurse. The nurse has all sorts of ways of letting him know that he better behave, or else. . . .

The interne is the nurse's main partner in interaction and he, in turn, needs her cooperation. She must bring to him all information about his patients and he issues orders to her concerning their treatment. The nurse feels that a young man just out of medical school can know very little about patients, certainly much less than she knows from her own experience with the sick.[19]

Although the interne and the nurse are both employees of the hospital, the interne considers himself a member of a free profession. He is trained to treat patients; he is expected to use his competence in the ward; he enjoys higher status and prestige than the nurse; he is expected to give her orders, and he bears the dignified title of "doctor." And yet he remains a "trainee." It is the ambiguity of these statuses that complicates the interne-nurse relationship.

The head nurse is usually older than the interne and expects respect for her age, which she feels is but a symbol of her long experience. A head nurse usually has been in the hospital for a number of years and "knows the ropes" in the organization.

Moreover, the interne stays at the hospital for only one year and on the nurse's floor for about ten weeks. It is the head nurse who best represents permanence and continuity on the ward, for she alone among the hospital personnel remains very long at the same station. Student nurses, medical students and house officers all shift around from floor to floor and from service to service during any single year.

The nurse's complaints about the interne usually refer to such traits as "immaturity," or "lack of competence." One nurse, an old hand at nursing, who had worked on both the private floors and the ward at Mount Hermon, said:

> They have to learn. This morning at the rounds, there's a woman who had a reaction after some medication, so the chief resident said, "Give her half a dose twice as often." So the interne says, "Why do you prescribe that, sir?" Only an interne would ask such a question. Isn't it simple to understand that if a woman has a reaction against some medication, you give her less of it at a time?

This nurse was sure that she understood the chief resident's order much better than the interne did. Another head nurse felt that nurses were not being given enough recognition for their knowledge:

> They don't consult the nurses enough. If nurses go on rounds, they hold the charts, they pass them to the interne, the interne to the chief resident, and then it comes back down the line and the nurse puts the chart back. All the nurse is there for, according to them, is to hold the charts.

Many nurses complained that they were not called in on Social Service rounds. One nurse told of a patient who was suddenly being discharged after four months in the ward (he had had his leg amputated). The nurse knew that the patient had previously been living in a rooming house and had no place to go:

> So I told the doctors and they got Social Service and now they have to keep him until Social Service makes the arrangements. This wouldn't have been necessary had I been at the Social Service rounds. Social Service would have been informed on time.

The interne, on the other hand, often feels that the nurse fails to recognize his authority, as in the following remark overheard at lunch:

> I had expressly ordered that no nitroglycerin be given until further notice, and she goes right ahead and gives her nitroglycerin. You'd think they have no head on their shoulders.

Whatever their negative views of one another, nurse and interne must nevertheless cooperate. They cannot withdraw from the paradoxical status relationship. William Foote Whyte, in a study of the restaurant, has shown that problems of contradictory status are aggravated where the relationship involves frequent interaction.[20] In the relationship between nurse and interne, frequency of interaction is an important variable.

We know that frequency of interaction strengthens sentiment[21] and often a hostile sentiment at that.[22]

> The doctor doesn't realize how busy we are. He will give the nurse an order instead of writing it in the order book; at the same time a student comes to the other side and wants something prepared, and the telephone rings and the nurse has to pass on a message; sometimes we wonder why we don't get mad around here.

The frequency of interaction is intensified by the fact that because of the crowded physical arrangement of the wards, doctors and nurses are often in each other's way (as we have seen before). "There isn't enough room. The staff men are standing around, blocking the doorway to the ward, the door to the exit, the pathway to the hall." This is a standard complaint. As one nurse said, "People become all irritated when they fall over each other."

Nurses also complain that the doctor (i.e., the interne) neglects to write the order in the order book. The nurse's insistence on this rule, viewed by some internes as sheer malice, stems in part at least from the half-conscious realization that writing minimizes interaction and therefore tension. It has been found that written orders in place of oral ones serve to minimize friction between restaurant workers beset by similar contradictions of status.[23]

The nurse is close to the interne in four ways: (1) spatially, because the nurses' station is small and the doctors have no station of their own;[24] (2) sociologically, because nurse and interne must communicate frequently; (3) professionally, in that both have "not quite" the status they vision for themselves, the nurse is a "not quite" authority holder over the ward and the interne is a "not quite" physician;[25] (4) task orientation, since the line between the nurse's responsibility for the ward and the interne's responsibility for his patients is often hard to draw.

The nurse tends to feel that the interne either invades her sphere of authority, or that he abdicates his own authority, expecting her to take over. "When they put in those new desks," one nurse complained, "they were for the doctors, but they're always at *our* desk."[26]

In the ward even more than at the desk the work of the nurse frequently overlaps with that of the interne.[27] Such overlap lends to complaints about real or imaginary infringement of status and authority. So one nurse says:

> Sometimes you can't even get to the patient; *they're* around them all the time.

Another complains of being expected to complete the filling out of requisitions for X-ray:

The doctors will fill out only one or two things; they will throw it on the desk. . . . I'm becoming the doctor's secretary. . . . *I don't know whether it is my job but I suppose it is not.*

Where the spheres of authority and responsibility are ambiguous, the nurse feels that authority is either usurped or abdicated at the doctor's whim. One nurse said:

> The doctor has to write the order in the order book, but sometimes he just tells us and we write it. You can't ask the doctor to stop examining a patient and come out to write the order. Actually, he doesn't realize the legal implications of this, for if the slightest thing goes wrong, the doctor may not remember having given the order because he was thinking of the other patient, and then the nurse is liable.

These frequent complaints associated with minor details of everyday routine reveal how much the overlapping of responsibilities disturbs the nurse's security. She seems to feel that her responsibilities are greater than her limited authority. As A. T. M. Wilson has noted:[28]

> In situations where responsibility is felt to be greater than the authority of a job, there is a considerable insecurity of those who must bear the burden of such disproportionate responsibility; and, as an inevitable consequence, they tend to deal with their insecurity by attempting to limit responsibility and increase efficiency through the formulation of particularly clean-cut regulations and rules. . . .

So one nurse explained:

> By the time the doctor writes orders in the order book, it is often too late for the order to go through. This has happened so often that *now there is a rule,* they have to have it in before four or it won't go through. . . .

Rules help the nurse to protect herself against responsibilities that she feels she cannot and should not live up to. They help to delimit (and therefore maintain) lines of authority. And they reduce the need for oral communication.

The frustrations that the nurse experiences in the nurse-doctor relationship breed mutual resentment. Internes complain that "when you have to deal with nurses, they're bitchy and administrative" or that "sometimes one doubts whether nurses know how to read." But the interne's relationship with the head nurse on a ward is a very temporary one and his main concern is with his future career. The nurse, on the other hand, is tied to the hospital in which she will continue to deal with a succession of such "youngsters," as she calls them.

The nurse's frustration is inherent in her professional role. Her authority is derived and will continue to be derived from work in the hospital and not from work outside the hospital. In her position as a subordinate to the physician, she cares about her own sphere of authority because she is hospital-oriented. The profession-oriented interne is seen as a "stranger"—who does not identify with hospital organization. Like any "stranger," he is guilty of "trespassing," and the frequency of interaction and the overlap of tasks seem all the more trying in view of the fact that the interne does not really "belong."

While the nurse insists on hospital rules, the interne is concerned with "the practice of medicine," and with the norms maintained by the medical fraternity. He is likely to regard administrative rules as unimportant.[29]

Studies of prejudice elicit an image of the "stranger" who is said to be "crowding in on us."[30] The stranger is looked upon as a parasite who "litters the beaches, messes everything up expecting others to clean up after them."[31] The interne is the target of a strikingly similar accusation:

> The nurses always have to clean up after the doctors; they always get everything disorganized and we have to spend our time reorganizing things properly.

By her insistence on rules and her refusal to be considered a "servant" who has to do the doctor's "dirty work"[32] the nurse is emphasizing that hospital organization is based on a "legal order"[33] in which the authority and responsibility of the members are defined and limited, rather than on a "traditional order" where the one who obeys orders is "subordinate with his total personality."

The nurse, in protesting the behavior of the internes, rebels against authority. But her rebellion is not directed at those in power but at those who seem to be powerful because they transmit orders. Indeed, the interne, although he "gives orders," has very little power and he himself is under the orders of his seniors and under constant pressure to do the work that is expected of him. One nurse, during a complaining tirade, gave a vivid description of an interne's plight:

> They have to be at an X-ray conference at 8:20. There is one round in the morning, then comes X-ray. Then come the staff men —that takes them till lunch—and at one o'clock they have a round again; and on some days they have special rounds in the afternoon. In between, the doctors run in and out to write orders in the order book. After dinner, when he might be able to work up patients, he goes on rounds again with the resident, that's the chart round. Then on Wednesdays they have GI rounds, it sometimes takes two hours; by this time it's five o'clock, the interne should go off duty but then he may have two patients to work up; after that he writes orders and this is often too late for the order to

go through. . . . After seven o'clock they have to go on rounds again, and sometimes they can't go till nine or ten o'clock. . . . Something should be done about rounds, I don't know how they manage. . . .

Although she seemed to be well aware of the fact that the interne has no say about the organization of work in the hospital, she still complained that some of the interne's orders are but a means of "passing the buck:"

> If a patient says, "I have to have an enema right now," and if it's eleven or twelve at night, instead of taking time to talk to the patient [to tell him that he doesn't need one], he gives orders to us. Once a doctor ordered five enemas at once just because the patients wanted it. . . .

The nurse who makes another powerless person responsible for orders she considers illegitimate has a counterpart in many other organizations. Henri De Man has observed,

> Characteristically [resentment against superiors] is primarily directed against the immediate chief, the foreman, himself a wage earner. . . . This is analogous to what we find in army life, where the private usually hates the sergeant much more cordially than he hates the divisional commander. In many instances we are told in so many words in the reports that the higher members of the managerial staff and the actual employer are not such bad fellows after all. . . .[34]

People who occupy positions that can easily be made to appear positions of power, while actually they are not, constitute an easy target for the rebellion of the underdog, just because they are powerless to retaliate. As such, they assure the harmlessness of the "rebellion," which leads to a release of tension, without, however, bringing about a change in the initial situation or in the social structure that gave rise to discontent.[35]

Such situations occur with such regularity in society that they produce similar stereotypes:

Stereotyped accusation against a member of the out-group:	What nurses have to say about internes:
He's only out for himself, always tries to get something for nothing.	[Internes are] very selfish; their attitude is: "I do my work, you do yours, and if you can do some of mine, that's fine too."
He wants to get ahead.	All the interne cares about is learn, learn, learn. He has no consideration for the patient.

| He dodges work. | They will fill out only one or two things and throw it on your desk. |
| They crowd us out. | The nurse can't even get to the patient sometimes. |

Such are the grievances of the underdog: directed with little effect against the nearest, most visible, target.

How, then, can these two persons, the interne and the nurse, bear with each other, especially since avoidance mechanisms are scant and can be only intermittently applied? What motivations keep each in his job? While the turnover among nurses is relatively high, it would probably be higher were it not for certain compensatory mechanisms.

The turnover of internes is institutionalized, and is a safety valve against violent disruption in nurse-interne relations. By the time tensions with the nurse accumulate, the interne is on the verge of leaving the ward. His expectation of departure helps cool his anger. "Thank God I'm getting the hell out of here soon," or, "I won't be sorry when I won't have to see *her* again"—such reflections ease present discomforts. The nurse also rejoices in advance to "see these boys go"; and, as the next group of internes comes in, she might say—as one of the head nurses actually did say a few days after the arrival of two new internes—"We have some very nice doctors here now; they're human beings, not children, like those who were here before." By the time a new head of steam has built up, these internes will be almost ready to leave.

Thus, the same "migratory status" of the interne that prevents him from assuming a stable status position and from identifying with the hospital, also helps to maintain a structure which might otherwise be seriously threatened.

But the nurse will continue to face the problem of "always" having to "clean up after the doctors," i.e., doing the doctors' dirty work. "Dirty work" is by definition humiliating. It is especially humiliating if it does not correspond to the self-definition of the role. The nurse tends to see herself (1) as a professional, or (2) as a "glamor girl."[36] To maintain this image and to impress it on others, she must defend herself as best she can against "dirty work."[37]

The head nurse delegates dirty work to student nurses and to nurses' aides. The student nurses, who, like the internes, view their present status as one of initiation and learning, accept these chores in anticipation of their future roles as graduate nurses when they will themselves be able to delegate dirty work to those under them.

The delegation of dirty work relieves the head nurse from an unpleasant chore and symbolizes her authority. "Delegation of dirty work is part of the process of social mobility."[38] It gives the nurse the feeling of "having arrived."

Characteristically, when delegating work to the student nurse, the head nurse often calls it "teaching," thus giving the most favorable connotation to the meaning of her work.[39] But there is still far too much "dirty work" left for her to do, at least in her own eyes: she claims that she is burdened with petty details instead of nursing. She can come to terms with this situation, as we shall see in Chapter V, by maintaining her authority over the patient and clinging to a professional ideology.

ELEMENTS OF RECIPROCITY[40]

Although she complains about "doing the doctor's work," the nurse also enjoys her vicarious participation in the doctor's job. Her expressions of hurt dignity are touched with boastfulness. When she complains that the doctor against all rules lets her write the order in the order book, there is pride in her voice, for the doctor's delegation of responsibility to her seems to make her almost as responsible and important as he is. The nurse "helps" the doctor, thereby borrowing, so to speak, from his prestige.

In the intensive interview, all the nurses, with the exception of the two nurses' supervisors (who did not have to take doctors' orders), claimed that nurses know more about patients than the doctors do and are indispensable to the doctor in his performance on the ward. "We know the patient. He will talk more freely to us than to his doctor," they would say, or "The doctor maintains contact with the patient through the nurse," or, again, "The nurse can act as a better interpreter to the doctor; the doctor doesn't have the time to listen to the patients."

Nurses are quite correct in these claims and those internes sensitive enough to take full advantage of assistance from the nurses acquire thereby much security in their own adaptation to the ward.

Everett C. Hughes has pointed out that:

> The common dignifying rationalization of people in all positions of a work hierarchy except the very top one is, "We in this position save the people in the next higher position above from their mistakes." The notion that one saves a person of more acknowledged skill, and certainly of more acknowledged prestige and power, than one's self from his mistakes appears to be peculiarly satisfying.[41]

This satisfaction seems to lie in the bond that is thus created. It is not the pointing out of mistakes in itself that provides satisfaction, but the interaction that results from it. The nurse who points out a mistake or who acts as an "interpreter to the doctor" wants her importance to be acknowledged. One nurse said of a "good doctor": "If he made a mistake, he was eager to apologize for it," but a "poor one" will "try to get out of it instead of saying, 'I'm sorry'."

29

To point out one's importance to a person higher up in the hierarchy, and to secure his acknowledgement of this importance, is one way of bridging status differences and achieving consensus. Other informal devices are joking and kidding, and "irregular deals" (types of assistance that circumvent formal rules).[42]

The relationship thus established is cemented by mutual obligations.[43] The physician must rely upon the nurse for information about the patient and for assistance in avoiding mistakes; the nurse in turn expects the physician to acknowledge merit in her performance. "Thus a number of minute social bonds are established by a series of alternating oscillations, in which a right is established in the offering and an obligation in the receiving."[44]

Authority in the hospital is based on obedience. (As one nurse said: "A good nurse must do what she's told even if she doesn't understand or agree.") There is little occasion for a nurse to express dissatisfaction and tension directly in her work. Therefore, she often resorts to in-group grumbling.

Complaining—like "pointing out mistakes," or for that matter like *any* initiation of interaction—is a call for consensus, an invitation to the listener to show sympathy and to share the speaker's point of view; and it calls for reciprocal confidence. While complaining is a symbolic affirmation of independence and strength, it may also be, as an observer of army life has pointed out, an "earmark of social solidarity."[45] It establishes a bond between the complainer and the listener by confirming to both that they have similar preoccupations.[46] It encourages exchange, and like other exchanges it cements relationships through the establishment of mutual obligations.[47]

Students of hospital organization have pointed to the lack of commensalism between doctors and nurses.[48] Absence of commensalism between groups is a characteristic feature of caste-like relations. At Mount Hermon, doctors and nurses used the same dining room but were never seen seated at the same tables. The spontaneous segregation of these groups, which reaffirms status prerogatives, also undoubtedly helps to strengthen consensus in the face of adversity. It allows people with similar grievances and complaints to get together for a short time each day and air them, thus fortifying themselves against the frustrations arising in work relationships where there is insufficient consensus.[49]

However, as Stanton and Schwartz have warned, the security which accompanies consensus "is so precious that . . . the parties tend to maintain it at the expense of their critical abilities. . . ."[50]

If the consensus established with peers is sufficiently satisfying, nurse and interne will be less inclined to make an effort to establish exchange and consensus with each other. Complaining, then, which reflects a lack

of exchange and consensus between nurses and internes, may relieve
certain frustrations, but only by further widening the gap between the two
groups. It is possible that the increased distance may lead to even more
discord, which in turn can only be made bearable by further complaining
—until there is a change of house staff on July 1st of each year.

There exists in the hospital no device by which the latent tensions
between doctor and nurse can be argued out in institutionalized conflict.
In the absence of such a device, the levels of complaint tend to be
quite high.

THE CONSENSUAL BASIS

One other element in hospital life binds together the entire staff: the
hospital ideology, which is "patient-oriented" and is transmitted to all.

A good nurse, we are told, is "one who thinks of the patient first . . ."
but some doctors "act as if the patient was a bother." A good nurse, a
physician says, should "understand the [patient's] problems and feelings,"
and the nurse generally prefers a doctor who is nice to the patient. "I
don't like a doctor who is interested in the case rather than the patient."
All nurses emphasize the slogans of their training, e.g., "to be interested
in the patient as a person," or "knowing the person as a whole, not just
the disease."

Internes employ similar language in response to questions. A good
doctor should be "sensitive to the needs of patients" and "honest with the
patient," and a good nurse should provide "comfort for the sick, sympathy
and understanding." "Empathy" and "rapport" were emphasized by one
interne as important qualities of both doctor and nurse.

Since the welfare and comfort of the patient was so emphasized, criticism (or praise) of another person's conduct was often couched in terms
of its effect upon the patient rather than upon oneself. One nurse complaining that the doctors too often order enemas to clear a gallbladder
series, said:

> They're unnecessary and it's a very uncomfortable procedure. It's
> not necessary to give three enemas and castor oil; castor oil is
> enough, but sometimes patients go through a lot of unnecessary
> things. . . .

That these "unnecessary" procedures make far more work for her she
did not say. Another nurse complains that some doctors are insincere
with patients:

> If a patient says, "I have palpitations," the doctor says, "Oh, I'll
> come back some other time." This is lying to the patient; they
> want to get on the good side of the patient. It happens often.

But she also notes that such "fobbing off" tactics make later trouble for her:

> The doctor says, "I'll give you this medication," and then he won't tell us; and the patient claims it from us and thinks we just don't want to give it to him.

Thus "patient-orientation" and "be honest with the patient" provide ideological justification for a defense of her own interests.

This ideology of patient-orientation, which is adhered to by all, can serve to legitimize criticism and complaints, and concern for self can be translated into concern for a third person. Use of the ideology has several consequences:

(1) It establishes a superficially unified view between nurses and doctors. Concern for the patient becomes a common frame of reference, a yardstick for measuring fitness and achievement.

(2) It marks both doctors and nurses as "professionals" bound by a system of ethics in which self-orientation is disapproved and other-orientation approved. The nurse shares the professional ethic of "altruism" and the medical ethic of "placing the welfare of the patient above . . . self-interest."[51] She feels elevated to the status of a medical person with an ethical outlook similar to that of the doctor.

(3) The patient's welfare is used as the supra-individual standard to which each party in the relationship can rally. Championing the cause of the patient equips each with self-righteousness and good conscience, and helps to legitimize a competitive spirit.[52] Both nurses and doctors will try to excel in virtue and righteousness and concern for the patient. These efforts of each on behalf of the same "cause" serve to strengthen the common norm and to make it a more lively concern of all.

(4) This displacement of concern from self to patient, however, tends to cloud the real issue, and conceal areas of genuine disagreement. "The patient comes first" is a very general statement and "general statements, or ambiguous ones . . . lend themselves to the false security of apparent consensus," which may bring about a "sense of isolation, . . . general frustration and panic, . . ."[53] when its hollowness is suddenly recognized in practical and immediate action. When a nurse bursts out: "I don't know why we don't get mad around here," and "I'd like to have the doctors realize the nurse's point of view, they're so busy with their own point of view," she breaks through the superficial crust of pseudo-consensus.

(5) What is the effect of this pseudo-consensus on the patient? Does he benefit from the competitive efforts to serve his needs? To a great extent, no doubt, but since the consensus is partly apparent, *The Patient* may often turn out to be a disembodied abstraction, often invoked but less often actually perceived.

Eight physicians and ten nurses were asked:

> Suppose you were a hospital administrator with unlimited means, both financial and as far as personnel is concerned, and you were asked to build a ward. What would you do?[54]

Only two nurses and two physicians advocated changes in the ward specifically for the comfort of the patients. The other six doctors proposed changes for the benefit of the doctor; and the other eight nurses proposed changes that would facilitate the nurse's work. Among them, one doctor and three nurses did suggest changes that appeared to be patient-oriented but were actually conceived to facilitate their own work. One nurse said:

> I would have a larger bathroom, and I would not have more than four patients in a room.

She indicated why:

> One patient asks for pills, then the others will have it.

In like vein an interne said:

> I don't like the big ward. I would like to have bedrooms. During the night one patient wakes up and goes to the bathroom. Then someone complains of pains; others want medication; and then the interne is called.

The ideology of patient-orientation does not conceal the desire of physicians and nurses that the ward be designed to decrease their own work loads. Also, assessment of the needs of patients is necessarily colored by the nurse's task of maintaining order in the ward, or the interne's need to acquire the necessary knowledge for the exercise of his profession. The ideology is ill-equipped to deal with the extra demands of the situation that nurses and doctors have to face in their respective social positions.

The nurse must manage the ward in such a way as to avoid trouble and in so organizing a ward, she would minimize the possibility of unrest. Ease of handling receives major emphasis.

Yet, there is a risk that the nurse in pursuit of the objective of orderliness and quiet in the ward may overlook genuine needs of the patients. The individual patient who demands attention is a threat to the peace.

The house doctor, as a man in training, is often primarily interested in the patients as an educational experience.[55] One resident said:

> I would have Social Service play a much greater role than they're playing now. They would be able to screen a patient before he came in to find out whether he belonged on the ward.

He referred to the circumstance that many patients, upon learning that surgery will be required, sign out of the ward only to reappear a day later on one of the private floors with a private surgeon. "We resent this," another resident said, "because we miss part of our training."

The ideology of patient-orientation does not always succeed, then, in hiding the pedagogical and technical interests of internes, especially in a situation of overwork and tension. Young physicians do not like to treat routine or "simple" cases. "The more complicated case is more interesting for the doctor," said one interne, expressing a preference for just those patients who, because of their poor condition, may make more trouble for the nurse. Another said, in a tone of complaint:

> In the X Hospital they squeeze their cases for medical interest. This hospital feels their primary obligation is to treat anyone who is ill and many who aren't.

Some physicians stated frankly that the ideology of patient-orientation interferes with the aim of learning. "They cater too much to the patients around here," one of them said.

> We have to get our work done and we have to be nice to people. It creates a problem. They want attention, but we are interested in medicine. . . . If you want to be a doctor you have to learn.

In the concrete reality of the job, the pseudo-consensus tends to break down. The patient tends to appear to the nurse as an object "to be disciplined" and to the interne as an anonymous "case"—either interesting or time-serving.[56]

Concern for the *Patient* is as important a prerequisite for membership on the Mount Hermon staff as allegiance to *The American Way of Life* is for citizenship. The Patient, with a capital "P", may be an effective symbol, like the common man, the worker, the whole child. But the individual patient tends to remain, in practice, an object or a "case." He is then seen not as the living human being who struggles, in his physical powerlessness, with the problem of his identity and autonomy; but as something to be "managed," like a thing. As one interne said ingenuously, "The problems that [doctors and nurses] work in are the same: total management of people."

All the integrating mechanisms that we have described—exchange, complaint, and a common ideology—help to provide relief from specific tension-ridden situations. They do not, however, provide correctives for the basic status contradictions that are so dramatically evident in the nurse-interne relationship.

NOTES

1. For an analysis of humor in hierarchically structured groups, see Rose Laub Coser, "Laughter Among Colleagues," *Psychiatry*, XXIII (Feb. 1960), 81-95.

2. The care of the patients is not *formally* delegated to the internes, i.e., the resident's name, not the interne's, appears on the patient's record. Failure to put on formal record the responsibility of the interne for the patient may create some uncertainty in the minds of the doctors as to *"whose* patient" the patient actually is, and may contribute to the situation discussed in a later chapter, that patients don't know who *their* doctors are.

3. Stanton and Schwartz (*The Mental Hospital, op. cit.,* pp. 195-197), describe consensus as the result of the most successful type of communication, in which the participants feel that the decision is completely unforced, in which there is no element of submissiveness, or defeat in argument; if there is any specific awareness at all it is one of discovery, of clarity, or of understanding.

4. An *arbitrary* decision, according to Stanton and Schwartz, *ibid.,* is one made by a person higher in the power hierarchy governing a person lower in it, without regard to the agreement of the latter.

5. For a more detailed analysis of the structure of the medical and the surgical ward, and their differential impact on personnel and patients, see Chapter IX. See also Rose Laub Coser, "Authority and Decision-Making in a Hospital: A Comparative Analysis," *op. cit.*

6. Visiting doctors also often hold the title of Professor at Holyoke Medical School.

7. The visiting doctor has more authority on the surgical than on the medical ward, for in surgery he is not only the teacher and consultant but is actually responsible for the operation which he performs or supervises. See Chapter IX.

8. Lyman Bryson, "Notes on a Theory of Advice," in R. K. Merton *et al.,* (eds.), *Reader in Bureaucracy,* Glencoe, Ill.: The Free Press, 1952, p. 203.

9. Cf. Oswald Hall, "Some Problems in the Provision of Medical Services," *op. cit.*

10. Medical students are not part of the house staff, although they are dressed in white and wear a name plaque preceded by the title "Dr." so that they can examine patients. They may be asked by internes to do a certain amount of work, but they are not assigned to the house staff all day long. They find themselves in a teaching situation, and whatever work they do is considered part of the learning process only. They are not expected to give any services to the hospital.

11. Conditions at time of research; they may well have changed since.

12. Although the residents have a heavy schedule also and are also on call several nights a week, they have a somewhat easier life. Often they live outside the hospital. If there is an emergency during the night, the interne will be called first and the assistant resident will be called only if needed in addition. Moreover, the assistant resident has a little more time to himself during the day, since he does not have to write out orders, prepare tests, or write long patients' histories, reports of physical examinations, and discharge summaries.

13. Cf. especially, Melville Dalton, "Conflicts Between Staff and Line Managerial Officers," *American Sociological Review,* XV (June 1950), 342-351.

14. This often constitutes a mechanism of *coöptation,* by which a representative of a group within the organization is taken into the administrative leadership; however, the "represented" group does not necessarily gain any

power because the coöpted member has to accept his role as a member of the administration. On the mechanism of coöptation, see Philip Selznik, *TVA and the Grass Roots,* Berkeley: University of California Press, 1949, *passim.*

15. Oswald Hall, "Some Problems in the Provision of Medical Services," *op. cit.,* p. 459.

16. The following typology owes much to Everett C. Hughes, "Dilemmas and Contradictions of Status," *Men and Their Work, op. cit.,* pp. 102-115, and to Chester I. Barnard, "Functions and Pathology of Status Systems in Formal Organizations," in William F. Whyte, (ed.), *Industry and Society,* New York: McGraw-Hill Book Co., 1946, pp. 207-243. Barnard distinguishes between "functional" and "scalar" systems of status. This typology cannot be applied here because we deal with two different lines of authority, that of nurses and that of doctors, existing side by side. Although both these systems are "functional," according to Barnard's definition, some problems arise that are similar to the contradictions between functional and scalar status that Barnard points out, because the persons in those positions are interacting with each other—across the lines that separate the hierarchies—in a superior-subordinate relationship.

17. Robert K. Merton and Alice S. Kitt have shown that people tend to behave not merely in terms of the group to which they belong but also in reference to the group to which they aspire. Not only membership groups but *reference groups* must be considered in the analysis of attitudes and interaction patterns. See "Contributions to the Theory of Reference Group Behavior," in R. K. Merton and P. F. Lazarsfeld, (eds.), *Continuities in Social Research,* Glencoe, Ill.: The Free Press, 1950, pp. 40-105.

18. The chief-of-service does not take part in activities on the floor except when he takes his turn with visiting doctors to go on rounds, counseling and advising the house officers. In this case he tends to play the role of a visiting doctor.

19. Training and experience are not the only factors that help to legitimize authority, and that can therefore be a source of contradiction of status. Chronological age or seniority can also furnish a basis for legitimation of authority. But in these respects also, the nurse, who is usually older than the interne and has been in the hospital for a longer time, feels that she deserves more prestige although she is expected to submit to the interne's orders.

20. "The Social Structure of the Organization: The Restaurant," *American Journal of Sociology,* LVI (Jan. 1949), 302-308.

21. Cf. George Homans, *The Human Group,* New York: Harcourt, Brace & Co., 1950, pp. 113 ff.

22. Lewis A. Coser, *The Functions of Social Conflict,* Glencoe, Ill.: The Free Press, 1956, esp. pp. 60-65.

23. Whyte, "The Social Structure of the Restaurant," p. 65. In a later chapter, I will deal with some differences in the nurse-interne relationship on the medical and the surgical wards. The fact that there is more oral communication of orders to the nurse on the surgical ward may be taken as an indication that the order book as a means to minimize frequency of interaction is less needed there.

24. For a theoretical elaboration of physical closeness in social relation-

ships, see Rose Laub Coser, "Insulation from Observability and Types of Social Conformity," *American Sociological Review,* XXVI (Feb. 1961), 29-39.

25. The "not quite" aspect of the nurses' role was pointed out to me by Hans Mauksch in a personal communication.

26. The social significance of space remains a problem in need of investigation. It has so far been considered primarily by the ecologists on the community level, but has not often been explored in other fields of sociology. William C. Loring, Jr. makes a contribution to this problem in "Housing Characteristics and Social Disorganization," *Social Problems,* III (Jan. 1956), 160-168.

27. Difficulties created by job overlap in hospitals are discussed by A. T. M. Wilson, *Notes on a Background Survey and Job Analysis,* London: The Tavistock Institute of Human Relations, Tavistock Publications Ltd., (n.d.), p. 4.

See also Rhoda Lois Goldstein, *The Professional Nurse in the Hospital Bureaucracy,* unpublished dissertation, University of Chicago, 1954, esp. pp. 45 ff. and 78 ff.

28. *Op. cit.*

29. "Some persons felt that [the temporary relationship between most doctors and the hospital] prevented the doctors from making a full emotional investment in the hospital job. Others felt that it kept the medical staff young and hopeful and thereby maintained their stamina against the resignation which prolonged contact . . . was likely to bring about. Probably both of these evaluations are correct." Otto Pollak, "Brief Communications: Staff Discomforts and the Social Organization of a Mental Hospital," *Psychiatry,* XIX (Aug. 1956), 309-314.

30. Cf. Georg Simmel, "The Stranger," in Kurt H. Wolff (trans.), *The Sociology of Georg Simmel,* Glencoe, Ill.: The Free Press, 1950, pp. 402-407.

31. For verbatim quotations of current stereotypes, see Leo Lowenthal, *Image of Prejudice,* unpublished monograph, New York, 1945.

32. On "dirty work," cf. Hughes, *Men and Their Work, op. cit.,* pp. 51 ff.

33. See Gerth and Mills, (eds.), *From Max Weber, op. cit.,* pp. 79 ff. and 196 ff.

34. *Joy in Work,* London: George Allen & Unwin, Ltd., 1929, p. 201.

35. Cf. Lewis A. Coser, *The Functions of Social Conflict, op. cit.,* pp. 39 ff.

36. See Chapter V for discussion of the nurse's self-image.

37. Hughes, *Men and Their Work, op. cit.,* pp. 51 ff.

38. *Ibid.*

39. Cf. "It happens over and over that the people who practice an occupation attempt to revise the conceptions which their various publics have of the occupation and of the people in it. In so doing, they attempt to revise their own conception of themselves and of their work." *Ibid.,* p. 315.

40. The following generalizations about nurse-doctor relationships are subject to considerable qualification, depending upon ward structure. See Chapter IX.

41. *Men and Their Work, op. cit.,* p. 316.

42. Cf. Melville Dalton, *Men Who Manage, op. cit.* It has to be understood, however, that such devices, while strengthening consensus and a spirit

of exchange, cannot come into being without there existing some basic understanding between the parties. We will see in a later chapter that banter between nurses and doctors is more prevalent on a ward where the nurse has more prestige and more autonomy, a position in which she is better able to use "equalizing" devices.

43. Cf. Marcel Mauss, *The Gift*, Glencoe, Ill.: The Free Press, 1955.

44. Claude Levi-Strauss, "The Principle of Reciprocity," in L. Coser and B. Rosenberg, (eds.), *Sociological Theory*, New York: The Macmillan Co., 1957, p. 90. See also, Alvin Gouldner, "The Norm of Reciprocity," *American Sociological Review*, XXV (April 1960), 161-178.

45. Frederick Elkin, "The Soldier's Language," *American Journal of Sociology*, LI (March 1946), 414-422.

46. On the ward, I learned that complaining both presupposes "rapport" and strengthens it. When nurses and internes began to express their grievances to me, I knew that the "ice was broken" and that I was being accepted.

47. Claude Levi-Strauss, *op. cit.*, describes this process in the meeting of two strangers in a French restaurant: "The [exchange of wine] is an affirmation of good grace which dispels the reciprocal uncertainty; it substitutes a social bond for mere physical juxtaposition. But it is also more than that: the partner who had the right to maintain reserve is called upon to give it up; wine offered calls for wine returned, cordiality demands cordiality. . . . There is no possibility of refusing the neighbor's offer of his glass of wine without appearing insulting. Moreover, the acceptance of the offer authorizes another offer, that of conversation."

48. Cf. Wessen, *op. cit.*

49. Conversations like the following can be overheard at the lunch table: Interne: "She [i.e., the head nurse] is the bain of my life. Every night in bed I devote thirty minutes to thinking about what I can do to take revenge." Other interne: "One thing you can do to her is embarrass her in front of a student nurse. That'll shut her up for the rest of the day."

50. *The Mental Hospital, op. cit.*, p. 195.

51. Parsons, *The Social System, op. cit.*, p. 472.

52. Cf. Georg Simmel, *Conflict and the Web of Group Affiliations*, Glencoe, Ill.: The Free Press, 1955, p. 39.

53. Stanton and Schwartz, *The Mental Hospital, op. cit.*, p. 197.

54. One of the eleven interviewed nurses was not asked the question because the interview was interrupted (cf. Table 2, p. 72).

55. Oswald Hall, in "Some Problems in the Provision of Medical Services," *op. cit.*, points out that the hospital is for the physician both a place where he treats patients and a place where he receives training.

56. Karl Mannheim (*Ideology and Utopia*, New York: Harcourt, Brace & Co., 1936, p. 175), points out that ideologies become distorted in content when embodied in practice, and tend to become very general and abstract as a common basis of legitimation.

CHAPTER III

First Admission to the Ward

U PON HIS ARRIVAL IN THE HOSPITAL AND AFTER HIS RELATIVES HAVE departed, the patient finds himself cut adrift in a strange new environment and faced with the problem of understanding himself and others in this unfamiliar context.

His general knowledge that he must "submit to competent persons around him because he lacks technical competence in dealing with illness"[1] does not forestall initial bewilderment. He finds that he is supposed to accept unquestioningly the procedures, routines and relationships of the hospital ward, but he is not apt to be in a frame of mind that would enable him to see clearly how the ward functions and to differentiate between the roles and attitudes of the many strangers whom he suddenly faces. He would be better able to play his "passive role," if he could maintain, or regain, an "active mind."

While the hospital is so organized as to encourage, demand, and institutionalize passivity in patients (a requirement reinforced by the cultural definitions in society at large), it makes almost no formal provision for encouraging the patient to maintain his self-image. Yet, a stable self-image is one of the prerequisites for his seeing and understanding ward relationships and ward functioning.

The patient who enters the hospital for the first time has much to learn. He must find out to whom he should address his questions. If he asks a nurse's aide or a student nurse, "When will the doctor come?" he will probably receive the answer: "He'll be here soon," a reply recognized by both nurse and patient as evasive, and the patient's anxiety will not be relieved. It might be relieved to some extent if the student nurse were instructed to say, "I have no say in the matter, but I am sure that the registered nurse, the one with a black band on her cap, has already notified the doctor, and I know that he always comes just as soon as he can." Such a candid explanation would help the patient to begin to put his confused thoughts in order.[2]

The patient must also learn which questions to ask and which questions not to ask. A patient who is very upset may ask many petty questions, unaware that these are only substitutes for an important question that he dares not or cannot articulate. His failure to ask for the right thing at the right time and place and his inability to suppress his anxieties tend to exasperate both nurses and doctors, who often say that "a patient shouldn't ask questions, everything is being done for him anyhow."

Similarly, the patient must learn to listen to questions and to understand them. There is a technical problem involved here: the patient must be ready to understand new terms. For example, if a nurse asks, "Did you pass water?" it will not do for the patient to say, pointing to his table, "No thank you, I still have some." Such misunderstandings are more frequent with patients who are first-generation immigrants, but they happen with other patients, too. Many of the expressions used in a hospital are alien even to American-born patients, yet hospital personnel tend to assume that everybody understands their professional abbreviations as b.m. for bowel movement or o.j. for orange juice.

Just as there are "ceremonial" and "factual" statements, so there are "ceremonial" and "factual" questions. If a registered nurse comes to a patient's bed and asks, "How are you this morning?" she does not expect the ceremonial reply, "Fine, thank you," or, alternately, "Not so good, what can you expect?"[3] She wants to know precisely how the patient has spent the night, or whether he was in pain, since she is trying to detect symptoms that she might then communicate to the physician. A nurse's aide, on the other hand, may ask exactly the same question but she is generally not interested in a detailed description of the symptoms, as she is not expected to take or initiate therapeutic action.[4]

To learn all this—what questions to ask, of whom to ask them, and to understand the meaning of questions addressed to him—the patient must understand the division of labor in the hospital. But this division of labor, as we have seen, is very complicated. Yet, the patient's own feeling of identity is related to the image he has of those around him,[5] and he can organize his own behavior in relation to them only if he knows who they are.[6]

The patient's sphere of action is also sharply circumscribed just at the time when his identity would seem to depend upon his being able to differentiate himself from others through personal choices and self-initiating behavior. Barker, Wright and Gonick[7] describe the reduced scope of the world of the sick person:

> [His] world becomes small. While formerly such determinants of behavior as appointments with friends, business engagements, and family responsibilities were tremendously important, they now become ineffective. . . . The things which influence the overt behavior of a person become limited to the requirements of a few people . . . and the demands of a few needs. . . .

The patient in the hospital cannot "branch out." He is restricted physically, as well as in his ability to make decisions, all of which limits his capacity to reorient himself.[8]

As long as the patient is at home, even if he is bedridden, he has some control over his surroundings.[9] He is kept posted by friends and relatives on the happenings of the day, and he tends to maintain some control over the family's daily schedule. He probably has his medication next to his bed and is himself responsible for taking it in the right order and at the right time.[10] As soon as he enters the hospital, however, he loses even this limited control over himself and over the people with whom he is accustomed to interact daily. Physical removal from his normal environment also means complete dissociation from his normal social role.

While such dissociation may impress upon the patient the emergency nature of his situation and his obligation to let others care for him, it also creates anxiety and the feeling, at least temporarily, that the world has lost the meaning it used to have.

During the process of admission to the ward the patient is being prepared for his new passive role by the attitudes of his own relatives and friends. Relatives or friends accompanying the sick person to the hospital, behave protectively as they would toward a child, and show an I-know-what's-good-for-you attitude that is seldom permissible among adults. When the wife accompanies her husband, she often assumes the role of mother toward him; and in the following scene a reversal of roles between parent and child is evident:

> An elderly lady [in street clothes] is sitting at a table in the waiting room, eating her lunch. A younger lady [her daughter] sits next to her in an easy chair. Mother hands a portion of melon to daughter.
> Daughter: "No, I won't eat it, you eat it."
> Mother: "Please dearie, I can't."
> Daughter: "Now you be a good girl and eat it. It's good for you."
> But the mother still refuses and so daughter shrugs and humors her by taking a bite or two. Nurse's aide appears.
> Daughter: "Go on, mother. You let the nurse take care of you. I'll wait here for you and see you later. You go now; I'll wait for you."

This reversal of roles is a further confirmation for the sick person that from now on he will be deprived of normal adult rights and obligations, and is being relegated to a child-like role.[11] This new dependent role involves a certain "loss of face." Upon entering the hospital the patient is forcibly reminded that he is not the person he used to be. He must now abandon a number of roles that he has more or less successfully played.

For any socialized actor—even for a passive-dependent personality —acceptance of this child-like status, with its attributes of inferior

41

status and its socio-emotional skewing, entails considerable adjustment.[12]

Any reassurances he receives, such as "everything will be fine," "don't worry, you'll be all right," are more than reassurances with regard to his physical condition; they also imply: "You will be the same person again; you will again be able to live up to your own expectations and those of others." Efforts at reassurance by relatives and friends, as well as the "bedside manner" of the doctor, help the patient to "save face."[13] As one patient said, "I believe a doctor should make the patient feel that he is himself."

The hospital patient also experiences some measure of abandonment. In his loneliness, he senses, often quite accurately, that his hospitalization is a relief for his relatives. The sickness of a person is a physical as well as a psychological burden for those around him. Taking a sick person to a hospital is for the relatives a dutiful way of discharging responsibilities.[14]

Some of the doctors at Mount Hermon occasionally recognized that the hospital served incidentally to relieve the family of responsibility. An interne, discussing an octogenarian patient with the Social Service reported:

> The daughter said, "Don't rush, keep her here as long as you have to." I think we should give that daughter a rest; she is caught with the responsibility.

Many patients, too, recognize this function of hospitalization and feel that their relatives are "relieved." In casual conversation on the ward as well as in the formal interview, patients often accounted for their hospitalization not so much in terms of medical needs as in terms of the relief to the family: "My daughter has her own kids to bother with" or "My wife has other things to do" or "My husband is sick himself."[15]

The patient at admission does not know what to expect. "Someone will be with you soon" or "Just relax, the doctor will come" is not a very precise reassurance to the person who wonders what they are going to do to his body. Some patients were able to articulate this feeling:

> I'm not afraid of being alone in the hospital; it's just the uncertainty.

> I was very apprehensive. I was frightened to death. I didn't know what to expect.

> [A good doctor is] a good speaker to you who explains you very good, explains everything what happens to you and what's going to happen. That's what I call a good doctor.

Not knowing what to expect, the patient fears the worst. And the process of hospitalization during the first hours after his arrival lends to such fears the support of reality. The series of procedures that follow immediately after admission are perceived by the patient as an attack on his body.

As a first step, he is deprived of body symbols. Although he may have been ambulatory at home awaiting admission to the hospital, he now has to surrender his clothes and his jewelry, and he may be given a hospital gown.

Depriving the patient of all his body symbols is a way of stripping status and self-assurance from him. It brings about assymmetry in his relationship with doctors and nurses, too. Nurses in their starched uniforms and wearing the insignia of their profession, doctors in white suits or coats, bearing the prominent stethoscope (and sometimes a little hammer, a flashlight, and other instruments as well),[16] are dressed for the occasion.

The contrast between the staff's display of body symbols and the patient's lack of them may be very humiliating for the patient. He may feel exposed and vulnerable. Everybody who is dressed in white may seem to have a right to manipulate his body, over which he himself has but little control. As one patient said, "You know they're going to poke and hurt you and no feelin' for you, nothin'."

But the patient soon undergoes an even more direct attack on his body. The nurse will place a thermometer in his mouth or rectum;[17] and he will be interviewed and examined physically by three doctors in turn—a student, an interne and a resident. He is told that he must use a bedpan until further notice; and frequently an enema is recommended. Blood is drawn from him at the first physical examination, a procedure which brings many protests and anxious comments: "They're taking an awful lot of blood from me, they're putting it in the blood bank" or "how much blood do they want?"

Loss of face, abandonment and physical pain often merge into diffuse anxiety.[18] "If nobody wants you, you have to worry," Mrs. Jones said, in response to my inquiries. Then she turned to her neighbor and said, "When you get old, you have no place to go." She started to cry. Another patient, suffering from ulcerative colitis, said: "It's the bleeding inside. That's the trouble." But then he pointed to flowers on his bedside table and said, "Maybe some people like me." The sense of abandonment is very real in the ward.

The patient's fears are grounded in real experience. He is alone among strangers; he is going to be physically hurt during examinations and tests and sometimes through an operation. If he is in the hospital for diagnostic examination, he may hear the frightening news that he has a terminal illness, or one presently incurable.

For the patient who doesn't know "what's wrong," the repeated examinations at admission are further source of apprehension. Not knowing that thoroughness in diagnostic work is part of the teaching program (and

43

therefore a reason for the high quality of medicine in hospitals associated with medical schools); not knowing that a resident must check an interne's work for accuracy; the patient may interpret such repeated examinations as a sign of the seriousness of his condition. Apart from tiring him out physically, they increase his anxiety. One resident clearly recognized this: "We really give them the works when they come here, we don't leave them alone a minute. And we can't tell them what they want to hear. We can't just say there's nothing much wrong. So when I have to go in for the third examination, I just check up on a few things and leave him alone. I figure if two men have fussed with him, that's enough. Or else I'll go in while one of the other boys is still busy, so I don't have to come back again." This resident dealt in an informal way with a problem that is not given formal consideration.

Leaving the patient in confusion about certain procedures may sometimes help to prevent an increase in anxiety (as when the patient is not told that repeated X-rays are necessary in view of the strong probability of cancer); but it may also intensify anxiety, as when the patient is led to fear that "something must be very wrong if so many doctors have to examine me."

Restriction of Communication

When the patient is admitted to the ward (especially if this is his first admission) his physical condition, his new (passive) social role, and the hospital admission procedures all tend to discourage him from "organizing himself." He finds it difficult to detach himself from his own feelings in order to recognize reality around him. But even if a patient were willing and able to acquire the necessary knowledge about ward life, how much of that knowledge would be actually available to him? Not very much. At Mount Hermon the social structure of the ward makes it difficult for patients to make the necessary distinctions among medical personnel and to understand the rationale for a number of hospital procedures.

At admission, the patient does not know that the first "doctor" who examined him was a student, the second an interne, and the third a resident. They are all "men in white." This blurring of the hospital hierarchy is deliberate hospital policy: every house doctor and every medical student wears a name plaque on which his name is preceded by the title "Dr." "Otherwise the patients would not let the students examine them," explains an administrator.

If the purpose of concealing role differentiation among doctors is to further the aim of the teaching hospital, the procedure may very well boomerang. The identity of the medical students may be concealed, but not their existence. Patients find out sooner or later that "the boys are here to learn;" and being unable to distinguish them, they often refuse to

44

be examined by any doctor. Many refuse to answer questions, refuse to have blood samples taken, see every procedure as experimental rather than therapeutic. A student reported:

> Did she hate to be examined. I gave her a physical and later when the interne and the resident came around she said I was her doctor and one examination is enough and she doesn't want students to experiment with her.

So by attempting to camouflage student activity in the ward, the hospital makes such activity appear "illegitimate," which only stiffens patients' resistance and seems to justify it.

Concealment of rank differences in the medical staff appears to have another function. It teaches students to act like doctors. In addition, by making students the "equals" of doctors in the eyes of patients, the medical group appears as a united team; this strengthens the solidarity within the professional group and fosters the development of the appropriate "professional" values among the students.[19] The newly admitted patient cannot penetrate this phalanx of professional solidarity, however.[20]

A Short-Circuit in Communication

A prerequisite for effective communication is that those who converse are aware of each other's assumptions and intentions so that they mutually can orient the content of their speech. Each must "put himself in the place of the other" in his imagination, while maintaining his own identity, and anticipate in a general way the other person's reaction. The expectation of the other person's response determines the content and manner of his communication. When, in Mead's terms, one person is not "ready to take the attitude of everyone else involved,"[21] communication breaks down.

In the medical interview, the doctor's role is "functionally specific," that is, he considers the interview instrumental. He is trying to obtain information concerning the patient's medical history and his symptoms past and present. The patient, on the other hand, sees the interview as an occasion for expressing himself: conversation with the doctor often seems to be an end in itself. Thus, patient and doctor lack consensus concerning the meaning of the relationship. The following partial transcript of an admission interview will illustrate the perils of communication where such consensus is lacking:

> When did you first notice this pain?

> When my sister died, six months ago. I'm that kind of person. I never say nothing if I don't like something. I got a son-in-law. He is a doctor and he said I should see a specialist. The specialist found nothing.

Doctor interrupting impatiently:

> When do you have pain?
> It's all here [pointing to stomach, chest, up to throat].
> How long after you eat does the pain start?
> When I eat, like just now [points to her supper plate]. I eat a little piece of toast, a little butter with it, not much butter. Sometimes I take an egg; I don't eat much. . . .

Doctor interrupts:

> Can you remember being sick when you were a child?
> My mother had eight children [leans out of bed and takes her wallet out of dresser and shows her own childhood pictures]. I had nine children myself [takes another picture showing a man in uniform out of her wallet]. That's my baby.

Doctor gets up and says: I'll be back a little later, and walks out.

This patient's behavior would be appropriate for an interview with a psychiatrist[22] since the patient's expressive action conveys information that the psychiatrist seeks, but in the medical interview the physician's goal (a concise medical history) can only be hampered by the patient's expressive behavior.[23]

In this interview, which is fairly typical of admission interviews, the patient failed to organize her responses to meet the expectations of the physician. However, the physician also often fails the patient. By failing to respond to any of the patient's advances, he passes up the opportunity to act as an agent of socialization, with the following attributes:

To the extent that the sick person is temporarily exempted from normal social role obligations,[24] the physician must make an effort to communicate with the sick person on the latter's terms in order to induce him to make an effort to meet the doctor on *his* terms. The physician, too, must "put himself in his imagination in the place of the other." By showing permissiveness toward the patient's expressive behavior, he may be able to motivate him to accept the doctor's definition of the relationship.[25]

The doctors on the ward do not, generally, see themselves as socializing agents. They tend to see medical attention and personal attention as incompatible. As one resident said, "The patients want attention, but *we* are interested in medicine." This limited perception of his role does not reflect personal unwillingness but tends to be the typical view in a ward where young doctors *have* to work and learn under continuous pressure of time. Given the pressure of time and hard work on the ward, the two aspects of the house doctor's role—that of student of medicine and that of socializing agent—are probably to some extent genuinely incompatible.

Therefore, physicians, even when they do perceive the twosidedness of their role, find it difficult to live up to both sides. An interne defined a good doctor as:

> First of all, capable of caring for his patients. Essentially he must have empathy with them and provide for many comforts which are not always related to his disease. This means a warm relationship with the patient and a closeness with the patient that you don't see on the ward.

But when the same interne was asked to define a good patient, he said:

> A patient must not take the doctor's time. . . . He should not ask the doctor for things that are the nurses' field, they should be brief and to the point instead of taking a lot of time.

I frequently observed at the admission interviews that the patient resisted most strongly; giving necessary information just when the doctor pressed for it most insistently. It was not always clear whether such resistance reflected fear or embarrassment or hostility. Probably all three elements were present. The following is a verbatim transcript of portions of an interview conducted by a visiting doctor the morning after the patient's admission to the ward.

> Doctor: How much meat do you eat?
> *Too much.*
> What is much?
> *Twice a week.*
> How much do you eat when you eat it?
> *Not much.*
> What do you call "not much"?
> *[Shrugs shoulders].*
> What is the relation of the size of the piece of meat to a package of cigarettes?
> Patient doesn't answer, but the expression on her face shows that she doesn't understand.
> Doctor repeats the same question a little louder.
> Patient: *A chop.*[26]
> A few minutes later:
> Doctor: Would you say you're constipated?
> *Not generally.*

(But subsequent answers seem to indicate the possibility that the patient does suffer from constipation.)

Attitude of patient:

> Patient looks surly, but after each answer she smiles with an expression of irony which seems to hide uneasiness. She seems to be saying, "what a bore" and "all these silly questions," but generally

her facial expression is tight and tense and seems to betray an effort to hide her feelings.

Tension was reinforced by the length of the interview. I was present for forty-five minutes, but the interview had begun before I arrived and had not concluded when I left. The interview took place during doctors' rounds, which meant that about ten people were standing around the patient.

One thing stands out clearly: the physician made no attempt to establish reciprocity with the patient, and the patient did not intend to inform the doctor. She "obeyed." She offered "answers." But most of them were not very useful or informative. In this interview there is no mutual respect between doctor and patient. Constraint is met with egocentric behavior.[27]

The six interviews at admission that I witnessed had all to be interrupted at some point because communication broke down.[28] The doctor would leave the patient with the words, "I'll be back a little later," go out to the back steps, and comment to me and to his colleagues (if there were any around) about the difficulty in getting the needed information—a comment usually accompanied by joking or hostile remarks. The physicians suggested that the interruption of the interview might "give him [i.e., the patient] a chance to pull himself together." But they, perhaps as much as the patient who remained alone, seemed to need this occasion to recuperate from the interview and to shake off a feeling of impotence by joking and complaining with a sympathetic listener.

The most frequent complaint voiced by the house doctor on the ward was that he could not get a "decent history" from the patient. When asked to define a "good patient," a resident said that "every doctor likes a patient who gives a nice history." Another young physician said that he expected in the patient "the intangible quality of being able to give a good history." One interne said that a good patient is "one who can give a reasonably good history of his illness, a description of what's wrong with him, eliminating things that are minor. Usually they insist on going into detail on some minor point." He realized, though, that the interview has a different meaning for the patient, for he added: "They feel they have to catch hold of something."

Although usually the staff succeeded in piecing the information together (if need be the visiting doctor may assist during his daily round), much time was wasted in the attempt. Sometimes the information obtained is inaccurate. Barker, Wright and Gonick maintain that a patient "is certain to give a more or less false report of his present and past symptoms."[29] Or information is often incomplete and must be supplemented by tests and repeated examinations. All this is the "cost" of lack of communication.

A patient who engages in expressive behavior with a physician, or who withholds information, is easily suspected of being, in the vernacular of the ward, "a crock"—i.e., a malingerer who is using hospital facilities illegitimately. Even the best intentioned doctor is inclined to concentrate his efforts upon the medically "interesting" patients, because doctors are "here to learn," and because time is limited.

"If the patient is elderly and has no outstanding characteristics, he gets routine care," said one interne. "He is taken care of, but no relationship takes place. . . . There is no rapport with the doctor." He mentioned three patients who were consistently overlooked and explained: "Nobody likes a complainer, a whiner." This may very well mean that a patient who most needs the doctor's attention and support is neglected in favor of a patient who is better able to meet the physician on his terms.

One patient seemed to believe that rapport was the secret essential ingredient in the establishment of a successful diagnosis:

> Dr. D. made a deep impression on me. He is a young fellow but smart, he's a gentleman, nice bedside manner. He took very deep interest. In March they made the same tests and examinations but there were different doctors. Now in three days they found out what I have.

This view of the relation between diagnostic success and bedside manner is certainly naive, especially since every case is discussed by the entire staff (including at least one visiting doctor), with final responsibility resting with the chief resident. Yet the patient is right to this extent: if rapport is good the physician gets information more quickly and is encouraged to push on in his endeavors because he feels that he can "get hold of something." Insofar as bedside manner helps the patient to regain self-confidence, it helps him to meet the doctor actively on the doctor's terms and to begin to treat the relationship as an instrumental rather than a primary one.

In one rather extreme instance no effective communication was ever established between the patient and members of the hospital staff. The failure was triggered by an unfortunate mishap, but no social repair was ever achieved: because of a confusion of identity between two patients bearing the same name, a patient from the medical ward was called out of the television room, (which was common to both the medical and the surgical wards) for examination by the surgical interne, an experience she found very upsetting. The mere fact of being taken to the surgical ward made her fear an operation which she had in no way expected.[30] Moreover, the physical examination on the surgical ward is more unpleasant, involving a pelvic or rectal examination. Patients who had witnessed the incident reported that the victim of this mixup had been "red as a beet."

After she returned to the medical ward, where she had to submit to medical interviews and examinations, she was so uncooperative that the physicians felt she was being hostile. Apparently not understanding the reasons for her hostility, they called a psychiatrist.[31] In the subsequent psychiatric interview (at which I was present), the patient refused to speak English. (The house doctor also reported that she refused to speak English "although she knew English very well.") Even when a Yiddish-speaking psychiatrist was called in and the patient was given an opportunity to speak in her own language, she made no mention of the episode of mistaken identity. Two days later she was discharged. No organic cause of her physical discomfort had been found.

We are in no position to judge to what extent, if any, the failure to establish a diagnosis in this case was related to the lack of communication between physicians and patient. The discharge of a patient was always decided upon with utmost care and after thorough deliberation. Nevertheless, even if there is only a slight possibility of structural factors interfering with diagnostic procedures, a thorough study of the relation between ward structure and medical achievement would seem to be warranted.

* * *

In spite of all these problems of communication, most patients eventually relate to physicians in a sufficiently satisfactory way for the doctors to perform their tasks adequately. Mount Hermon has an excellent reputation, and deservedly so. We must therefore ask: By what mechanisms are patients adapted to the ward? In what ways are the difficulties of the first days of patienthood overcome?

NOTES

1. Cf. Parsons, *The Social System, op. cit.,* pp. 439-446.
2. The fact that laymen cannot distinguish the various status positions of nurses seems to be frustrating for the latter also. *The Modern Hospital* for November 1956 (Vol. 87) prints the following letter in its column "Small Hospital Questions": "We now have working on our floors some trained practical nurses, some nurse's aides, and some attendants who perform only minor nursing duties. They all have distinctive uniforms and are divided according to function. Some of our people are disturbed because patients' visitors and others think of them all as simply 'nurses.' Even some of our doctors are uncertain, sometimes, about some of the distinctions. Is there any way we can positively distinguish the 'nurses' from the 'helpers' so that this confusion will not exist? [signed G.E.T., Colo.]" (p. 47). Since people depend for the maintenance of their self-image to a large extent upon the way they think others see them, nurses might gain considerable security by having patients know them the way they want to be known. This may well be a positive factor in the nurse-patient relationship.

3. The stereotyped answers to ceremonial greetings differ according to cultures, and symbolize patterned relationships in these cultures. Eastern European Jewish patients, especially first-generation immigrants, usually answered, "I haven't slept all night, I never sleep," or "Don't ask," while acculturated Jews or non-Jewish patients more frequently said, "I'm fine." Generally, it is considered bad-mannered among Eastern European Jews to say "I'm fine," since this sounds like bragging; the complaining answer is considered a sign of modesty. But even more important is the relationship which the answer symbolizes: it invites sympathy and further questioning, thereby intensifying the relationship. In American culture, on the other hand, both pessimism and personal involvement are fended off. The answer "I'm fine" does not call for comment, and therefore limits the relationship to its segmental aspect. As Erving Goffman has remarked, "Greetings . . . serve to clarify and fix the roles that the participants will take during the occasion of talk and to commit participants to these roles." ("On Face-Work," *Psychiatry,* XVIII (Aug. 1955), 213-231.)

That ceremonial greetings reveal something about the cultural meaning of the relationship has been noted by Daniel Lerner, who quotes Frenchmen as replying to the question, "Comment ça va?" with "On se défend." ("Interviewing Frenchmen," *American Journal of Sociology,* LXII (Sept. 1956), 187-194.)

4. Indeed, questions often derive their meaning from the role of the person who addresses them. This may lead to misinterpretations if a person has an ambiguous or dual role. For example, when a visiting doctor asks an interne, "What do you think of this patient's condition?" the interne thinks his competence is being tested, while the senior may actually want to know his opinion.

5. Some hospitals make a special effort to remedy a patient's lack of orientation on admission. We are told that in the Middlesex Hospital in London, for instance, "the patient is given a booklet which tells him of all the arrangements made for him by the hospital and includes such useful hints as how to disintinguish staff and students by their coats and overalls." Wendy Hall, "This Is the Way Patients Should Be Treated," *The Modern Hospital,* 86 (Feb. 1956), 56-58.

6. "The attitudes of the other players which the participant assumes organize into a sort of unit, and it is that organization which controls the response of the individual." George Herbert Mead, *Mind, Self and Society, op. cit.,* p. 134.

7. *Op. cit.,* p. 240.

8. Cf. Renée Fox, *Experiment Perilous, op. cit.,* pp. 118 ff.

9. On the difference between the patient at home and the patient in the hospital, and on the problems facing the patient after admission, see Leo W. Simmons and Harold G. Wolff, *Social Science and Medicine,* New York: Russell Sage Foundation, 1954, esp. pp. 176-187.

10. Cf. ". . . Suppose you are sick and go to the hospital. You are moved out of *your* home and *your* bed into *their* hospital and one of *their* beds. You are stripped of accoutrements—familiar bottles on the bedside table—those things which gave you a sense of self-sufficiency. All of your symbols of power are gone." Thomas R. Ford and Diane D. Stephenson, *Institutional Nurses:*

Roles, Relationships, and Attitudes in Three Alabama Hospitals, Tuscaloosa: University of Alabama Press, 1954, p. 21. (Emphasis in the original.)

11. Parsons and Fox, "Illness, Therapy and the Modern Urban Family," *op. cit.* These role expectations should be distinguished from the psychological phenomenon of regression which is also present. Many writers have analyzed the mechanism of regression in illness (see Barker, Wright and Gonick, *op. cit.*).

12. Parsons and Fox, "Illness, Therapy and the Modern Urban Family," *op. cit.,* p. 38. (Emphasis in the original.)

13. On the maintenance of "face" as a condition of interaction, see Erving Goffman, "On Face-Work," *op. cit.*

14. Cf. "The observer can, indeed, often sense a feeling of great relief on the part of the relatives that at last the patient is over the threshold and 'from here on the nurses and medics are responsible.' " (Leo Simmons and Harold G. Wolff, *op. cit.,* p. 178.)

15. The following jocular exchange was overheard while a discharged patient and her husband were waiting for the elevator. Another patient to the husband: "So, you're taking her home, mazel-tov." He: "What's so good about taking her home? She lies down and wants this and that and I have to run around and do the work." He smiled as he spoke and his tone was light, but such bluntness is certainly exceptional. In this permissible jocular form, the husband expressed feelings that others hide from the environment or from themselves.

16. The medical students (and there are between three and six of them on the ward), especially during the first days after their arrival, often are not content with a stethoscope but display their other instruments elaborately.

Maxwell Jones in *The Therapeutic Community, op. cit.,* p. 40, describes the doctors in the following terms: "We do not dress to conform to the usual concept of the professional man. We have all avoided the white coat, prominent stethoscope, and aggressive percussion hammer as extensions of our body image. . . ." Although this is a mental hospital, we have observed in another general hospital, located in the same geographical area as Mount Hermon, that house doctors came to patients' beds in street clothes, with at most a little tool bag in their hands. In the same hospital also, one nurse's aide was dressed in street clothes, bringing in the food and acting as "hostess" for the patients.

17. "When the Smile with the starched uniform pops the capsule into your mouth, you begin to think that something really serious is about to take place. You realize that members of the hospital staff now rule your life. . . ." (Ford and Stephenson, *op. cit.,* p. 22.)

18. In a study of severely burned patients, David A. Hamburg, Beatrix Hamburg and Sydney deGoza found that "patients interpreted their injuries as a threat to the capacity to be loved by others." ("Adaptive Problems and Mechanisms in Severely Burned Patients," *op. cit.*)

19. Cf. Mary Jean Huntington, "The Development of a Professional Self-Image," in *The Student Physician, op. cit.,* pp. 179-187.

20. Cf. "The professional etiquette is a body of ritual which grows up informally to preserve, before the clients, the common front of the profession." (Everett C. Hughes, "Institutions," in Alfred McClung Lee, (ed.), *New Out-*

line of the Principles of Sociology, New York: Barnes and Noble, 1946, p. 273.)

21. *Mind, Self and Society, op. cit.*, p. 151.

22. The stage setting of the medical interview at admission bears in one respect some resemblance to the setting of the psychoanalytic session. The patient is lying down, the doctor sits beside him and is a stranger. This physical arrangement provides additional encouragement for the patient to shut out reality. It is an arrangement which the psychoanalyst finds most useful for obtaining free associations and repressed material from the patient. As Lawrence S. Kubie has said, "The purpose of [the couch] is primarily to facilitate the production of free associations." (*Practical and Theoretical Aspects of Psychoanalysis*, New York: International Universities Press, 1950, p. 50.)

Some of the questions that the doctor asks easily revive in the patient memories of traumatic events and crucial relationships and further reinforce the temptation to take the interview as an occasion for expressive communication. One patient, asked about the cause of her father's death, said: "I rubbed his stomach. For six months, every day, I rubbed his stomach. I felt it grow under my hand [makes a movement with her hand on her own stomach to illustrate]. He died in my arms." She then broke out in tears and the interview had to be interrupted. The revival of such memories also helps to detract the patient's attention from the purpose of the interview.

23. Parsons mentions in another context that cases "may arise where primary interest is expressive on one side and instrumental on the other." He gives the relationship between performer and audience as an example. There is, however, a difference between these cases and the complications arising in the medical interview. In Parsons' example, as well as in the psychiatrist-patient relationship, there is complementarity of expectations despite a divergence in motives, but in the special physician-patient relationship discussed here such complementarity is lacking. (Parsons, *The Social System, op. cit.*, p. 84.)

24. *Ibid.*, pp. 433 ff.

25. The last paragraph paraphrases the analysis of the role of the socializing agent in Talcott Parsons and Robert F. Bales, *Family, Socialization and Interaction Process*, Glencoe, Ill.: The Free Press, 1955, pp. 58-59.

26. Though patient speaks English fluently, the physician's vocabulary and his pace of speech seem unfamiliar to her. Doctor's attempt to use a "familiar" illustration ("What is the relation of the size of the piece of meat to a package of cigarettes?") further widens the gulf since cigarettes are probably not so familiar to this 73-year-old lady as to the doctor.

27. Cf. Jean Piaget, *The Moral Judgment of the Child*, Glencoe, Ill.: The Free Press, 1948, *passim*.

28. It would be interesting to test Weber's contention that no relationship can exist where the meaning is not shared by the participants. Research on this problem could be designed to find out at what point in the interaction reciprocity and communication break down to the extent of severing the relationship. This could be done by observing for a certain period all admission interviews and examinations and noting how frequently and at what occasions physician and patient have to part.

29. *Op. cit.*, p. 230.

30. In other cases, too, it was evident that the surgical ward represented a threat. Medical patients were often "boarded out" to the surgical ward in cases of overpopulation in the medical ward, since the surgical ward was less crowded. Patients who were not informed of the reason for their transfer, told me of their anxiety.

31. Burling, Lentz and Wilson, *op. cit.*, p. 131, have remarked that some people feel that psychiatry is used as a "grab-bag" to which patients are referred when the physician can think of no solution. More specifically, I found that psychiatrists were called in most cases when communication broke down. Moreover, patients with "uninteresting" (or low-prestige) diseases were sometimes accused of belonging to a mental hospital rather than to this one. This indicates that psychiatry is sometimes assigned cases that seem unworthy of medical attention.

PART II

THE SOCIALIZATION OF
PATIENTS

"Going downhill involves no sustained mus-
cular effort, only an agreeable process of
putting on the brakes in order not to finish
by running and tripping head over heels;
it is really nothing more than just letting
yourself go; and thus the gait of these
people had something loose-jointed and
flighty about it, which communicated itself to the appearance of the whole group
and made one almost wish to be of their
lively party."
Thomas Mann, *The Magic Mountain*

CHAPTER IV

Father and Student

T HE WHOLE DUTY OF THE PHYSICIAN, SAYS SIGERIST, IS NOT DISCHARGED by "restoring the patient anatomically. . . . His problem is not solved until he has dislodged the patient from his isolated position in society and reinstated him as a useful member of his own community."[1] In this way the physician is an "agent of socialization." In treating the patient, he acts as a representative of both the small society of the hospital and the large society to which the sick person must be restored. While treating physical symptoms he must assist the patient first in adapting to the sick-role, then in progressively unlearning it.

". . . There's Another One Every Day"

The patient's mastery of the environment and of self depends to a large extent on external support and such support is likely to be more effective if it is given by a person with whom the individual can form a lasting relationship while in the hospital. Through the constancy of interaction he might be able to develop a consciousness of other and self that would help him to perceive his own role and differentiate the meaning of events.[2]

Since each patient is assigned to one interne, one might expect the interne to be an effective agent of socialization for the sick person during a process of consistent and continuous care. However, medical students, internes, and residents deal with the same patients. Under these circumstances patients have great difficulty in identifying "their" doctor.

Mr. Strong, asked after his operation who his doctor was, replied, "I don't know. There are so many of them." Mrs. Crane, five days after her admission, replied to the same question: "There are so many, you know. Well, I think there is one who takes care of me more. I don't remember his name." Mrs. Reilly, ready to leave after a four weeks' stay, answered: "Oh, what's his name, isn't it funny that I should forget it? Not that it makes any difference because he isn't just the only one to take care of me." Mr. Bloomfield said: "How should I know? There are dozens of them."

There are many doctors, and they are a very mobile group. On the medical wards the chief resident (who serves both male and female wards), leaves after six months to go to the private services. The assistant resident spends six weeks in charge of each of the medical wards, and then after a total of three months, is transferred to other services in the hospital. The tenure of the interne is equally brief. Fourth-year medical students spend approximately three weeks each on the male and female wards. The situation is much the same on the surgical wards, except that the chief resident there remains in charge for the whole year. "I had a few doctors," said one patient; "they went upstairs. Now we're having a new crowd, I don't know their names."

The fact that the patient does not have his own doctor adds to his insecurity. "They keep you for days and days. . . . Your own doctor tells you what's going on. Here they keep making tests and nobody tells you anything." Another patient wondered which doctor would operate on her:

> All these doctors were standing around me and one of them called out: "Who is the one with the varicose veins?" And then he said to another one: "You take care of her." I wonder, is he the one who is going to operate on me? He looked so young, so inexperienced. . . ."

The desirability of a more or less constant and regular doctor-patient relationship was stressed frequently by staff psychiatrists. They often recommended that a patient be allowed to have his "own" doctor and that everyone should make sure that he really knows who his "own" doctor is. Constancy of interaction seems to be all the more important because of the symbolic status of the physician for the patient. Given the pressure of work and the structure of the ward, the recommendation of the psychiatrists could have but little effect.

". . . He Is a Father to Me"

The patient tends to see the doctor as a protecting parent. J. C. Flügel has noted three factors that especially contribute to the displacement upon doctors of feelings originally directed to the parents. They are: the special knowledge possessed by the doctor in matters of vital concern where others are ignorant, the urgency of the situation into which the doctor is called, inducing a childlike state of mind that often accompanies illness.[3]

If Flügel is correct, we would expect in the patient the development of an ambivalent feeling of love and fear of the "powerful" doctor similar to the love and fear of the "powerful" father. The doctor symbolizes both hope and fear; he will either effect a cure or send the patient home uncured. He is loved as a potiential protector and hated because he occasions the patient's fears.[4]

In response to the question, "How would you describe a good doctor?"

many patients contrasted the good doctor to a bad doctor, thereby giving expression to both their admiration and their hostility:

> The main thing: talks nice to me. Gives me hope. Some doctors will come in and give prescriptions and run out.

> When the doctor takes interest. . . . Some doctors, they come in and don't look at you. . . .

> One who knows what he is doing . . . who is sociable; some come in and don't talk.

> If he considers his patient and doesn't rush him to go home. . . .

> . . . He is not too good a doctor. He is a mechanic. He is a Harvard graduate . . . gave me a speech and that's all. . . . There was another one, he was a sociable and talkative man, he used to talk to me nice.

The patient has good reason to make the house doctor the object of his hopes and fears. The house doctor makes many important decisions about him: the types of tests to be administered, whether surgery should be recommended, how long he shall stay in the hospital, etc. Some of these decisions extend into the post-hospitalization stage; the house doctor has some say, for example, about whether a patient should be sent to a nursing home.

The interne also mediates between the patient and his family. During visiting hours the patient cannot give his family a progress report, because he has only limited knowledge about himself. Nor can the family bring authoritative news directly to the patient. All important news must be dispensed by the doctor and he can strongly influence the attitude of the family toward the patient. If he is interested in the patient, he may impress upon the family the part they can play in the therapeutic process. If he is not interested, he may convey the idea that the patient is a "nuisance," whose physical condition does not warrant the "to-do" the patient expects.

What the doctor tells the family often transforms their behavior toward the patient. Mrs. Copman was, understandably, not told that she had cancer. But as soon as the physician informed her family, she became the center of attention of several sisters and brothers, her own children, and many grandchildren, nieces and nephews; all of whom crowded the small TV room every day, staying long beyond visiting hours, and hovering about her with affectionate personal attentions. Mrs. Geltman, too, who on the day of her arrival had said that "nobody wanted her," was showered with presents on the day after the diagnosis of cancer had been established and communicated to her family. The altered attitude of her family toward her manifested itself even in her appearance. On the day of her arrival she wore a new pure-silk robe, a present from her son as she proudly informed the other patients. In sharp contrast, when Mrs. Goldstein, whose itching condition could not be diagnosed, was sent to a nursing home from the hospital, she was sent in a taxi hired by the hospital; she wore a shabby cotton dress and she was not accompanied by her daughter or by any other relative or friend. The physician had made it quite clear to her daughter that they were not interested in a patient who, in their opinion, was not seriously ill.

The physician is obviously not responsible for the attitude of family members, but by conveying to them his judgment of whether the patient is "a nuisance" or a "seriously ill" person who deserves all possible attention, he can reinforce and legitimize a predisposition in family members toward the patient. A latent attitude may find expression under the sanction of the doctor's authority.[5]

A certain similarity appears here again between the role of the house doctor and the role of the parent. Just as the parent mediates between child and society[6] so does the house doctor mediate between the ward patient and the community outside.[7]

Although the patterning of the doctor-patient relationship after the parent-child relationship is understandable, and a dependent relationship *may* develop, certain other aspects of the interne's role on the ward of a teaching hospital tend to tear down the father image that the patient may have formed initially (or may have been ready to form).

"They're Nothing But Students"

Who are the "omnipotent" doctors? In physical appearance alone many of them qualify poorly as father figures for elderly patients. They are young. Some of them are not yet out of medical school, and even those who are M.D.'s are on the ward in order to learn the practice of medicine. As a rule they are unmarried or childless and have few social responsibilities outside the hospital.

The increasing duration of medical training makes for a "prolonged adolescence" in the interne, who is physically and mentally mature enough to assume adult responsibilities but is not able to assume the economic and social responsibility of supporting a family. A resident, the father of two children, said to another resident's wife: "If my family had to depend on me for support, they would starve."[8]

The young doctor in training, whether married or not, is usually not yet emancipated from his family of orientation because he is not yet economically independent. If he has children, he is usually unable to assure their complete maintenance. Moreover, since he is not yet "on his own," his status as physician is only anticipatory. In the cultural definition of the American family, he deviates from the role of the "head of the family."

Because of the length of medical training, a man in his late twenties is still "learning his adult role": one patient, Mr. Geoffrey, commented at discharge: "I found out they're nothing but students with their gadgets in their pockets. To me they look like high school boys."

Patients on the ward also soon come to resent the fact that the young doctor in training looks upon them as objects of study. "They keep you for days and days and practice on you," one patient complained. Another one said:

When you're sick it's no good being a guinea pig and being experimented on all the time. They never leave you alone a minute. It's intravenouses all the time and poking all over you and everybody asking the same questions all over again.

Medical students must learn the technique of examining and interviewing patients. They must also learn how to make intravenous injections and how to tap blood. The patient, dreading these procedures, perceives them as "experimentation on his body." "Mother doesn't like it here," a young woman was heard saying to a nurse. "She doesn't like all these experiments. She doesn't like what people are doing."[9]

Because the purpose of tests is not explained to them, patients often begin to doubt that blood has to be taken for medical reasons. They think (and pass the word) that it is being taken only for purposes of training. Mrs. Eman complained:

So much experiment. I don't mind giving three times water, giving three times blood, but enough is enough. It wasn't necessary. It was all right for the doctors to find out, but not for me.

And Mrs. Wolsky, after two weeks in the hospital, refused one morning to let the assistant resident take blood. She ducked under her blankets and yelled: "I don't want a student to touch me." Later she explained: "They took blood yesterday; how much blood do they want?" Mrs. Goldman said at discharge: "They've taken an awful lot of blood from me. I told them I haven't got no more." Later in the interview she returned to the topic unbid: "When the doctors come, I tell them I don't have no more blood."

It is in their rebellion against the learning process that some patients partly recapture their identity. They now tend to focus their hostility on the doctor-in-training because (as the one "who takes their blood" and "gives them shots")[10] he seems to confirm their fears of injury. The "development of focal attention and emergence of reality,"[11] is in part a result of "negatively" repeated events, i.e., of examinations and other procedures to which the patient is repeatedly subjected. A partial reality perception emerges, not out of a consistent relationship with the physician, but out of a routinized procedure that the sick person tends to see as a

consistent attack on his body. Many patients, unable to achieve an adjustment to the doctor, develop instead a defense against him.

The "Interesting Case"

A patient who is medically interesting is liable to be "bothered all day
long," as one nurse said:

> When they think of teaching, the patient is the last one to be con-
> sidered. They go on all evening. It's a burden for the nurse and
> it's a crime for the patient.

The nurse's perception is of course colored by her particular position
on the ward,[12] but there is no question that to teacher and students there
are two types of patients; interesting ones and uninteresting ones. Mr.
George was interesting:

> When I was here in March I have seen 20 to 30 doctors. After two
> to three weeks I was sicker than when I came. I told them I
> couldn't take it any more.

So was Mrs. Reilley: "I sure don't like being looked over by everybody
like they were in a museum."

The interesting patients are seen frequently by many different doctors
and students. The uninteresting patients get routine attention and they
are often passed over on rounds with the visiting doctor. These patients
feel rejected. At her discharge, Mrs. Goldstein, who had been admitted
to the hospital with the symptom of "generalized itching," said, "Nobody
answers. They don't talk to me. I'm a stranger. They like to take care of
people they know; [crying] nobody did nothing for me." Because she was
not ill in an interesting way, she was given a minimum of attention.

The majority of patients, probably, are "interesting" in the beginning
and then become routine cases once the diagnosis is established and the
therapeutic process decided upon. Renée Fox quotes a patient from another
hospital: "You doctors! How fast your demeanor changes! There was a
time when you all considered my case interesting, and you'd come to see
me one after the other. Now I'm not an interesting case any more. So you
all rush by like locomotives."[13]

At Mount Hermon also, physicians are well aware of this. One doctor
said:

> The first three days after they come in, we all crowd around them,
> take them from one test to another, they hardly get any rest. And
> after three days we let them lie there and don't even look at them.

For a few days the patient sees literally dozens of "doctors" around him
(including technicians and students) without knowing exactly who his
"own" doctor is. Once he has ceased to be "interesting," and the therapy

has become a matter of routine which the interne alone can handle, he probably learns the name of the interne in charge of him. But now he finds that the interne is not motivated to spend much time with him.

No wonder that patients often feel either "used" or "neglected." Neither as an interesting "specimen" nor as a "routine case," can they generally form a meaningful relationship with a person who symbolizes authority in the hospital.

". . . They Look Like High School Boys"

For some patients, condescension toward the house doctors thinly veils their hostility. A patient will say, "they wouldn't know too much, they're internes," or "as a rule, these fellows here aren't real doctors," or "they're nothing but students . . . they look like high school boys." Mr. Loeb resentfully explained:

> I didn't let them tap my blood because I could tell these boys were fishing. They didn't mean business, they didn't know how. Just fishing.

Other patients seem to have successfully converted their antagonism to the doctor into a friendly attitude of superiority. Here is part of a conversation in the television room:

> See this doctor walking down the hall? He's so funny; yesterday he was dying for a corned-beef sandwich. Mrs. Rothstein got him one.

> Where did she get hold of a corned-beef sandwich?

> She called up her husband he should bring one. You should have seen him, he was drooling for a corned-beef sandwich. Mrs. Rothstein said she couldn't stand looking at him drooling like that, so she called up her husband.

The roles have been reversed. Mrs. Rothstein, an "opinion leader" on the ward, succeeded, through her "mothering" action in belittling the doctor so that he appeared "funny" to the other patients and could be described as "drooling" like a baby.[14] Doctors are human, too, and like patients can be very hungry.

Such transformation of hostility into condescension is a well-known mechanism of defense in a social relationship in which outright hostility is socially unacceptable and psychologically inhibited by fear of retaliation. If the image of omnipotence of the person one fears and respects breaks down, as in the collapse of the image of the heroic father, hostility changes into contempt.[15] The "all-powerful" doctors become the "boys."[16] The doctor who could be (for many older patients) a son,[17] is seen as someone in need of help and encouragement. Mrs. Reilly, who at first complained about the frequency of examinations, discovered that she could he helpful:

> I guess I feel different about the place. I don't mind any more the boys coming up to examine me. I figure if I can help them out, it's all right.

Mr. Loeb took more the attitude of the instructor or "teacher's helper." After an interview with the house doctor under the guidance of a psychiatrist, he said: "I taught these young boys something. I told them all about the mistakes they made last year, so they could learn. They're still young."

Many patients come to terms with their hospitalization and their subordinate position by transforming some of their feelings of hostility and contempt into condescension. By making allowances for the young doctor's needs the patient becomes, in his own eyes, an important member of hospital society.

Thus, the sick person, who has temporarily lost his usefulness in his home environment, finds a new way of being useful in the ward. He may be temporarily inferior to others in knowledge and in authority, but he achieves a measure of superiority in the role of pseudo-parent, and a measure of importance in this world of White Authority where the doctors seem to depend on him for their training. Just as the nurse derives rewards from "pointing out mistakes to the doctor,"[18] the patient derives a reward from feeling indispensable as a helper.[19]

Through the mechanism of transforming hostility into condescension, which contains an element of sympathy, the patient is able to extend the range of his socially approved behavior and thus strengthen his own self-consciousness.[20] Patients who say, "I figure I help them out," align themselves with the hospital in its emphasis upon the value of teaching and with the larger society which attaches great importance to education. Nobody can argue with the assertion that "the boys have to learn." There is agreement between doctors and patients that learning is good; and that those who are learning have the right to make mistakes, the right to practice ("They make mistakes but they have to learn to be able to help the next one"). Learning requires permissiveness. On this common ground, patient and interne meet, and so even though the interne often fails in the direct task of orienting patients toward hospital life, he may still serve to some extent as an unwitting agent of socialization.

"The Good Doctors: They're the Visits"

Once a day there appears on the ward the visiting doctor. He seems to be *the* one in "authority," for he teaches and counsels all the house doctors. As one patient said:

> I like the rounds. The specialist explains to them. That's very good. . . . Students and internes listen to him.

Another said: "The big doctors know what it is and give them instructions what to do." Or again:

You have the advantage of visiting doctors, specialists. They examine you and pass on opinion. Not so much pass on opinion but
describe to the students.[21]

For patients who are readmitted several times (the old timers who
usually communicate their feelings to the newcomers), the most "stable"
doctor is, paradoxically, the visiting doctor. He gives his service to the
ward for several months each year, so that his occasional presence often
marks some continuity of medical care for patients who are readmitted.
Moreover, he may happen to be the patient's own family doctor or
specialist when at home, or he may be the doctor of friends or relatives in
the patient's home community. And patients often boast of their special
inside knowledge. One patient reported (incorrectly) that Dr. Turk's wife
was a teacher at Wilbur College. "Do you know her? It's funny that I
can't remember her name." Another proudly stated: "Dr. Brown comes
around too, sometimes. He is my family doctor." "You know Dr. Turk?"
another woman asked. "He's a wonderful person; he wanted me to come
for lunch at his house." And Mrs. Cane, who announced every day that
her son had previously interned at Mount Hermon, said one morning with
shining eyes: "Dr. Brown came to see me; he's the boss of this hospital; he
liked my son. When he heard I was here, he came right down to see me."
Other patients, to whom the visiting doctor is a total stranger, become
"acquainted" with him through the reports of the "old-timers."

However, as was noted earlier, the visiting doctor in observance of
hospital etiquette does not interact with the patient on the ward, even if
he happens to be that patient's private doctor at home.[22] Patients, generally
unaware that the visiting doctor's aloofness is a function of hospital organization, division of labor and professional solidarity, may be deeply disturbed by this. Mr. Levenstein, who had been admitted with a congestive
heart failure, complained:

I went to Dr. X. He took my $20 and said I should go to the hos-
pital. He sent me to the emergency ward. The next day he didn't
recognize me. He didn't come up to me. He came to the ward and
didn't know me. [Weeps] A student may be a better doctor. After
you take all my money you walk in and pass by and don't say even
"Hello, how do you feel?" A smile costs no money.

Patients can seldom, then, establish personal contact with the visiting
doctor, but they often continue to relate to him vicariously, and to idealize
him. It is the idealized image that guides perception in the following remark:

Most of the time they [i.e., the house doctors] have a specialist with
them; he examined me. . . . Two of the doctors looked up at him. I
saw them.

65

It is very likely that patients are able to "de-fuse" their ambivalent feelings by channeling their positive feelings of respect and admiration toward the visiting doctor, and most of their negative feelings of hostility and mixed feelings of condescension, toward the house doctors. As this ability to cope with their feelings and express them in behavior grows, patients achieve some measure of gradual adaptation to the ward.

There is some evidence in our data that this channeling of feelings is the result of a process in time. In the formal interviews, twenty-four patients spontaneously expressed hostile or condescending feelings about the teaching situation, or expressed their admiration for the visiting doctor in contrast to the house doctors. These twenty-four patients were compared with the other twenty-six patients who did not express any such feelings. It turned out that there is significant difference between "old-timers" and "newcomers," thus supporting the hypothesis that these feelings are more manifest after more frequent exposure to the hospital (Table 1).

Table 1

Frequency of Admission by Specific References to Teaching Situation

Mention inferiority of house doctor or superiority of visiting doctor, or emphasize "learning"	Patients interviewed were at their:	
	First Admission	Recurrent Admission (2 or more)
Yes	7	17
No	15	11
General Hostility	1	0

This table seems to indicate that "first admissions" do not express these feelings as frequently as "recurrent admissions," thus suggesting that the "defense mechanism" discussed in this chapter tends to be the result of a *process*. In a subsequent chapter (Chapter VIII) we will see, however, that frequency of admission is also associated with the patient's emotional dependence on doctor and hospital; it will seem that such "adjustment" is not without its dysfunctional consequences.

* * *

The preceding pages have focused on the doctor-patient relationship. Although each patient must evolve his own defenses and make his own adaptation, and though we must make allowance for individual psychological differences, the patient does not stand alone. He is greatly helped in the formation of defensive adaptive attitudes by the other patients in the ward.

1. *Man and Medicine, op. cit.,* pp. 74-75.

2. In a study of children in a foundling home and in a nursery, René Spitz has found that children who are not given the opportunity to form more or less permanent relationships with an adult are hampered in their manipulation of inanimate objects, as well as in their interactions with other people, and have a tendency to withdraw into passivity. (René Spitz, "Hospitalism," *The Psychoanalytic Study of the Child,* Vol. I & II, pp. 53-73 and 113-117, respectively; also "Anaclitic Depression," *ibid.,* Vol. II, pp. 313-342.)

See also Ernest C. Schachtel, "The Development of Focal Attention and the Emergence of Reality," in *Metamorphosis,* New York: Basic Books, 1959, pp. 251-278.

James M. Baldwin has also emphasized the importance of the "recurrence of the object" for the consciousness of self and other: "The identification of the recurrent object as being the same object as that before experiencd—that is the mark of this higher individuation. With it the additional element of meaning known as persistence of the object is much developed. . . . A crude identity or immediate-sameness is given in each second or later individuation, and the value of this in the later progressions toward the richer meaning of the object is that of persistence. . . ." (*Thought and Things,* Vol. I, London: Swan Sonnenschein & Co., 1906, p. 151.)

3. J. C. Flügel, *The Psychoanalytic Study of the Family,* London: The Hogarth Press, 1935, pp. 120-121.

4. The psychoanalytically oriented reader will probably hold the opinion that we deal here with the projection of the patient's own hostile wishes onto the doctor. I do not deny that this mechanism may be at work here, but I want to emphasize that one aspect of the mechanism of projection has been neglected in psychoanalytic thought. The attributes that the individual ascribes to the other person are not only (and not necessarily) his own; they may be the "complement" of his own feelings. According to Baldwin, the individual may not only ascribe his own feelings to others, but he may see in the other person the agent who causes these feelings. (See James M. Baldwin, *Mental Development,* New York: The Macmillan Co., 1895, esp. p. 126 and pp. 334-340.)

5. Frequently the love and protection the patient craves is accorded him by his family when there exists a physical threat. For many elderly people, who feel useless to their relatives and unloved by them, becoming sick is a form of blackmail, as if they were to say: "See what becomes of me?" Being sent to the hospital is an indication of their need of more support and love. (On the problem of illness as a refuge, see Barker, Wright and Gonick, *op. cit.,* pp. 238 f.)

6. On the parent as a mediator between the society and the child, see Erich Fromm, "Sozialpsychologischer Teil," *Autoritaet und Familie,* Max Horkheimer, (ed.), Paris: Librairie Félix Alcan, 1936, pp. 87 ff.; Parsons and Bales, *Family, Socialization and Interaction Process, op. cit.,* esp. Chapters II and III.

7. Not only the family but also the wider community is involved. One patient had this to say: "The doctors were discussing it aloud in front of every-

body. I walked out, I was so mad. Because where I live there are lots of people who come here and they come back and talk about everything and before you know it everybody around home is going to talk about my having cancer. . . ."

8. Peter Blos lists the following as being the three major goals of adolescent development: (1) emancipation from the family, (2) acceptance of the sex role, (3) achievement of economic independence. (*The Adolescent Personality*, New York: Appleton-Century-Crofts, 1941, p. 275.)

9. These routine procedures, like blood tapping, were applied only if justified medically. However, students are not yet skilled and therefore may hurt the patient more than a skillful nurse would.

10. Cf. Patient A: "They shot the President of Panama." Patient B: "They go on shooting these days just like they shoot needles into you." [Smiling]: "It's true, all they do is shoot needles into you, a dime a dozen."

11. Schachtel, *op. cit.*

12. Cf. Chapters II and V.

13. Renée Fox, *Experiment Perilous, op. cit.*, p. 183.

14. Incidents like this one are rare on the ward (but provide the occasion for much conversation and laughter and may well become part of the ward folklore). The doctor who accepts food from a patient violates professional etiquette, since his act reduces the social distance between doctors and patients. In this case the "doctor" was a fourth-year medical student whose socialization into the profession was not yet completed. It is probable that the patients did not know this. But even if they did know it, they referred to "the doctor" when they passed on the story, the better to emphasize, perhaps, the role reversal that had taken place.

Note that the role reversal is brought about by means of jocular talk. On the functions of jocular talk on the ward, see Chapter VI.

15. Cf. "[The adolescent] finds out that his father is no longer the most powerful, the wisest, the richest of all; he becomes dissatisfied with his father, learns to criticize him and to categorize him socially." (S. Freud, "Zur Psychologie des Gymnasiasten," *Gesammelte Schriften*, Vol. XI, Leipzig-Wien: Internationaler Psychoanalytischer Verlag, 1928, pp. 287-290.) Burling, Lentz and Wilson, *op. cit.*, p. 27, also mention the disparaging attitude of the patient toward the doctor.

16. This expression is of current usage on the ward, but in the plural only. If referring to a specific doctor or student, patients usually speak of "the doctor."

17. The actual age difference between patient and doctor is of secondary importance. Mrs. Rothstein, who took the motherly attitude, was 36, while the "doctor" was in his late twenties. What is important here is the *perception* of the patient. Once the doctor is perceived as someone who is still subject to socialization, he becomes a "boy" in every respect. Here, low status in one sphere is used to ascribe low status in other aspects of the role personality.

18. With regard to the function of pointing out mistakes to someone higher in status, see p. 29.

19. Cf. Renée Fox, *Experiment Perilous, op. cit.*, pp. 150 ff.

20. James M. Baldwin, *Social and Ethical Interpretations in Mental De-*

velopment, New York: The Macmillan Co., 1897, p. 225, says: "Reflective sympathy reaffirms the social value of the reaction, utilizes it, and in discovering the relations of persons for itself, in a reflective and critical way, goes on to refine the reactions and embody them in the institutions of social life."

21. John Romano, in a paper on "Patients' Attitudes and Behavior in Ward Round Teaching," makes a similar point and quotes a patient who said that the presiding physician "made me feel important—almost as important as these damn red splotches on my skin." Romano suggests that the rounds be used as an educative technique for the patient and for improvement of rapport between doctor and patient. (*Journal of the American Medical Association,* 117 [1941], 664-67.)

22. See Chapters I and II.

CHAPTER V

Mother or Career Girl

The Mothering Nurse

If the physician, often a quasi-father figure, stands somewhat aloof from the patient in his professional authority, why cannot the nurse, a quasi-mother figure, help to bridge that gap and thus serve as an important agent of socialization in the ward?

The nurse often regards herself, and is regarded by others, as a mediator between physician and patient.

"How d'you expect to maintain contact with the patients if not through the nurses?" one nurse asked a resident who expressed disdain for nurses, and she reports that "he didn't have anything to say to this."

On the ward, where the patient does not have his "own" doctor, and where house doctors and medical students are forever moving on, the nurse does seem to be in the best position to mediate. Several factors, however, reduce her effectiveness as a socializing agent.

A number of excellent extensive analyses of the nurse-patient relationship are available.[1] In this chapter attention will be focused on those aspects of the nurse's role that tend to limit her effectiveness in helping patients come to terms with illness, hospitalization and discharge. In a later chapter certain differences between the medical and surgical wards in the effectiveness of nurses will be explored.[2]

The English term "sister" (like the German "schwester" and the French "soeur") suggests a personal closeness in the nurse-patient relationship. In a similar vein, the expressions "nursing the sick" and "nursing the baby," denote at least a metaphorical similarity between care of the patient and nurture of the child.[3] The emphasis is upon protection and emotional gratification.

A large number of the patients interviewed made no mention of "professional" qualities in defining a "good nurse" but stressed her supportive role. Thirty-eight out of fifty-one patients interviewed said that a good nurse takes a personal interest in patients: she should "help people all she can," she should be "understanding and listen, not be impersonal," she should "give attention to the patient," etc. Mr. Russ elevated these expectations:

> You give him a smile; it's just like the medicine. A little talking, a little more friendly, warm. That's how I feel about it; you can trust the person. That's why it is a schwester, so you have confidence.

Mr. Goldman remembered a "good nurse":

> When she takes good care—like when she gives you a pill and some drop leaks she takes a handkerchief to wipe it while I was lying down.

Nurses, too, recognize "tender care" as a role obligation. They refer to it as T.L.C. (tender loving care), thus institutionalizing, or even routinizing it.[4] Tenderness, then, is a recognized and accepted aspect of nursing, but both the status of the nurse in the hospital and her own self-image as a professional interfere with her ability to give T.L.C. unequivocally.

The Professional Nurse[5]

The concept of "professional role" implies: (a) what Parsons calls "functional specificity"—that is, a very well-defined service to perform[6] and (b) work of high prestige. Functional specificity implies for the professional person a limited degree of personal involvement and a specific allotment of time to the service. Such limitations on personality and time, however, conflict with the "sisterly" or "motherly" care that the nurse is expected to give.[7]

The "professional" role thus tends to conflict with the "sisterly" role.[8] The extent of "loving care" that the patient will get will depend on the relative emphasis nurses place on these two role components. Some of the eleven nurses interviewed gave more emphasis to one, some to the other, in answering the question, "Why did you want to be a nurse?" Two nurses saw themselves as "helpers." For example:

> My mother had been ill a great deal when I was young, and ever since I was a child I thought maybe I can help someone feel better.

The other nine nurses claimed to have been attracted by the status aspects of nursing.[9] Of these, six were unequivocally profession-oriented:

> One reason was that I didn't want to go to college. I was tired of school, but then I didn't want to be just a secretary or so and I wanted to be with people and I was good in science.

While three were attracted by the "glamour of the occupation":

> Originally because I had always grown up with the idea of being a nurse; it was very glamourous.[10]

Although the number of formal interviews with nurses is too small to yield reliable evidence, the responses tend to support the impression that "glamour-oriented" nurses share a common look with the profession-oriented. In response to the question, ". . . If you were asked to [plan] a ward, what would you do?" all three of the nurses who stressed the glamour aspects of their occupational choice suggested physical reorganization of the ward to improve the efficiency of nurses. And of the six nurses who were attracted by the professional aspects of the occupation: two made proposals that would benefit nurses, while two suggested changes that would favor both nurses and patients. Only one of the profession-oriented nurses suggested changes that would be entirely for the benefit of patients. In contrast, neither of the two nurses who had chosen nursing as an opportunity to care for people, suggested changes that would benefit nurses only:

Table 2

Nurses' Motivations for Occupational Choice by Proposals for Changes on the Ward

Proposed Ward Changes Would Benefit:	Nurses' Motivations for Occupational Choice		
	"Glamour Girl"	"Professional"	"Helper"
Patients	0	1	1
Patients and Nurses	0	2	1
Nurses	3	2	0
No Answer	0	1	0

At Mount Hermon nurses are given little opportunity to apply what medical knowledge they have acquired to the care of the patient. Professional pride and pride in work would lead nurses to derive particular satisfaction from participating in medical practice, which is the most "important" work in the hospital. Yet for several reasons (only one of which will be mentioned here), the nurse is likely to be excluded from medical activities on the ward at Mount Hermon.[11]

In this teaching hospital, medical students perform a number of routine medical procedures, such as tapping blood, taking blood pressure, and giving injections, all jobs that, in non-teaching hospitals, are assigned to nurses. One nurse who had previously worked in a small private hospital recalled that:

> The nurses didn't medically know as much as I did but they were called upon in an emergency to do things that I would never be called upon to do here. The doctors were more liberal with them than they are here with us. *They could draw blood there where we can't here. The patients there depend a little more on the nurses than here.* Here, even though the patients depend on the nurses,

72

they know that the doctor is around all the time. . . . [emphasis ours]

No wonder that at Mount Hermon many nurses complain that medical students are "stealing the show." During the formal interview six nurses mentioned the medical students as a source of frustration: "We have to cater to the medical students," or "They slow work down, they're under-foot . . . they add to the general confusion." "They're getting in the nurses' way," or "The nurse can't even get to the patient sometimes because the doctors and students are there all the time."[12]

Unable to exercise her professional-medical skills, the nurse turns for status-enhancement to other aspects of her role. For the head nurse especially this means organization and management.

Managerial tasks are clearly second best, and typical complaints arise about the burden of "petty details." We remember the nurse who said:

> [A doctor] will give the nurse an order, a student comes to the other side and wants something prepared, and the telephone rings and the nurse has to pass on a message. . . .

There is a note of importance in this complaint, but little glamour or professional pride. "The nurse more and more is taking the position in our society and in this hospital of being an organizer," one nurses' supervisor said proudly, but she added that she would prefer that this task be per-formed by somebody else.

> The best thing would be to have a manager, organizing, directing the traffic, organizing the supply on the floor. The manager doesn't have to be a nurse, this system would release the nurse . . . then the nurse could actually do nursing.

Table 3

Nurses' Motivations for Occupational Choice by Complaints About "Details in Work" and "Medical Students"

	Professional*	Helper
"Too many details in work" or "Students are in the way."	8	0
None of these	1**	2

* The three "glamour-oriented" nurses, who are included in this group, respond in the same way: two of them complain that the medical students are in the way, and one feels burdened by too many details.

** This nurse differs from the other profession-oriented nurses in that she was the only one who gave "material security" as the main reason for her occupational choice.

Complaints about "medical students" and about "petty details" are not, as might be expected, voiced by the nurses who would rather help patients, but significantly seem to be expressions of discontent at being barred from professional activities.

How do the nurses handle these frustrations? How do they maintain a strong self-image? Mostly by subtle redefinition and emphases. One nurse, describing how she would post each day on the doctors' bulletin board a list of medical procedures to be followed by the medical students, explained:

> . . . and then usually the medical students check them off. Sometimes they pay no attention to the list, it depends on the group of students. . . . *We have to check on them and make sure they have done things.* [emphasis ours]

Another nurse, speaking of certain tests:

> The doctor knows what the test involves: someone must draw blood on a patient and then on another patient to have a control with a white blood count. But the doctor will order only one, and *if the nurse doesn't check up* the test will have to be done over again. . . . [emphasis ours]

These nurses speak as if the nurse is the supervisor of medical students and even of the house doctors. Language is indeed a powerful tool for shaping reality. So nurses (like patients) refer to the house doctors as "the boys." But when referring to their own work, they do not speak of "cleaning up" but rather of "taking care of the equipment."

Such are the "devices by which men make their work tolerable, or even glorious to themselves and others."[13] All sorts of workers select for their job descriptions or job titles the most favorable designations. "Schoolteachers sometimes turn schoolteaching into educational work, and the disciplining of youngsters and chaperoning of parties into personnel work. Teaching Sunday School becomes religious education, and the Y.M.C.A. secretary is 'in group work'."[14] So at Mount Hermon when being a "good organizer" means picking up trash it is described as follows:

> Being observant goes along with having an inquiring mind. That's really important. I'll go on the ward and see things and nobody sees it. This is a good example: everybody will be falling over something and nobody will pick it up.

The nurses address these status claims to both doctors and patients. How are such claims received in the hospital?

What Doctors Expect of the Nurse

Unfortunately, we have too few standardized interviews with doctors at Mount Hermon to draw firm conclusions about what doctors expect of nurses. But the interview material, as well as other observations, tend to confirm the findings of Albert F. Wessen that doctors judge nurses in relation to their own work rather than in their independent relation to patients.[15]

Five of the eight physicians interviewed did mention the supportive role of nurses, such as "understanding patients," but only one physician defined the work of a good nurse exclusively in terms of comfort to the sick. All the others mentioned qualities pertaining to "professional" performance, such as "foresight," "management," "efficiency," etc. One doctor saw the nurse as an "assistant to the doctor," and three required that she "carry out orders" and "do her routine work well." These responses suggest that doctors tend to emphasize the subordinate or professional qualities of the nurse more than her patient-supportive qualities.

If this assumption is justified, the nurse who wants to improve her "professional" image and perhaps promote herself from "one who obeys orders" to a "doctor's assistant," will pay more attention to her relationship with doctors than to her relationship with patients. Her own profession-orientation is reinforced by doctors' expectations.

How the Patient Sees the Nurse

Patients have little opportunity to witness the nurse's professional skills, especially on the medical ward, where the surgical procedures of applying dressings, putting a patient on drainage, etc., are seldom or never required. Patients also have little opportunity to witness a nurse's decision-making power. Most of their requests for treatment or explanation are met with: "You [or "I"] will have to ask the doctor," or "Doctor's orders."

A nurse is permitted to give patients very little information. Patients are not told their weight, their temperature, their blood pressure. "The theory is that the patient should know as little as possible about himself," one nurse explained, and the rules of silence are followed strictly.[16]

In the absence of very strong evidence that the nurse's job involves much professional skill and authority, patients find little reason to correct their

Table 4

Patients' Definition of a "Good Nurse"

Qualities	No.
Supportive qualities only	39
Professional qualities only	2
Professional and supportive qualities	1
Task performance and supportive qualities	3
Other	2
No answer	4

self-oriented judgment of the nurse's essential task, which they see as one of lending personal reassurance and emotional support to their lives.

Forty-three patients said that a good nurse has to be related to the patient in a "kind" or "personal" manner. Of these, thirty-nine did not mention any other qualities whatsoever. Only three patients mentioned professional qualities ("She has to know almost as much as the doctor") and three patients made task performance ("efficiency") an important attribute.

How Nurses Relate to Patients

The two nurses who said that their selection of the nursing occupation was motivated by a desire to "help" did not complain of being "burdened with petty details" nor did they object that the medical students were "in their way" (Table 3). Apparently, nurses who really want to be with patients are able to derive satisfaction from the relationship they can establish with them. At Mount Hermon we occasionally observed nurses sitting with patients, talking with them or playing a game—but not very often. A few patients commented upon the "kindness" and "helpfulness" of some nurses. However, a nurse's motivation to give bedside care would have to be very intense to counteract the actual pressure of work and the feeling that the ward "belongs" to medical students and house officers for the purpose of medical teaching. The institutionalized emphasis on instruction makes it easier for a nurse to gain work satisfaction as an administrator at her desk or as a counselor to student nurses.

The registered nurse could be a source of great comfort to the patient, especially right after his admission. She could explain to him the reasons for the repeated examinations; she could answer his questions and reassure him that she is available to provide for his needs. These activities would raise the nurse's prestige in the eyes of the patient and also give her a feeling of being needed and of helping the patient to orient himself in his new hospital environment.

But when doctors (as well as administrators) praise the "efficient organizer," the attention of the nurse is geared toward "running things smoothly" and toward minimizing disturbances, which, in turn, affects her relationship with the patients. For example, a nurse does not usually answer a patient's call immediately, especially during the first day after his admission. She is not thereby showing "callousness," as some patients are wont to believe. She adopts delay as a method of teaching the patient that she should not be called for trivial matters. That these tactics are taught to student nurses is clearly shown in the following dressing-down administered by a head nurse:

> It's 11 o'clock and you aren't even through with the beds. Mrs. V. took all your time? That's no excuse. Just go about your work and ignore all her little demands. If she insists, tell her you have no time

right now, or better still, don't tell her anything and walk over to the next bed. She'll learn. Getting through in the ward is your responsibility and handling a demanding patient is your responsibility also. [Turning to the observer:] You really have to teach those kids. They'll be stepped on. They have to learn to organize their work.

Ignoring a patient's call is more than a mechanism of self-protection, however. It is a means of establishing authority with the patient also. Another device for minimizing disturbances on the ward is the appeal to rules and regulations and to "doctor's orders," an appeal that the nurse feels should put an end to a patient's argument. Unfortunately, this device tends to boomerang by lowering the status of the nurse in the eyes of the patient. He will learn to comply with a nurse's wish for order and quiet, but he is confirmed in his view of the nurse as a powerless person who only obeys doctor's orders, and can make no decisions on her own.

In attempting to protect herself against just this attitude of the patient, the nurse often attempts to make a show of authority. But all too often she uses her authority "negatively," i.e., to withhold rather than to give, in order to force the patient into conformity with her definition of "smooth running" of the ward. She fails to see that the patient's frequent calls, his attempts to explore his environment, afford her the opportunity to use her authority in helping him to understand it.

Given the predominance of the professional orientation among the nurses, their effectiveness as agents of socialization would seem to be most closely related to the amount of professional skill and of positive decision-making they are permitted to exercise. A comparison of medical and surgical wards tends to bear out this assumption (see Chapter IX).

NOTES

1. For patient-nurse relationships in general hospitals, see Burling, Lentz and Wilson, *op. cit.,* esp. Chapter 7; George Devereux and Florence R. Winter, "The Occupational Status of Nurses," *American Sociological Review,* XV (Oct. 1950), 628-634; Ford and Stephenson, *op. cit.;* Rhoda Goldstein, *op. cit.;* and A. T. M. Wilson, *op. cit.*

2. Cf. Chapter IX.

3. Cf. Devereux and Winter, *op. cit.*

4. Cf. "My idea of a good nurse is to give a lot of T.L.C. to a patient." (Third-year student nurse, on the verge of being graduated.)

5. For historical background of the changes undergone in the occupation of nursing, see Burling, Lentz and Wilson, *op. cit.;* also, Ester L. Brown, *Nursing as a Profession,* New York: Russell Sage Foundation, 1937; Mary M. Roberts, *American Nursing: History and Interpretation,* New York: The Macmillan Co., 1954.

6. "The area of professional authority is limited to a particular technically

defined sphere." (Talcott Parsons, "The Professions and Social Structure," in *Essays in Sociological Theory, Pure and Applied,* Glencoe, Ill.: The Free Press, 1949, p. 189.)

7. Isidor Thorner has well formulated this dilemma: "The nurse is faced with the problem of achieving a compromise between the functionally specific impersonality of her role and the therapeutically beneficial expression of interest, warmth, kindness, and sympathy elicited both by the condition of the patient and his expectations of what constitutes proper feminine conduct." ("Nursing: The Functional Significance of an Institutional Pattern," *American Sociological Review,* XX, Oct. 1955, 531-538.)

8. For the difference between secondary and primary relations, see Charles H. Cooley, *Social Organization,* Glencoe, Ill.: The Free Press, 1956, Ch. III; and Talcott Parsons' excellent exposition of Toennies' concepts of *Gemeinschaft* and *Gesellschaft* in the *Structure of Social Action,* Glencoe, Ill.: The Free Press, 1949, pp. 686 ff. See also Kingsley Davis, *Human Society,* New York: The Macmillan Co., 1949, pp. 289-307.

9. Cf. "The term profession is a symbol for a desired conception of one's work and, hence, of one's self. . . ." (Hughes, *Men and Their Work, op. cit.,* p. 44.)

10. Those who were originally motivated by the quest for glamour and those who originally sought status enhancement from a "professional role" are likely to merge into a common type after exposure to the realities of the hospital world. The nurse who is attracted to the occupation by its alleged "glamour" is more likely to enjoy the authority of her uniform than to stress the dispensing of affection and loving care.

Devereux and Winter, *op. cit.,* have argued that the status problem of the nurse is comparable to that of the lower middle-class in that personal insecurity leads to the tendency to cling stubbornly to "respectability" for fear of being downgraded socially. When the nurse finds during her hospital experience that the glamour she sought is not as easy to come by as she imagined, she will be motivated to shift to symbols of professional status. Hence the tasks that appear to be most compatible with concern for "glamour" are those that involve administration and management rather than psychic support of patients.

11. For an analysis of nurses' positions in the structure of a general hospital, see Wesson, *op. cit.*

12. Such complaints occur repeatedly, but most frequently in the medical ward. In the surgical ward the nurse has to take more active part in the care of patients. Differences in nurses' roles on the two wards are described in Chapter IX.

13. Hughes, *Men and Their Work, op. cit.,* p. 48.

14. *Ibid.,* p. 43. For a more detailed analysis of the ways in which the nurse comes to terms with her work, see pp. 40-50 of this book.

15. Wessen, *op. cit.*

16. There may be good reasons for not giving a patient information that is conducive to creating anxiety. But there is little provision for giving information that may help to relieve anxiety and increase a patient's understanding about his condition. Doctors often don't have the time or patience to talk at

length to a person about his illness. One nurses' supervisor said: "Doctors have been pretty brusk. 'You have to have your thyroid out,'—it's very serious to the patient even if it isn't serious." Such news might be much less upsetting if the nurse had been allowed to talk to him in detail about his illness and its prognosis.

CHAPTER VI

Brothers and Strangers

A NEW PATIENT FINDS AN IMPORTANT SOURCE OF SUPPORT IN HIS RE-
lations with other patients,[1] and especially with those who have been in the
ward for some time and those who have been hospitalized frequently.

Patients who have been admitted to Mount Hermon several times are
apt to take a proprietory attitude toward the hospital. For example, Mrs.
Brown, when asked whether this was her first experience with the hospital,
replied:

> I've been here once before, but when I came here, I knew the place.
> My mother had been here several times and my husband, he was
> both on the medical and surgical wards. My father died here. This
> is like home for me.

Patients like Mrs. Brown talk freely about their previous associations
with the hospital to other members of the ward. Even as they are still
waiting for admission to a bed, they may be heard in the television room
explaining to other patients some of the details of hospital life, and making
sure that their seniority is recognized at every introduction. Elderly Mrs.
Stone, waiting to be admitted to the ward, called out to a younger woman
who was attempting to open the door to an outside porch: "It opens the
other way. I know this. I was here when they built it." Then she turned to
an even younger patient and boasted: "I was here when you weren't even
born. This is my fifteenth admission. . . . I know how it goes around here.
They take good care of you."

Mrs. Stone was always ready to share her long-accumulated knowledge.
To one of the younger patients who was aggressively refusing her lunch
she said: "Just leave it, honey. Don't talk so much. Just leave it, they're
used to it here." And to another new patient, who nervously asked a
nurse's aide, "Where's the bathroom, where's the bathroom?" she explained: "Pass the water, honey, pass the water, that's how they say it."

Thus, through old-timers like Mrs. Stone, new patients begin to learn
the ward jargon and to interpret its meaning. They gradually find out that

the house doctors are called "the boys" and that "the boys are here to learn." They are told that "the boys around here are nice, everybody is nice." They hear that "the poor boys are overworked," and they are briefed on recent happenings.

A patient soon learns from his fellow patients that he is not supposed to complain;[2] he learns that the hospital is not entirely threatening and discovers that life there can be entertaining and amusing as well. He is reassured to realize that sickness in the hospital is an expected condition, and that "here in the ward they're all the same and they can talk." Separated from friends and relatives though he may be, a patient can generally say by the time he is ready to leave the hospital: "Here on the ward I feel I'm not alone."

Although it is from the old-timers and the "hardened recidivists" that the new patient receives the most instruction, the patient population of the ward is so fluctuating that nearly everybody has a chance, sooner or later, to know more about the place than some other patient "who has just come in." Even a patient who is very anxious about himself may be able to assume an air of assurance before a still more recent arrival. So Mrs. Doyle, still worrying about her prospective operation, offered support to Miss Nagel, who didn't yet know what was wrong with her.

Guidance and Support

Almost every patient is capable at times of "helping others along," but in each ward there are usually one or two who may rightly be called "opinion leaders." One such leader was Mrs. Rothstein.

Within five or ten minutes after Mrs. Rothstein would walk into the television room, several other patients would come drifting in; and soon after she left the television room it would be abandoned again. She knew most of the patients by name and would introduce them to each other. She would volunteer information to me when I was talking with another patient, if that patient was unable to provide it. She knew the names of most of the doctors as well as certain other information about them, which she shared generously. The other patients liked to be with her and accepted her advice gladly.

Mrs. Rothstein had been hospitalized previously and had been a regular visitor to Mount Hermon's outpatient department. She was known to the visiting doctor who discussed her case with the house doctors. She had come to the medical ward from the emergency ward, where she had been admitted with a severe attack which was part of a syndrome that persistently defied diagnosis. She had been sent to the emergency ward by her family doctor in the hope that new light might be shed on her condition if she could be seen during the acute stage of the attack.

Puzzling as Mrs. Rothstein's condition was, she was spared many of the anxiety-provoking circumstances that confront the average patient at admission: (a) she was an "interesting" case and therefore enjoyed more than the usual attention of several visiting doctors; (b) she was given immediate attention (since she came to the emergency ward) without having to wait for the routine admission procedure; (c) she had been admitted previously and the hospital was familiar to her; (d) she was familiar with several other departments in the hospital, and hence knew where she was in relation to the rest of the building.[3] For all these reasons Mrs. Rothstein felt *relatively secure in the hospital atmosphere.*

Mrs. Rothstein came from the community that Mount Hermon hospital serves. She was active in community organizations, and on the ward she encountered other patients from her own neighborhood; within a few days she had organized car pools for visiting relatives and was giving reassuring information about other patients to their relatives. Hence, Mrs. Rothstein was *a link between the hospital and the community,* providing support and guidance for those who felt the impact of the separation from their customary environment.

As one who had been admitted to Mount Hermon hospital previously, she was also a link with the past, *a representative of tradition.* Howard Rowland asserts that "practically every ward has enough carriers of gossip to keep tradition alive and to transmit it to newcomers."[4] To be a gossip carrier in a hospital would appear to be an essential prerequisite for an "opinion leader" on the ward.

Finally, Mrs. Rothstein, because she knew some of the visiting doctors from outside the hospital, was able to consider herself "in on things," and so took on the role of *hospital representative* to other patients.

When Mrs. Rothstein was transferred from the emergency ward to the medical ward, she asked to be given, if possible, the choice of a bed, and she chose one in the right-hand far-off corner. Knowing the physical structure of the ward from previous experience, she secured for herself the best "strategic" location, a spot that assured her maximum opportunity for interaction with other patients. From this vantage point she could overlook the entire ward and keep an eye on nurses, doctors, and patients walking in and out.[5]

Mrs. Rothstein's bed was the only one in the ward that was placed diagonally, and the only one that afforded a patient the opportunity to look out of a window—a minor detail, to be sure, but one whose importance should not be underestimated. Being able to look out of the window is more than a welcome distraction. Through its symbolic significance, it may help the patient to maintain some degree of relatedness to the outside world.[6]

Mrs. Rothstein's condition was not satisfactorily diagnosed and the acute pain did not return. After several consultations it was decided to refrain from troubling her with experimental medication. She would have been discharged after a few days had it not been for the fact that she developed a

82

pulmonary cold with low temperature. Under these circumstances the doctors could not assume the responsibility of discharging her. So for three weeks she stayed in the hospital, sitting in the television room a large part of the day and the evening, walking back and forth between the ward and the television room, and talking gaily to other patients.

Mrs. Rothstein was as *unrestricted in her movements* as the limitations of space and hospital regulations permit. The nature of the illness is obviously a limiting factor in the patient's capacity to function as a socializing agent. The ambulatory patient is in a much better position than is the very sick patient to participate in the life of the ward. This illness factor can be overstressed, however; even a bed-ridden patient can participate quite fully in ward life. At one time the most popular person on the surgical ward was a woman who was completely immobilized after surgery. On the male medical ward during the same period, the "life of the ward" was a man who was immobilized with a coronary condition.

Other personal characteristics contributed to the acceptance of Mrs. Rothstein: she was "average" in economic, occupational and educational status among the ward patients.[7]

Mrs. Rothstein's qualities mutually reinforced each other. Feeling herself to be a representative of the community and of tradition added to her sense of security, which was further enhanced by the relative lack of restrictions on her movements. In addition, her acceptance by the other patients increased her feeling of importance as an "old-timer" who "belonged."

Her security permitted her to maintain ego-identity. My very first impression of Mrs. Rothstein, as she "entertained" in the TV room, was of a woman completely at home. In my notes I find: "very supportive in her behavior toward others in the ward, gives newcomers information on ward life, deals out candy and plays the role of 'hostess' in friendly manner." She was out-going, verbal, pleasant and motherly.[8]

In the waiting room she told one patient, back from surgery, "Should you sit like this, dangling your legs? You better sit here, with your legs up." The patient complied. To another patient she said: "You should know better than hanging around here in your condition. Why don't you go to bed?" The patient thereupon walked meekly out of the TV room. Later, in bed, Mrs. Rothstein pointed to her neighbor's tray and asked: "Why don't you eat? If they give it to you, it means you must have it for your health. It's good for you."

She was free with advice yet neither moralistic nor "bossy." She shared with the other patients the common gripes about hospital routine and other annoyances:

> You can't sleep in this place. The woman next to me was moaning like anything, never stopped. And then there was one across the hall, you should have heard her carry on all through the night. . . . I'm telling you! So then I just fell asleep; at 6 o'clock they wake

83

me up: "Would you like to wash, Mrs. R?" Wash! At 6 o'clock in the morning! So after they made my bed, I went right back to sleep. Then they woke me up, so I thought there's something else, some medication or the rounds, but it turned out I got a telephone call.

Mrs. Rothstein demonstrates here a solidarity with her fellows, who are also annoyed with hospital staff and with "deviant" peers. "Nothing's wrong with me," she concludes, "but by the time I get out of here I'll be exhausted." This summation of her sleepless night is her way of saying: "Look here, I know what this place is like, but it does have its funny side, too." Such jocular comments abound in the conversation of opinion leaders; and much of the general conversation on the ward consisted in jocular talk and jocular griping. By a continuous endeavor to overlook or make light of their individual plights, patients were able to bring about a social synthesis of their individual experiences which greatly strengthened ward solidarity.

Laughter in the Ward

Although some patients are more gifted than others in highlighting the "comic element" of their experiences,[9] most of them when sitting together in the television room or conversing in the ward, tend to fall into jocular conversation.

Here is a sample of conversation in the television room: "Did you hear what happened yesterday? I'm telling yah, it was a riot. The funniest thing!"

The story is then told of the mixup between two Mrs. Ann Broseman's, which resulted in the wrong one, poor Mrs. Broseman from the medical ward, being taken from the TV room by an interne from the surgical ward and being subjected to an elaborate physical examination in the surgical ward.[10]

In the meantime the nurses in the medical ward were looking for Mrs. Broseman. They were all excited and worried because they *are* responsible for the patients, you know. Well, finally they got her. She was raving mad and red as a beet. She came here for high blood pressure in the first place. Well, it must have gone sky-high after that!

This incident touches on certain threatening aspects of hospital life, for these are fears, common to all, that some confusion in administering medication might occur. But by making the story seem funny, the storyteller implies that even if such fears were realized, even if the confusion occurred, it would have ridiculous rather than disastrous consequences.[11] And the ridiculous victim ("red as a beet"), damaged in dignity, but not in body, proves that those fears were groundless.

This story also channels and releases hostility against the nurses and

84

introduces a comic reversal of roles. It is the nurses, not the patients, who are "excited and worried." Such a reversal of roles is a frequent element in comic representations.[12]

Humor that reassures by contrasting one's own plight with the greater plight of others elicits what is called in German *Schadenfreude*. The story of Mrs. Broseman's mishap brings the laughter of relief that it was she, and not those present, who lived through the disagreeable experience. In the confirmation of one's own safety there is a sense of elation, and the humorist invites her listeners to join with her in a triumph of invincibility.[13]

There is explicit reassurance in this story, too. The speaker without having to take an attitude of "I know it all," or "just listen to me, girls," reassures the listeners that the nurses were searching for their patient because "they *are* responsible," and "they finally got her."[14] Thus does the storyteller partly offset her debunking account of the excited and worried nurses. The patients can rely, after all, on their protection and concern. Thus this jocular report was a message to other members in the group that they may relax with safety.[15]

Jocular talk not only reassures, it also socializes in other ways. Jocular griping transforms socially inadmissible complaints into approved forms of striking back at ward routine. It helps both the complainer and his listeners to come to terms with their condition and with ward life. "I never complain," one patient said. "What good would it be anyhow? No use complaining. . . . Got to take things as they are. Take life as it is. Some people magnify things. Others make them smaller. That's the better way." In her jocular talk to other patients, this patient "made things smaller" not only for herself but for the other patients as well. She interpreted hospital life for them:

> I couldn't sleep all night. The lady next to me had a nightmare and was shrieking. Across the hall there was one who had gotten a needle and she yelled till the ceiling came down, I'm telling yah. So I walked out to have a smoke and there in the television room was the family of one who had died across the hall. They were crying and lamenting.[16] I'll be glad to get home to get some rest. If I stay here longer, I'm going to get sick.

The joke that the hospital makes you sick or wears you out is a standard one. Through such standard jests, personal experiences are transformed into sentiments that can be shared by all. The jocular gripe is the collective expression of an individual complaint.

Peter Blau, in his *Dynamics of Bureaucracy,* observes that complaints are nearly always made to a single person while jokes are often told to a group.[17] What Blau says about jokes applies also to the jocular gripe, which performs the functions of both complaint and joke, but differs from both.

Speaking privately to me, a patient complained: "Dinner was no good. What I cook is better." Ten minutes later, in the television room, before a group of other patients, she said: "Those hamburgers were as hard as rocks. If I'd bounced them against the wall they'd come right back." Both the speaker and her audience laughed heartily. Why was criticism of the food so differently expressed in the two situations?

(1) Alone with me, the patient talked about herself and her own cooking. But in the presence of several patients she chose to expand her personal experience into a general one. Her humorous image permitted all of them to participate imaginatively in a more objective test of the meat's quality.

(2) The group laughter in the TV room was liberating laughter.[18] "What is fine about humor," Freud says, "is the ego's victorious assertion of its own invulnerability."[19] In the complaint the patient admits his vulnerability; in the jocular gripe, as in other types of humor, he overcomes it. In addition to the humorist's triumph over his own weakness— the peculiar quality of gallows humor—there is here the added gratification in the *collective* character of the triumph.

The jocular gripe is peculiarly fit as a mechanism of adaptation to the hospital for it helps the patients, who are particularly vulnerable, to regain their identity through collective triumph over their weakness, and at the same time to release their grudges in a "substitute complaint."

(3) The joined laughter in the TV room brought about a quick consensus among the patients.[20] And consensus in turn stimulates and reinforces laughter. The laughter or the smile that accompanies jocular griping expresses in part the delight that accompanies consensus.[21] One aspect of in-group consensus noted by Bergson is the feeling that "only we" know what our laughter means. Consensus strengthens the boundaries between the group of laughers and outsiders,[22] in this case between the patients and those in authority, the doctors and nurses. The annoyance most of us feel sometimes when we hear people laugh in the next room is an annoyance at being "left out." Much jocular humor among the patients achieves this exclusive consensus. So nurses and doctors, who have access to the most intimate parts of the patient's body, are denied access to his mental life.[23]

(4) Jocular talk is the standard fare of sociability. Personal complaints are tabooed on the ward. As Simmel noted, "The purely and deeply personal traits of one's life, character, mood and fate must . . . be eliminated as factors in sociability. It is tactless . . . to display merely personal moods of depression, excitement, despondency—in brief the light and darkness of one's most intimate life."[24]

The patient who complains considers himself more important than others and thereby violates the "democratic structure of sociability" of which Simmel speaks. Corroborating evidence comes from a patient who said: "There is always one who's crabbing. He thinks he's better than others, but a patient is a patient in the hospital. . . . Even when you're a doctor and you're a patient, you're just another patient."

But the patient who eschews personal complaint and invites others to laugh with him brings about, or strengthens, a feeling of equality on the ward, a state of reciprocity, the simplest and purest form of social relationship. Although both statements describe the same experience, the social difference between "I suffer from insomnia" and "a hospital is no place to rest" is very great. The first is, in Piaget's terms, an egocentric statement.[25] The second states a general condition to be shared—and perhaps transcended—by the patients.

The jocular gripe differs not only from the personal complaint but also from the joke. Jocular gripes, and jocular talk generally, contribute more than does the joke to the reinterpretation of events and to the solidarity of the participants. As H. H. Fowler defines the terms joke and humor, the comic quality of the joke lies in the surprise element of the punch line, which makes a demand upon the *intelligence* of the listener; while humor (which includes jocular talk), finds the comic in the observation of *actual events* and evokes the *sympathy* of the listener.[26] Although both jokes and jocularity may evoke the sort of laughter that strengthens social cohesion, jocular talk cannot be resorted to in the complete absence of social cohesion, for it presupposes a common experience between speaker and listener which is the basis of the sympathy that it elicits.[27] A joke needs only a *listener,* a jocular gripe calls for a *participant.*

In the following accounts by a patient of the same experience—one addressed to a group of those who are "in the know" and the other addressed to a newcomer on the ward—the importance of shared experience is manifest:

To a group of women in the television room, all of whom had been in the hospital for some time and were complaining about the commotion in the ward:

> They never let you sleep here. One thing you can't get is sleep. . . . They never leave you alone. Not even right after my operation. Four nurses would stand around me and come up all the time asking, "Do you feel all right?" "Do you have any pain?" "Do you want a pill?" "Do you want some water?"—when all you want is sleep.

This brought general agreement and remarks like "you said it," "yeah, sure, that's just how it goes," etc., from her listeners.

Later that afternoon, the same patient told her story in the television room again, but this time a newcomer, admitted only a few hours before, was present.

Newcomer: I wonder what they're going to do to me.
Patient: They're really nice here, you know. Like after my operation, four nurses were standing around me ask-

ing if I was in pain or was there anything I wanted. I didn't want anything, but it felt good just the same, to know they care. You don't have to worry around here.

The newcomer might have been more perturbed than relieved to learn that "they never leave you alone," for she was not yet in a position to interpret this familiar gripe which brought a smile only from the initiated.

There is reason to believe, despite her complaints, that the patient who complained of too much attention enjoyed the care and reassurance of the nurses when she woke up after her operation. We are inclined to think that "she put on an act." In Flügel's words, "at least one of the most important functions [of humor] is to attract the attention of our fellow beings and to elicit an appropriate reaction from them."[28] As in every other artistic creation,[29] there is a make-believe element in the jocular remark: the term "make-believe" expresses well the bond that the act creates between speaker and listener.

So far, I have considered some functions of jocular talk for the participants. What effect does jocular griping have upon the social structure of the ward? At least three consequences appear to flow from the prevalence of humor on the ward:

(1) Complaints tend to be reduced to a minimum through a taboo enforced by the patients themselves and through the substitution of jocular griping, which helps to shape the behavior of patients in the ward according to the expectations of doctors and nurses.

Disapproval of the complaining patient is shared by most doctors, nurses and patients, according to responses obtained in the interviews with all three groups. This common disapproval of complaint is an integrating element in the ward. Thus the patients themselves, by teaching and helping each other to suppress and modify complaints, help to enforce the norms of doctors and nurses.

(2) The jocular treatment of incidents that would ordinarily call forth complaints provides patients with what Bergson calls a "corrective for an imperfection."[30] In the minds of those who are exposed to an undesirable situation, it is being remedied or reduced through its jocular interpretation. A change in the definition of the situation transforms the dangerous into the harmless, or the frightening into the amusing. So humor helps to make the hospital acceptable *as it is*.

(3) But this involves a possible dysfunctional consequence of jocular talk in the ward: the "corrective for an imperfection" occurs only in the patients' perception, and an unsatisfactory situation may persist unaltered as a source of concern. The early waking of patients in the hospital is a case in point. Jocular talk is a compromise, and like the correction offered by the compromise of a neurotic symptom it is apt to express inadequately the conditions that call it into being and to satisfy very inadequately the individual needs.[31]

In conclusion: jocular talk and jocular griping on the ward allow the patients to reinterpret for each other with concision and economy their experiences, and at the same time to entertain, reassure, convey mutual interest, and pull the group together by transforming individual experience into collective experience. Freud has pointed to the *psychic economy,* which humor makes possible for the individual.[32] Here I would like to stress the contribution humor makes to *social economy,* a contribution not to be lightly regarded, in a group whose membership is continuously changing, a group made up of many small transient sub-groups that form and re-form during the day in the ward and in the television room. In this shifting milieu, a well-told story may in a few brief minutes contribute more to the support of the frightened sick than well-planned lectures and discussions.

Solidarity in the Ward

The difficulties that the new patient encounters (which were discussed in Chapter III)—the loss of important ego-sustaining symbols and activities in a new and strange environment—are partly overcome by the mechanisms of socialization that exist in the life of the ward. Of the agents of socialization, the "opinion leader" employing, among others, the devices of jocular talk and jocular griping is only the most immediately apparent. Many other patients also serve in the ranks.

The plight of patients is greatly alleviated by the support of other patients, especially the support given to the newcomer by those who are already "in the know." Patients readily acknowledge the comforting aspects of ward life. Of the fifty-one patients interviewed at discharge, only eight spoke of the ward as exclusively a source of discomfort. Seven patients mentioned pleasures as well as pains when speaking of ward life, and twenty-eight respondents praised the ward without qualification.

Table 5

Favorable and Unfavorable Comments About Ward Life

In answer to the question, "Do you like the ward?"	
Yes	28
Yes and No	7
No	8
No answer or indifferent	8
Total	51

The eight patients who made only unfavorable comments about the ward complained mostly about the commotion and unrest. Mr. Hailos, who felt that "there is too much noise in the hospital . . .," said:

89

It would be better if the patients had more privacy: when the surgical patients come in they make noises and complain and if there are many patients of this kind it isn't pleasant.

Mrs. Wood felt the same way:

One night there was a very sick woman next to me and that had a very bad effect. She cried and yelled; later the nurse took her out. . . .

Mrs. Levy, one of the seven patients with a mixed reaction to the ward, begins in a similar fashion:

Better if you can afford to go private. All that's here is sick people; that makes you uncomfortable. I don't sleep well; one person cries; . . . . Many things going on. The ward is not comfortable.

But she continues without a pause:

Private is lonely. When you're alone, you have too much time to think, you always remember the past, not the future. . . .

The majority of the patients derived some satisfaction from their temporary life among peers. Of the total of thirty-five patients who said that they liked the ward (at least in part), twenty-nine said that they liked to be with people (Table 6):

Table 6

Reasons for Liking the Ward

Reason	No.
Like to be with people	29
The ward is efficient	1
No comment	5
Total expressing satisfaction derived from ward	35

Mr. Flowerman said:

I enjoyed the ward . . . everybody was happy, we were full of jokes. My sister asked me how do you feel, I said I'm enjoying myself, we chatted around, it was a pleasure.

Mr. Goldman said:

It's long hours in the hospital and if you have nobody to talk to it's no good.

For people who have temporarily lost touch with the reality situation of their ordinary lives, ward life may provide a new external framework within which the self may find its bearings.

New values, new relationships, reshape individual experience. Mrs. O'Neill was perhaps most articulate about this:

> [The ward] has taught me something too: to appreciate my blessings; there is always someone with bigger troubles than your own. I like people, I study them, I study myself too. . . . The patients all help each other.

Mrs. Bowman said:

> We had a nice bunch of girls there, that's why the ward is good, you always have some company there and get chummy with each other like you'd known each other for years.

Ward life may help establish ties among patients who, although previously strangers, come from the same community and have common acquaintances. When two patients discover that they live in the same neighborhood their husbands may begin to pool rides to the hospital when visiting. Or a patient may discover that he knows another patient's mother; or two patients may find that their husbands belong to the same union local. It is usually the more verbal patient (the opinion leader), who discovers such outside contacts; not only for himself but for other patients also.

The bonds formed in the ward are reinforced when patients can link new acquaintances with mutual friends outside the hospital. Mrs. Brown said:

> They have a nice bunch of women there, I have their 'phone numbers, I'm going to call them, I got many invitations. All of these people may become your best friends; I met a few who know my family and my husband's family.[33]

The break that occurs when the patient leaves his normal life at home and enters the restricted hospital life is gradually repaired in many cases by the re-establishment of continuity between these two spheres, with the help of other patients.

But does adjustment to the ward, community of the sick, help the patient to make the step back to the community of the well? By cultural definition, the sick role requires identification not with other people in a similar role, but with those who are well. At home the patient is generally strongly motivated to stop being a patient and become again the equal of his relatives and friends who move about and meet their social obligations. It is true of home-bound invalids that "the sick are tied up, not with other deviants to form a 'sub-culture' of the sick, but each with a group of non-sick, his personal circle, and, above all, physicians. The sick thus become a statistical status class and are deprived of the possibility of forming a solidary collectivity."[34] And this is true, too, of patients on the private floors. But in the ward it is not true. Patients there *do,* indeed, constitute a solidary collectivity, a "sub-culture." They have at least two things in common: the condition of being temporarily handicapped, and their submission to the same nursing and medical authorities. As patients they seek solace from each other, and their sickness is the very basis of their belongingness.

But does such identification with the sick prevent the patient from relinquishing the sick role as quickly as he might? Not necessarily. There is a double aspect to the sick role. One who wants to be a "good patient" must not only follow instructions, but must also try to get well quickly. A patient who identifies with other sick people on the ward may select the second aspect of the role of the patient, or ignore it. He is helped by other patients to learn submissiveness, but he also sees his new friends getting better and being discharged—a reminder of what he himself has to prepare for.[35]

NOTES

1. About solidarity and interaction among patients, see Renée Fox, *op. cit.*, pp. 139 ff.; William Caudill, Fredrick C. Redlich, Helen R. Gilmore and Eugene B. Brody, "Social Structure and Interaction Processes on a Psychiatric Ward," *op. cit.*; Howard Rowland, "Interaction Processes in the State Mental Hospital," *op. cit.*, and "Friendship Patterns in a State Mental Hospital," *op. cit.*

2. On the problem of socialization by the peer group, see "Informal Social Organization in the Army," *American Journal of Sociology*, LI (March 1946), 365-370, (anonymous).

3. Rules and regulations are less restricting for the secure than for the strange patient. One day, when Mrs. Rothstein was ready to be discharged, she was standing dressed in street clothes in front of the elevator. "I'm going down to the outpatient department to get me an appointment," she explained. "It takes hours if I wait for them to get it for me. Of course, I'm not supposed to do this, you know. You're supposed to wait till they wheel you out of here, but I know this place, so I'll quickly go down and come back and nobody will know and it'll save me a lot of time."

The importance of a patient's familiarity with the building and the physical lay-out has been recognized by Ford and Stephenson in their study of three Alabama hospitals, *op. cit.*

4. Rowland, "Interaction Processes in the State Mental Hospital," *op. cit.* On some functions of gossip, see Rose Laub Coser, "Insulation from Observability . . ." *op. cit.*

5. Bernard Berelson *et al.*, point out that there is "greater interaction through more strategic locations" of opinion leaders in *Voting*, Chicago: University of Chicago Press, 1954, p. 110.

"Given the freedom to choose, the members of a primary group will arrange themselves spatially in ways that reflect and implement their social relationships," Robert O. Blood and William P. Livant, "The Use of Space within the Cabin Group," *The Journal of Social Issues,* XIII (#1, 1957), 47-53.

6. Ilona Karmel begins her novel *Stephania* (Boston: Houghton Mifflin Co., 1953) with the episode of rivalry for the bed near the window.

7. She possessed the qualities which Berelson *et al.,* attribute to informal leaders: showing interest in others, being strategically located, and not being too different in socio-economic status (Berelson *et al., op. cit.,* pp. 110 ff.).

8. According to experimental studies on leadership, these qualities distinguish leaders from followers. Cf. L. H. Moore, "Leadership Traits of College Women," *Sociology and Social Research,* 1932, pp. 44-54; Theodore M. Newcomb, *Personality and Social Change,* New York: Dryden Press, 1943; Catherine M. Cox, *The Early Mental Traits of Three Hundred Geniuses,* Stanford, Calif.: Stanford University Press, 1926, quoted by Cecil A. Gibb, "Leadership," in Gardner Lindzey, (ed.), *Handbook of Social Psychology,* Cambridge: Addison-Wesley Publishing Co., Inc., 1954, II, p. 887.

With regard to the personality trait of surgency, which is "defined in terms of talkativeness, cheerfulness, geniality, enthusiasm, expressiveness, alertness and originality," see also Gibb, *ibid.,* pp. 888 ff.

9. See bibliographical article by J. C. Flügel, "Humor and Laughter," in Gardner Lindzey, (ed.), *Handbook of Social Psychology, op. cit.,* II, pp. 709-734, and Rose Laub Coser, "Some Social Functions of Humor," *Human Relations,* XII (#2, 1959), 171-172.

10. A more serious aspect of this incident has been noted in Chapter III.

11. For a very sensitive account of such counter-phobic behavior, see Renée Fox, *op. cit.,* especially pp. 170-177.

12. Henri Bergson has pointed to the fact that a reversal of roles is a frequent element in comic plays, *Laughter,* London: The Macmillan Co., 1911, p. 95. Ludwig Jekels, in an article "Zur Psychologie der Komoedie," makes the point that while the theme of tragedy is the hostility of the son against the father, in the comedy the theme is frequently reversed: the father is being deprived, in the comic play, of his "fatherly" attributes and invested with the weaknesses of the son—meaning, "You are only a human being, just like me." (A. J. Storfer, [ed.], *Almanach des Internationalen Psychoanalytischen Verlags,* Vienna: 1927, pp. 190-198.

Gregory Bateson points to a reversal of roles in the ceremonials of primitive tribes, through buffoonery for the man and magnificent ceremony for the woman, in a society which, in everyday life, glorifies masculinity and assigns to women the passive role. (*Naven,* Cambridge, England: Cambridge University Press, 1936.)

13. The joy caused by the sudden realization through humor that one is superior to the other person has been pointed out by many writers, from Hobbes to Bergson and Freud, and does not need special elaboration here. It is expressed in the German proverb, *"Wer den Schaden hat, braucht fuer den Spott nicht zu sorgen."*

14. On humor as a means of reconciling social ties and social antagonisms, see A. R. Radcliffe-Brown, *Structure and Function in Primitive Society,* London: Cohen & West, Ltd., 1952, pp. 90-116.

15. Donald Hayworth, "The Social Function and Origin of Laughter," *The Psychological Review,* XXXV (1928), 367-384.

16. Even death is trivialized and transformed into a collective will to live. Cf.: A "favorable influence is at work in the hospital ward. A sense of the actual nearness of death pervades the atmosphere there, and this serves to strengthen the instinct of life in all patients. One might, as a matter of fact, expect that in a hospital, where one sees such a tremendous amount of suffering, one would the more readily reconcile one's self to death, which ends pain. But such is not the case. Nowhere is the desire for life more definitely felt. No patient is sufficiently objective to give himself up as actually lost." (Paul Federn, "Weariness of Life in Hospital Patients," *Mental Hygiene,* XVI, Oct. 1932, 636-49.)

17. Chicago: University of Chicago Press, 1955, p. 92.

18. It is not necessary to elaborate here Freud's explanation of how the feeling of liberation consists in a release of tension and aggression. See "Wit and Its Relation to the Unconscious," *The Basic Writings of Sigmund Freud,* A. A. Brill (trans.), New York: The Modern Library, 1938, pp. 733 ff.

19. Sigmund Freud, "Humor," *Collected Papers,* London: The Hogarth Press, 1950, V, p. 217.

20. Cf. "The joke is a shortcut to consensus," Tom Burns, in "Friends, Enemies and Polite Fiction," *American Sociological Review,* XVII (Dec. 1953), 657.

21. Stanton and Schwartz, *The Mental Hospital, op. cit.,* p. 196.

22. Bergson, *op. cit.,* p. 6.

23. David Victoroff describes what he calls "le rire d'exclusion de celui dont le rire accuse la disgrâce, tandis que la joie qu'il manifeste correspond à l'accueil que se font réciproquement les rieurs au moment où leur unanimité forme ou reforme le groupe. Plus souvent, le rire oppose non pas un groupe à un individu, mais deux groupes, chacun excluant l'autre. . . ." (*Le rire et le risible,* Paris: Presses Universitaires de France, 1953, p. 156.)

24. *The Sociology of Georg Simmel,* Kurt H. Wolff, (trans.), *op. cit.,* pp. 46-47.

25. Piaget, *op cit., passim.*

26. According to Fowler, the motive or aim of humor is discovery, its province is human nature, its method is observation and its audience is sympathetic, while the motive or aim of wit is to throw light, its province is words and ideas, its method is surprise and its audience makes use of intelligence. (*A Dictionary of Modern English Usage,* Oxford: Clarendon Press, 1952, p. 241.)

27. This difference between the "pure" joke (whose comic element is provided by incongruity more often than by content) and humor that conceals a complaint is given support by a study on "Laughter In Psychiatric Staff Conferences." The authors found that for the first laugh in each session, twice as many scorings were made for incongruity as for disparagement; however, disparagement laughs rose as the conference lengthened (Anne T. Goodrich, Jules Henry and D. Wells Goodrich, in *American Journal of Orthopsychiatry,* XXIV, 1954, 175-184.) Although the authors of this paper only state but do not explain the difference in the occurrence of incongruity and disparagement

jokes, there is reason to believe that the latter were made more readily after some cohesion had been established among the staff members in the beginning of the session.

28. "Humor and Laughter," *op. cit.*, p. 730.

29. Cf. "The funny story is an artistic thing even as is the novel, the movie or the drama. . . ." Hayworth, *op. cit.*, p. 379.

30. *Op. cit.*, p. 87.

31. Cf. the discussion of safety-valve institutions by Lewis A. Coser, *op. cit.*, pp. 41-47.

Cf. also Victoroff: ". . . Le 'ridicule tue.' Mais prenons bien garde: c'est un assassinat d'un genre tout particulier qui transforme la réalité sans aucune intervention matérielle efficace et rend même inutile toute intervention de ce genre. La fonction sociale du rire dans les sociétés modernes serait comparable, à cet egard, à celle que la magie exerce dans les sociétés pré-civilisées: les procédées magiques dispensent de toute action matérielle et technique ou réduisent l'action matérielle à son minimum. . . . Le rire comme la magie—et sans qu'il y ait nécessairement un rapport de filiation de l'un à l'autre—semble répondre à ce profond besoin qu'a l'humanité de transformer la realité sociale, sans passer par l'intermédiaire de l'action techniquement efficace." (*Op. cit.*, p. 166.)

32. Freud, *Wit. . . , op. cit.*, and Freud, "Humor," *op. cit.*

33. It may be objected that such friendships among patients prevail mainly in a community hospital, and especially one serving a close-knit community. This is undoubtedly so. However, I have had occasion, after the field work for this study was completed, to gain some impressions in a teaching hospital with but weak community ties: there also, even in a four-bed room, friendships were formed quickly and outlasted the period of hospitalization.

Burling, Lentz and Wilson, *op. cit.*, pp. 30-31, also stress this point in their description of several different types of hospitals. See also Fox, *op. cit.*, esp. pp. 139 ff.

34. Parsons, *The Social System, op. cit.*, p. 477.

35. Moreover, the ward provides a favorable setting for mechanisms of recovery which Hamburg, Hamburg and deGoza, *op. cit.*, have found to be important in their study, namely: (1) mobilization of hope; (2) group relationships; (3) establishment of rudiments of independent activity by doing small things for each other; (4) humor; (5) restoration of self-esteem.

PART III

THE ADJUSTMENT OF
PATIENTS

"This prudence, this habit of feinting with
their predicament and refusing to put up a
fight, was ill rewarded. For, while averting
that revulsion which they found so unbear-
able, they also deprived themselves of those
redeeming moments, frequent enough when
all is told, when by conjuring up pictures of
a reunion to be, they could forget about the
plague. Thus, in a middle course between
these heights and depths, they drifted
through life rather than lived, the prey of
aimless days and sterile memories, like
wandering shadows that could have acquired
substance only by consenting to root themselves in the solid earth of their distress."

Albert Camus, *The Plague,* II, p. 66

CHAPTER VII

A Home Away from Home[1]

THE FORMATION OF FRIENDSHIP TIES AMONG PATIENTS ON THE WARD soon begins to make patients feel "at home." Mrs. Golder, for instance, said, "it's wonderful here, it's a regular party. . . . It seems home to everybody."

Because the patients have suffered a partial loss of ego identity, they seek reassurance and recognition through self-expressive behavior. The primary relationships established on the ward, like those that characterize family life, may come to be considered ends in themselves, and very frequently outlast the time and the place in which they are first formed.[2]

For some patients, as has been seen, Mount Hermon embraces an element of tradition that claims their allegiance. For still other patients, who had nobody to take care of them outside, the hospital was a substitute for a family. Mrs. Norstin, for example, did not want to go home when discharged. "I'm surprised my doctor sends me home," she said. . . . "I'm helpless when I go home. . . ." Mr. Morris felt the same way: "The trouble is this, I have nobody to take care of me. . . . It's only a week and here they discharge me." And Mr. Flowerman explained: "I lost my wife. . . . Someone has to take care of me. . . . If I had my wife, I wouldn't go to the hospital, I'd lay down in bed and call the doctor. But here, you get every day clean linen. They give you this and this and this. . . ."

Even to some of those who have families, hospital care seems preferable. Mr. Levinstein said: "You get better care, there are the nurses, the doctors; ask a woman, she can't tell you nothing." And others, too, spoke of the greater attention and courtesy they could expect in the hospital.

Once their initial fears have subsided, many patients, feeling protected and taken care of, decide that "this is as good as" or "better than" home. Their meals are brought to them, their beds are made, their hygiene is supervised. They can now indulge in a legitimate passivity and gratify desires that in ordinary life they would have to repress in order to live up to their responsibilities.

Many of the fifty-one patients interviewed at the time of their discharge,[3] spoke of the hospital as a place where they could feel protected and secure rather than as a place where specific, well-defined tasks had to be accomplished.

But some other patients emphasized that the hospital was better equipped to do a specific job. Miss Peterson, in explaining why she preferred the hospital to home, said, "They are more equipped, their research is further advanced, there is always something new coming into a hospital." And Mrs. Frederick, who tended to view the hospital as a place of healing only, said that she would rather be home since "there is nothing [the hospital] can do for me now."

Miss Peterson, Mrs. Frederick, and certain others saw the functions of the hospital as *limited* and *instrumental,* while patients like Mr. Levinstein, who emphasized the "care and attention" received at the hospital, seemed to look upon the hospital as a source for the gratification of *primary* needs.[4] The patients interviewed divided almost equally into these two groups.

Table 7

Patients' Images of the Hospital

Hospital is a place to:	No.
Give care and attention	21
Do a job that cannot be done at home	19
Answer not applicable to these categories (or NA)	11

Do the two categories of patients that emerge here (see Table 7) possess distinctly different orientations toward hospital life? If so, the desires of one group for primary satisfactions, and of the other for instrumental achievements, should appear in patients' responses to other questions dealing with relationships in the hospital structure. For example, the attitudes toward hospital staff might be expected to diverge in a similar way, with some patients expressing primary attitudes toward doctor and nurse, and others judging them on their professional competence.

Certainly for any patient the most important person in the hospital is the doctor. What does the patient expect from him? Two basically different images of the doctor emerge from the patients' responses to the question, "What is your idea of a good doctor?" They are (1) the professional man, and (2) the omnipotent figure, or dispenser of protection and love.

Twenty-two patients in some part of their answers pointed to the necessity of scientific and professional competence. Said one: "He should be understanding, polite and know what he studied, what his profession is, that he understands what he is trying to diagnose." Mr. James, an uneducated and not very articulate patient, found it easier to define the bad doctor: "A bad one is careless, independent, he thinks his reputation makes up for him. A good doctor don't overlook much, weighs things carefully."

Twenty-seven patients spoke of the doctor not as a trained professional, but as a man who will gratify primary needs, either through the provision of kindness and love or through inherent omnipotence. "The main thing: talks nice to me, gives me hope . . ."; "when the doctor takes interest. A smile doesn't cost nothing. . . ." Mr. Rubin related his experiences with two private doctors:

He is not too good a doctor. He is a Harvard graduate, a sporty guy; gave me a speech, that's all. There was another one; he was good; he was a sociable and talkative man; he used to talk to me nice.

These patients felt that a "good doctor" is one who "talks nice," and who makes them "feel good." Some other patients expected from the doctor omnipotence and omniscience—a personal *mana,* not an acquired skill. The most striking description of the magical medicine man came from a 70-year-old arthritic lady who told of a "good" doctor that she encountered fifty years ago when she first came to America:

When people came to him, they went back happy. He just looked at a patient, they make him talk, people went back all cured. He didn't even give them medicine, or maybe one medicine or two medicines and people went back happy and so cured. If a patient came to him, he write everything on a postal card and he keep it for years. He didn't have any equipment like they have now and every patient was cured.

Not all those who expected omnipotence from the doctor waxed so lyrical. Some simply said that *all* doctors "know more, know better," or that the doctor always gives "right advice." "In my whole life I've never known a doctor to be wrong," said one.

In the following table the criteria of medical or professional competence have been classified as "instrumental," while criteria of "omnipotence," and of love and kindness, have been called "primary" since these traits serve to satisfy affective needs (Table 8).

Table 8

Patients' Images of "The Doctor"

A good doctor can be judged on the basis of:	No.
Instrumental criteria	22
Primary criteria	27
N.A.	2

Again the answers divide almost equally between "primary" and "instrumental" orientations, with a slight majority of "primary" responses. Moreover, these definitions of a "good doctor" correlate significantly with the definitions of the hospital's function (Table 9). Patients who felt that the hospital needed to do an efficient job were more likely to expect a doctor to display professional competence while those who expected "care and attention" from the hospital tended to expect "solace" or "omnipotence" from a doctor.

Table 9

Patients' Images of Hospital by Images of Doctor

	Patients' Attitudes toward Hospital		
	Instrumental	Primary	N.A. (or not applicable)
Patients' Attitudes toward Doctor:			
Instrumental	16	1	5
Primary	3	19	5
N.A.	0	1	1

Of the nineteen patients who expressed an instrumental attitude toward the hospital, seventeen expressed an instrumental attitude toward the doctor; and of the twenty-one who expressed primary attitude toward the hospital, nineteen expressed a primary attitude toward the doctor. These associations suggest that the instrumental-primary division is a meaningful one.[5]

On the basis of their answers to these two questions, we may classify the respondents into three types:

I. *Instrumental:* Those who gave only instrumental responses (including those who gave one instrumental and one inapplicable response).

II. *Primary:* Those who showed only a primary orientation in their answers (including those who gave one primary and one inapplicable response).

III. *Mixed:* Those who gave one instrumental and one primary answer.

If this classification of patients proves useful, there should appear a significant difference between "primary" and "instrumental" patients in their adaptation to hospital life. Let us consider three of the demands that the hospital makes upon patients:

(1) That he forfeit his reliance on family and friends in the matter most important to him at the moment, his health. From the time he enters the hospital, those who have been closest to him will be "visitors," while the strangers on the hospital staff will have intimate control over him.

(2) That he accept the "routine" and "order" of the hospital as defined

by nurses and doctors and that he accept the hospital setting *as is,* an established order beyond his control and not subject to his interference.

(3) That he attempt to be a "good patient." This means, to the doctors and nurses, that he will not complain, or demand very much personal attention.

Patients with a primary orientation toward the hospital or the doctor might be expected to comply with demands more readily than patients with an instrumental orientation. Responses to a series of questions designed to test attitudes toward these demands tend to confirm this expectation.

(1) In an attempt to find out to what extent patients forfeited their reliance on family and friends and gave up, generally, their nonpatient role, I asked: "What do you miss most while you're in the hospital?"

(2) In an attempt to find out whether patients accepted the hospital setting as given and defined by others, I asked: "Are there any suggestions that *you* would care to make for a possible improvement of the patients' comfort?"

(3) Finally, in probing the respondents' images of the "good patient," I tried to find out whether they believed that patients should submit to rules and regulations without making any personal claims.

Feeling of Deprivation

The hospital ward offers to many patients an "escape from freedom."[6] There they can legitimately withdraw from social obligations, activities, and strivings which prevail in the "outside world." "Here I can stay in bed with all my problems," Mrs. Kit said. . . . "This is the sixth time. This is just like my home, I just make up my mind to come back."[7]

Small amenities of daily life—a cup of tea, a glass of water, an extra pillow—are easily obtainable. The major daily chores—the making of beds, the bringing in of meals, the clock-regulated administration of medication—are taken care of by the nursing staff in routine fashion. A patient has few responsibilities of his own; he cannot decide for himself what to eat, what medication to take, whether to take his own temperature.

Mr. Goldman said: "I got everything, I don't need nothing, you press the button, the nurse is right there." The same conditions, however, seemed intolerable to Mrs. Thompson, who said:

In a place like this you get mad and have to do things whether you want to or not, abide by rules, . . . they take your freedom away from you. I got stuck here for six weeks. So many restrictions on you.

The answers to the question "What do you miss most while you're in the hospital?" may be classified under three headings:

(1) Some patients said they missed most activities or people closely associated with their roles outside the hospital. Mrs. Thompson missed her

"freedom." Miss Terrini (who lived at home with her mother and supported her), missed her "mother." Mr. Thomas missed his "little boy, 8½ ." Mrs. Miller missed "husband and daughter;" 68-year-old Mrs. Mann missed her grandchildren; Miss Bluestein, a high school girl, missed her friends; and Mrs. Wood, missed "husband, child and household" and said "work is waiting for me. . . ."

(2) Some patients said that they most missed certain things to assure their bodily comfort, such as food, liquor, and smoking, and belongings that can be considered body extensions, especially clothes. Mr. Flowerman, (who enjoyed the attention he was getting in the hospital and defined a good doctor as one who could "talk nice to me"), said that what he missed most was "smoking." Mrs. Stephanos missed food. Mrs. Goldman, aged fifty-one, said "I like nice clothes to wear. . . ." Mr. Finkelstein, who lived at home with his daughter and her family, exemplified those patients who show concern with their own bodies. Asked what he missed most, he said:

> First thing, I have a good bed [at home]. Second thing, I got a
> bathroom next to me. Third thing, I eat too much in the hospital.
> Today they had some kind of lamb, that's all I ate, meat, vegetables,
> bread, a cup of tea, that's all.

(3) Some patients said that they didn't miss anything. When Mrs. Kit, to whom "the hospital is just like home," was asked whether there was anything she missed while in the hospital, she said: "No, I don't miss nothing;" and Mr. Goldman, who lived with his wife and was a foreman in a shop, said: "I got everything, I don't need nothing; you press the button, the nurse is right there."[8]

The distribution of responses to the question, "What do you miss most while you're in the hospital?" is shown in Table 10:

Table 10

Types of Deprivation Experienced by Respondents

Patients say they miss most:	No.
People, activity	24
Intake, belongings	11
Nothing	9
N.A.	7

For a total of twenty of these patients, family, friends, and home activities were not in the foreground of their thoughts. We may reasonably assume that these patients were less concerned with "non-hospital reality" than were the twenty-four patients who said they missed most people or activities associated with home and good health. These twenty appear to have forfeited, for the time being, their reliance on family and friends and on their own activities.

As Table 11 shows, this differential awareness of wants is related to the patients' differential orientation towards hospital or doctor:

Table 11

Attitudes Toward Hospital or Doctor by Types of Deprivation Experienced

Miss most:	Attitude toward Hospital or Doctor			
	Instrumental	Mixed	Primary	N.A.
People, activity	*14*	2	8	0
Belongings, intake, nothing	4	2	*13*	1
N.A.	3	0	4	0

Respondents whom we have classified as "instrumental" in their orientations toward hospital or doctor were more likely to miss "people" or "activity" than respondents whom we have called "primary"; conversely, patients who said they missed "people" or "activity" were more often than not instrumental in their orientation, while those who reported missing nothing or being concerned with their bodies more frequently tended to display primary attitudes toward hospital or doctor.

This suggests that a patient who enjoys the "care and attention" in the hospital and expects solace from doctors is more likely to meet successfully the implicit demand that he "forget about" his outside duties and responsibilities and forfeit his reliance on relatives and friends.

Acceptance or Criticism

Working on the assumption that the rigid routine of the hospital that deprives patients of the possibility of interference and decision-making also provides order and security for those whose self-image has been impaired, I tried to find out from patients to what extent they abided by rules and regulations because they were forced to, and to what extent they considered the rules "good." I hoped to distinguish between those who questioned the daily routine of the hospital and those who, in Erich Fromm's words, "wanted to do what they had to do."[9]

I asked the patients whether they had any suggestions for the improvement of patients' comfort. Twenty-three patients could suggest nothing for the improvement of patients' comfort, even after being probed;[10] but twenty-three others (many of them only after being probed) offered some suggestion for a change in ward routine. Suggestions ranged from "larger washroom," "better television set," "more visiting time," to "less talk among nurses," "brighter coloring on the walls," "waking at a later hour."

Table 12

Respondents' Willingness to Make Suggestions

"Do you have any suggestions for possible improvement of patients' comfort?"	
Yes	23
No	23
N.A.	5

As Table 13 shows, respondents who had no suggestions to make for the improvement of patients' comfort were more likely to have a primary attitude toward hospital or doctor, while those who made some suggestions tended to have an instrumental approach:

Table 13

Attitudes Toward Hospital or Doctor by Willingness to Make Suggestions

Suggestions:	Attitudes toward Hospital or Doctor			
	Instrumental	Mixed	Primary	N.A.
Yes	14	2	7	0
No	4	2	16	1
N.A.	3	0	2	0

Out of the eighteen instrumentally-oriented patients who answered the question, fourteen had a concrete suggestion to make, while out of the twenty-three primary-oriented patients who responded, only seven had a suggestion to offer.

Mr. Flowerman is representative of the patient with a primary orientation who had identified with those in authority. (He enjoyed the attention he received in the hospital, expected the "good doctor" to "talk nice," and missed "smoking.") He said: "I would like to smoke. But it wouldn't be right. If I were in charge, I wouldn't let anybody smoke either." When asked whether he had any suggestions for improvement of patients' comfort, he seemed not to understand the question. When he was probed, "Suppose you were on the board of directors of the hospital, could you think of any recommendations?" he said: "Everything is as it should be. They have a television here; of course, now it's out of order. What more could they do? They have a waiting room, what more could you want? They change beds for me. . . . At home you can't get that attention, you can't change your bed every day."

Six patients, in backing up their unwillingness to make suggestions, emphasized their acceptance of authority: "The hospital is being run how they see fit," "Patients shouldn't talk," "I don't think a patient should make suggestions," "Everything is as it should be," "The doctors know what's best," and "[Patients have] to obey orders." *All of these patients were of the "primary" type.*[11] The emphasis all these patients place on the appropriateness of their subordination to hospital routine lends additional support to the conclusion emerging from Table 13, that patients who seek to satisfy primary needs in hospital or doctor are more likely to accept ward routine.

Submission or Autonomy

I asked the question, "What is . . . a good patient?" in an attempt to find out whether patients shared with doctors and nurses expectations about the passive role of patients. I wanted to know which respondents would grant a patient in the hospital ward some degree of autonomy and which respondents considered hospital rules and regulations to be inviolable absolutes requiring total submission. In his *Moral Judgment of the Child,* Jean Piaget[12] distinguishes between "heteronomous" and "autonomous" authority. People who have a heteronomous conception of authority feel that rules and regulations emanate from a power *outside* of the social relations within which they are applied. To these people, rules are immutable, unquestionable, and totally binding. On the other hand, persons who have an autonomous conception of authority feel that rules arise in the course of social interaction and can be changed, through agreement, by those who participate in the "game." Rules can be judged and evaluated and changed by those to whom they apply.

Autonomous behavior, according to Piaget's theory, consists in (a) self-sufficiency of the individual, (b) his ability to judge "good" and "bad" deeds from the perspective of the actor involved, and (c) his ability to interact with others on the basis of reciprocity.[13]

One or another of these criteria of autonomy appears in a number of the responses to the question "What makes a good patient?" Three types of answers, then, may be properly classed as stressing "autonomy:"

(1) Some respondents felt that "you got to help yourself," that a patient should be ". . . self-sufficient as much as possible." Mrs. Hardman said that "the patient has to do a lot himself. . . . They can't follow completely," and Mrs. Bowman said, "a good patient is one who understands the doctor . . . [he must] know what it's all about."

(2) A number of respondents, refusing to lay down an absolute standard of "goodness" in a patient, noted that the point of view or the condition of the individual patient must be taken into account. Mr. Hailos felt that "that depends on the age . . . it also depends on their education. . . ." Mrs. Nathanson stated:

I say this much, the patient can be good when she isn't suffering. When the patient is suffering she can't be good, she wants relief and I can't blame her. I've seen some pesty patients, they holler and yell but they feel that someone can help them. If there's any spark of life in you, you try to fight, but if you are desperately ill, you can't fight.

Mr. Flowerman's discussion of "the good" patient makes wide allowance for human sympathy. He said:

According to the illness he has. A man lies with me; he has had a leg off; he has diabetes, you can't ask anything of him; he is blind. You have to take from that patient whatever he gives you. He started to cry at night. I thought I wouldn't live through the night. When he started to cry, I thought: now he understands his situation, now he is in his right mind. . . .

Mr. Geoffrey also related a patient's behavior to his ability to make judgments:

If a patient knows what's the matter, if they take off a piece from his finger [shows his finger which was partially amputated previously], he knows what's wrong, he can be a good patient; but if his stomach hurts him and it's inside and he doesn't know what's going on, he can't be a good patient.

(3) Some respondents said that the "good patient" should be "considerate," "cooperative," etc. Although at first sight, these answers seem to belong to the heteronomous "obedience" dimension of classification, I feel reasonably justified in interpreting them as calling for reciprocity. Mrs. Smith, who believes that a patient should be "nice . . . it takes two to be nice, it takes two to make a bargain, you got to be understandable that a person can only do so much," is saying that, to be good, a patient must enter imaginatively into the position of the other partners in the relationship. Miss Curl emphasized this quality, too. She expanded her initial statement that: "[a good patient] tries to get along with doctors and nurses," to say: "Try to help them out as much as you possibly can. . . . They're busy people. . . . There are people who say they're going to die and they don't realize that there are other patients who are sicker. . . ."

It seemed to me that answers of respondents who consider a patient "good" if he is "cooperative," "considerate," etc., should be classified, along with the first two types of responses, as "autonomous." Although in everyday language "cooperation" may often be a polite euphemism for "obedience," on the ward those patients who spoke of cooperation seemed to differ significantly in their intentions from those patients who felt that a good patient should "keep quiet," or "keep his mouth shut," or otherwise avoid trouble.

Indeed, in sharp contrast to all three types of "autonomous" responses were the answers of those respondents who would not allow the patient any leeway for making decisions. According to Mrs. Norman, a patient should "do what he is told." Mrs. Cherry said that patients are good when they "lie in bed and keep their mouth shut. . . ." Mrs. Kane also thought a good patient "is one who keeps his mouth shut;" and Mr. Walnut decreed that he must "just behave himself." To these respondents, only the most submissive behavior is appropriate for a patient.

If we divide the respondents into two groups, those who expected some degree of autonomy of a patient and those who expected complete submission, we have the following distribution, (Table 14):

Table 14

Patients' Images of a "Good Patient"

A patient should be:	
To some degree autonomous	27
Completely submissive	20
N.A.	4

Comparing these answers with previous answers, we find that those who were instrumental in their orientation toward hospital or doctor were more likely than were those with primary attitudes to grant some degree of autonomy to patients.

Table 15

Patients' Images of Hospital or Doctor by Images of a "Good Patient"

	Patients' Orientation toward Hospital or Doctor			
	Instrumental	Mixed	Primary	N.A.
A good patient should be:				
Autonomous	17	2	8	0
Submissive	3	2	15	0
N.A.	1	0	2	1

Respondents who expected some autonomy of good patients were more likely to look upon the hospital as a place to "do a job" or more likely to judge the doctor by his professional competence than were respondents who expected patients to be submissive to hospital demands. The latter were more likely to expect from the hospital and the doctor gratification of primary needs of attention, care, or protection.

The Price of Adaptation

In the preceding pages I have explored the relation between patients' attitudes towards doctors and hospital and their acceptance of the rules and restrictions imposed by the hospital structure. As might have been expected, patients with primary attitudes appear much more likely to accept hospital norms. Although patients with primary orientation toward hospital or doctor seem, then, to be particularly adaptable to the sick role in the ward, such adaptability also has *dysfunctional* consequences.

In the hospital structure, where a doctor is endeavoring to be "more of a doctor" and a nurse tries to be "more of a nurse," a patient is expected to be "less of a patient" as hospitalization draws nearer to the end. Only because they are supposed to contribute to his speedy recovery, and make it possible for him to abandon the sick role, are the restrictions that are imposed on the sick person justified. A good patient, as defined in society, is certainly one who submits to medical and nursing authority; but he is also one who gets well quickly and then is ready to take up everyday activities.

In the hospital (as elsewhere in our culture) a patient who makes a speedy recovery is praised as being a "good girl" or "good boy." Not only does this convalescence indicate that he has been obedient to doctors' instructions, but it also shows a readiness to move out of the sick role and to assume again a life of social usefulness. Someone who "refuses to get better" is considered a bad patient. Thus a patient who suffered a relapse explained: "I was a bad boy today. Three days ago the doctor said I can go home in a few days. Today I started bleeding again."

Now it seems reasonable to suppose that complete adjustment to the requirements of the hospital may make it more difficult for a patient to move as expected out of his sick role. The patient who had a relapse just before he was scheduled to be discharged, had made a "good adjustment" to the hospital, in the estimation of his doctors and nurses. He himself said, "The first two weeks I was here, I was very impatient to go home. But now I figure it's better to be here; this way, I'll really get better. After all, *they* have so much experience, *they* know better, *they* are running the hospital."

Clearly, this patient accepted the norms of the hospital, but he appeared to relish the idea of continuing to play the sick role. It is significant that at discharge he said with a contented smile: "[At home] my wife has my bed all made for me."

We cannot say with any assurance that this patient's relapse was the result of his psychological unwillingness to leave the sheltered hospital atmosphere. Yet of many patients on the ward, the doctors would say, "He likes it here too well," or "This patient has hospitalitis; each time we tell her she can go home, her blood pressure shoots up sky-high." Although such patients were generally liked by doctors and nurses because, they were "so sweet," or "so good" or because they "never complain," this approval was never unmixed with skepticism.

A patient who "enjoys it here too much" arouses some suspicion. He contradicts the cultural definition of a patient, who should, as the etymology of the word indicates, "suffer." Moreover, a sick person who refuses to move out of his sick role, or who comes back again and again, robs doctors and nurses of the satisfaction and credit of a job well done.

A patient who likes the ward is easily suspected of not being very sick. Sometimes this suspicion is justified. One patient admitted:

> I just came in because I wanted a check-up. From time to time I want my diet straightened out. It gives me a fresh start. As a matter of fact, I don't mind going to the hospital. I like the ward.

Such patients are getting a free ride: they are getting something for nothing; and they hurt the self-esteem of doctors and nurses whose efforts to help them seem to be in vain.

Staff concern about patients who "like" the hospital was voiced by a nurse who said: "[The patients] should have more diversional therapy . . . but when you make things too pleasant, they won't want to go home."

To try to gauge how willing a patient might be to assume again his non-patient role, I asked at the end of the formal interview, when the discharged patient was in his own street clothes and ready to go home: "What will be the first thing you'll do when you get home?"

I used almost the same categories in classifying the answers to this question that I used in classifying the answers to the question, "What do you miss most while you're in the hospital?"

Some respondents wanted, first of all, to be with *family or friends,* or to carry on *activities* they had neglected while sick. Thus Mr. James said: "Look around at my things . . . I'll try and get a good stick so I can go out in the yard [to see how the beans and tomatoes are growing]." Mrs. Brown said, "Kiss my son and squeeze him. He's three. . . . I have another one who's only one." Mrs. Peterson said that she would make different arrangements around the house "so that things will be organized," and Mr. Taylor said he would "talk to my folks, I miss them a lot."

Other patients answered in terms of *bodily gratification* or *complete passivity.* Mrs. Abrams was going to "take a bath." Mr. Finkelstein was going to "lie down," and Mrs. Stephanos wanted to "rest, feel everything I have." The distribution of answers is given in Table 16:

Table 16

Anticipated Post-Hospital Experience

"What will be the first thing you'll do when you get home?"		
Patient anticipates:	Interaction or action	18
	Bodily gratification or passivity	29
	N.A.	4

Those patients, more than half, who did not speak of taking up their social obligations or resuming their relations with family or friends, were more likely than the others to look to the hospital or doctor to gratify primary needs. They seemed generally unready to envisage taking up social life outside the hospital again.

Table 17

Patients' Images of Hospital or Doctor by Anticipated Post-Hospital Experience

| | Patients' Orientation toward Hospital or Doctor | | | |
	Instrumental	Mixed	Primary	N.A.
Patient prepares for:				
Interaction or action	15	1	2	0
Bodily gratification or passivity	5	3	20	1
N.A.	1	0	3	0

Those patients who considered hospital and doctor in their instrumental function, however, were also more apt to speak of some activity or some relationship with those from whom they had been separated.

Sometimes patients are quite aware of the price of adaptation to the hospital. Renée Fox quotes a patient as saying:

> This place keeps drawing you in toward itself, and the world outside starts to get smaller and smaller—farther and farther away. . . . I wouldn't want to adjust perfectly to any place. And particularly not to this place.[14]

Now we see that although acceptance of hospital norms and a primary orientation toward the hospital or doctor may facilitate adaptation to the ward, they may also make it difficult for patients to leave the sick role and the ward and take up again their normal lives and work.

Lack of acceptance of ward demands may have larger implications. In an experimental study in a mental hospital, it was found that patients who, at admission, resisted the hospital, and displayed "the strongest outward-directed drive," were generally diagnosed as the most likely to recover. "The presence of this drive should be highly evaluated from the standpoint of the ultimate aim of the hospital, even though it may be very inconvenient for the purpose of making the patient accept the temporary stay in the hospital."[15]

The Paradox of Rationality

It has been seen that the role of the patient contains contradictory imperatives of passivity and effort. The patient who best adjusts to the demands of hospital efficiency may prove to be least well prepared to take up the activities and social intercourse appropriate to recovery; for the passivity appropriate to hospitalization may inhibit active efforts to re-enter the demanding responsible world of the non-sick. Similar role contradictions, it is interesting to note, are found in all "rational" types of social organization.

In the preceding pages the orientation that I have called "instrumental" might equally well have been called "rational," in that it is concerned with the effective relation between means and ends. It will be remembered that some patients saw the hospital as designed to do a "job" that could not otherwise be done; they saw it as an effective means to secure the desired end of effecting a cure; similarly they judged the doctor's qualifications in relation to his healing function. Patients who looked upon hospital or doctor in this manner should certainly be called "rational."

However, "rationality" is an ambiguous term which contains warring elements; and it is this very conflict of "rationalities" that seems to account for the apparent contradiction in the demands upon the patient.

"We understand as substantially rational," says Karl Mannheim, "an act or thought which reveals intelligent insight into the interrelations of events in a given situation."[16] The patients classified earlier as "instrumental" in their orientation tended to be "substantially rational."

These patients were less ready, however, than other patients to relinquish autonomous judgment of hospital procedure. Subordination of their judgments to the demands of the organization would be what Mannheim calls "functionally rational" in that it leads to optimum adaptation to the demands of a structure that is designed to bring about the desired cure. "Everything that breaks through and disrupts this functional ordering is functionally irrational."[17] A patient who wants to make suggestions to hospital staff and organization may contribute to the disruption of the functional ordering of hospital procedure.

Mrs. Thompson, a 50-year-old Negro woman on the surgical ward, is a case in point. She defined a good doctor as one who "can tell you what's wrong instead of running back and forth." She said that she missed most her "freedom, and home-made cooking." She complained that "you have to do things whether you want to or not, abide by rules, accustom to new habits, they take your freedom away from you." She suggested that to improve the ward they get "first of all, a new cook. And some doctors who handle you easy and not as if you're made out of iron." The doctors said of Mrs. Thompson that she "had the whole floor upset," and that "she's making trouble for the nurses." The nurses felt that "she's a trouble-maker, she's giving the doctor a hard time."[18] At discharge, when she was about to go to a convalescent home, she remarked: "I'm not used to anybody waiting on me, fussing over me." Her "substantive" rationality was "functionally irrational."

The demands made on patients appear to be rationally ordered and logically consistent, but they entail a difficult psychological transition from one state to another. Patients are asked to let others take care of them as a means of getting better; at the same time they are expected to become self-sufficient as quickly as possible, so as to be able to carry out the obligations of a normal life. It is not always easy, however, for a person who has given up his substantial rationality in the hospital to recapture it when his health is restored.

It may be argued that in modern society we are all subject every day to such contradictory demands. As we move from one sphere of activity to another—the family, the job, voluntary associations, etc.—we must alternate between situations in which we must make our own calculated decisions and situations in which we must conform to the decisions of others. But such shifts, often accompanied by a change in the social environment, occur rather regularly and predictably and allow the individual, at least for a small part of each day, to reflect upon the consequences of his choices. But the patient during the whole length of his stay in the hospital is not expected to make his own rational choices. By the time he is discharged he may have "unlearned" the making of choices. Motives once internalized may continue to operate when they are no longer functionally adequate.

Mannheim says, "It is clear that persons who are confronted more frequently with situations in which they cannot act habitually and without thinking and in which they must always organize themselves anew will have more occasion to reflect on themselves and on situations than persons who have adapted themselves once and for all."[19] Conversely, it seems likely that a person's ability to "reorganize himself anew" may be weakened if he suffers long and frequent exposure to an environment which demands unquestioning and unreflective behavior.

NOTES

1. See Rose Laub Coser, "A Home Away from Home," *Social Problems,* IV (July 1956), 3-17.

2. The term "primary" is here used to indicate total rather than segmental involvement of the personality, and affective and diffuse rather than affectively neutral and specific attitudes. (Cf. Davis, *Human Society, op. cit.,* pp. 295-297; and Parsons, *The Social System, op. cit.,* pp. 65-66.)

3. Patients were asked, "When you're sick, would you rather be home or in the hospital?" For interview schedule, see appendix. In elaborating their answers, most of those interviewed expressed feelings and opinions about the hospital, its functions, and life on the ward.

4. Eleven out of the fifty-one patients did not elaborate on their preference for home or hospital; their answers were classified as "not applicable" to the categories discussed.

5. This and all following associations hold, if controlled by age and sex. See Appendix II.

6. In the waiting room, Mrs. Bowman said to me: "You look tired, you know, you ought to get away from it all some time. . . . Get away completely, lie back and relax and not think of anything and have people take care of you, give you a back rub." Probe (smiling): "Maybe I ought to come in here for a week?" Mrs. Bowman understood that hint, for she was embarrassed: "Well, no [pause]—I just got my back rubbed, it feels so good, you know." She went on: "This is my third time here. I was at the X Hospital and previously at Y. But here they're much nicer. If you ask for something, they'll bring it to you."

7. Mrs. Kit's hospital record indicated that when interviewed, she was in the hospital for the ninth rather than the sixth time. Olga W. McNemar and C. Landis obtained a correlation of only .50 between patients' reports of frequency of illness and their hospital records. ("Childhood Disease and Emotional Maturity in Psychopathic Women," *Journal of Abnormal and Social Behavior,* XXX, 1935, 314-319.)

8. Edward Liss says: "The cultural techniques" of patients "give way first. Those are the interests that have evolved through social relationships at home and in school. Next to go are the social relationships, and what is left is the primitive insistence upon and interest in food and affection." ("Convalescence," *Mental Hygiene,* XXI, 1937, 619-622.)

9. Bruno Bettelheim noted that in a concentration camp the inmates after some time accept the norms of those in command. (See Bruno Bettelheim, "Individual and Mass Behavior in Extreme Situations," *Journal of Abnormal and Social Psychology,* XXXVIII, 1943, 417-452.) See also Goffman, "The Moral Career of the Mental Patient," *op. cit.*

10. It is interesting to note that the idea that a patient has no say is so internalized that more often than not the question was not understood. Whenever a patient seemed not to understand, he was probed with questions about those things that were frequent objects of complaints, like not sleeping enough, being waked up early, inadequate food, etc. If even after probing the respondent mentioned no changes in hospital routine that he would find desirable, he was classified as having nothing to suggest.

11. Five of these patients displayed primary attitudes with regard to both hospital and doctor, and one displayed a primary attitude toward the doctor while his image of the hospital was not ascertainable.

12. *Op. cit.*

13. For a further development of the concept of "reciprocity" and "autonomy," see also Charles Odier, *Anxiety and Magic Thought,* New York: International Universities Press, 1956.

George Herbert Mead has elaborated especially on this aspect of reciprocity in social relations: "The child who plays in a game must be ready to take the attitude of everyone else involved in that game. . . . The child taking one role must be ready to take the role of everyone else. . . ." (*op. cit.,* p. 151).

14. *Op. cit.,* p. 184. (The complete quote was taken from Fox, *Ward F-Second and the Research Physician,* Unpublished dissertation, Harvard University, 1953, p. 87.)

15. Tamara Dembo and Eugenia Hanfmann, "The Patient's Psychological

Situation upon Admission to a Mental Hospital," *American Journal of Psychology,* XLVII (July 1935), 381-408.

On the problem of patients' attachment to the hospital see also Norman Reider, "A Type of Transference to Institutions," *Bulletin of the Menninger Clinic,* XVII (March 1953), 58-63. See also Elizabeth Proehl, "The Transition from Institutional to Social Adjustment," *American Sociological Review,* III (1938), 534-540.

16. *Man and Society in an Age of Reconstruction,* London: Routledge & Kegan Paul, Ltd., 1940, p. 53.

17. *Ibid.,* p. 54.

18. The interne in charge, who did, indeed, have a hard time with her, somehow appreciated her sense of autonomy. He had this to say a week after her discharge: "Did you see Mrs. Thompson coming back for a check-up? You know, it's funny, for all the trouble she gave me, I was glad when I saw her. I said hello to her like to an old friend. I kind of miss her on the ward. She sure kept me on my feet."

19. *Man and Society. . . , op. cit.,* p. 57.

CHAPTER VIII

The Hospital-Oriented Type:
A Social Role

Hospital Orientation

In the preceding chapter we dealt with a configuration of attitudes toward the hospital. It appears that those patients who look for primary gratification in hospital or doctor tend to be hospital-oriented in other respects as well. They were less likely than the other patients to miss relatives, friends, and home activities; they were more likely to be content with the ward, and could offer fewer suggestions for changes in it; they tended to feel that the good patient should submit meekly to orders. And they arrived at the moment of discharge less well prepared than the other patients to anticipate giving up their patienthood.

One might be tempted to divide patients into "active" and "passive" character types, were it not for the fact that many patients who gave "passive" answers behaved on the ward in a very active manner. Many of them were outgoing, helpful, joking (very much like Mrs. Rothstein, whose profile was drawn in Chapter VI). It seems better, therefore, to call patients of this kind "hospital-oriented" to distinguish them from those who were "outside-oriented."

These appear to be configurations of attitudes. Patients who were hospital-oriented in their answers to all three questions: "What do you miss most?" "Do you have any suggestions?" and "What makes a good patient?" were much more likely to express primary attitudes toward hospital or doctor and less ready to anticipate going home than were patients who were hospital-oriented on only one or on none of these questions. If we assign to each respondent a score, arrived at by allotting one point to those who missed activities or friends, one point to those who offered suggestions for changes in the ward, and one point to those who ascribed "autonomous" behavior to a good patient, combined scores will range from 0 for the most hospital-oriented, to 3 for the most outside-oriented. As Table 18 shows, patients who score 3 or 2 are more likely to be instrumentally oriented than patients who score 1 or 0. Those who score 0 are primary-oriented without exception, and passive in their non-patient role anticipation.

Table 18

Scores of Acceptance of Hospital Setting, by Instrumental vs. Primary Orientation and Anticipation of Nonpatient Role

Score:	3	2	1	0
Orientation toward hospital or doctor:	I M P	I M P	I M P	I M P
Anticipation of non-patient role:				
Active	6 0 1	8 0 1	1 1 0	0 0 0
Passive	0 1 1	4 0 3	1 2 7	0 1 9
No Answer	0 0 0	0 0 0	1 0 2	0 0 1

I—Instrumental P—Primary
M—Mixed

Conversely, the instrumentally-oriented patients are more likely to score 3 or 2, while the primary-oriented patients are more likely to score 1 or 0; and patients who anticipate some activity or interaction after leaving the hospital are more likely to score 3 or 2 while patients who expect passive gratification after discharge tend more frequently to score 1 or 0 (Table 19). Therefore, it seems justified to divide the sample into three main groups: those who are mostly "outside-oriented," those who are "hospital-oriented," and those who are "intermediary" (Table 19).

Table 19

Configurations of Hospital vs. Outside Orientation

Orientation toward hospital or doctor:	Instrumental				Mixed				Primary			
Score:	3	2	1	0	3	2	1	0	3	2	1	0
Anticipation of non-patient role:												
Active	6	8	1	0	0	0	1	0	1	1	0	0
Passive	0	4	1	0	1	0	2	1	1	3	7	9
No answer	0	0	1	0	0	0	0	0	0	0	2	1

Many personal factors—character structure, individual history, family life, etc.—are undoubtedly related to the type of adaptation a patient

118

makes to the hospital. However, here I shall limit discussion for the most part to social-psychological and sociological factors. I shall try to relate the orientation of patients to (1) some aspects of the *role* in the larger society outside the hospital, (2) the *frequency* of exposure to the hospital, and (3) the type of *social structure* to which patients are exposed in the hospital.

The Elderly

In our society the aged, like the sick, are considered to be exempt or deserving of exemption in certain ways from the responsibilities and obligations of the productive adult.[1] And indeed, the sick role is often associated with old age. We tend to marvel at the man who at an advanced age is *nevertheless* in excellent health. We tend to shake our heads and exclaim at the young person who is very ill "and yet so young!" The physical deterioration of the body with age is matched by a social definition of the old person as one who "deserves" to be cared for. The older person is usually expected, even compelled, to give up his life-long occupation, around which his self-image has formed.[2]

The age of the ward population is relatively high, and is an important factor in the adaptation to the sick role in the hospital. Among the respondents, hospital orientation is correlated with age (Table 20).

Table 20

Patients' Outside or Hospital Orientation by Age

Type of Adaptation:	Number of Interviewed Patients at Each Age Level:		
	Under 40	40-59	60 and over
Outside-Oriented	6	7	6
Intermediate	1	5	4
Hospital-Oriented	1	7	14

It turns out that 14 out of 24 of the oldest patients who were interviewed are hospital-oriented, as compared with 7 out of 19 of the middle-age group and only 1 out of 8 of the youngest group. This tendency is consistent with the primary-instrumental typology as well as with the variables used to measure adjustment to the hospital in Chapter VII. Chart III, comparing Hospital-oriented to Outside-oriented, illustrates this consistency.[3]

This is not surprising in view of the fact that a great many of the older people in our culture have relinquished or lost their positions in the active life of society.[4] The older person is not expected to work for his maintenance. As a member of the family he is considered, and often made to feel, useless. He is restricted in his exercise of substantial rationality, since the realm of activities upon which he has to reflect has become limited.[5]

Chart III

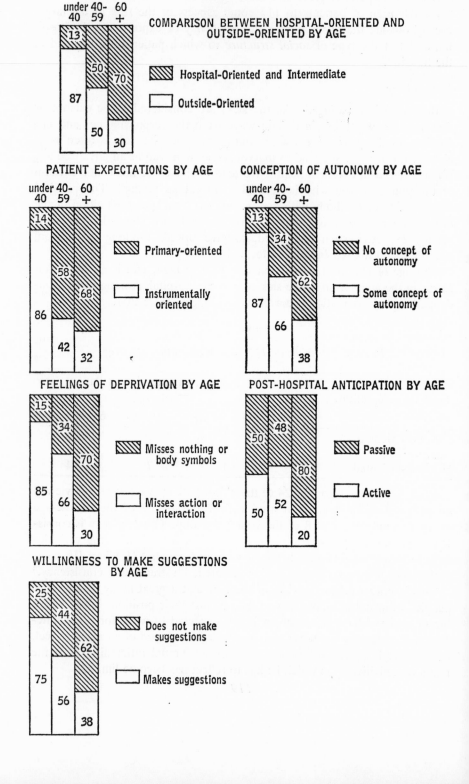

COMPARISON BETWEEN HOSPITAL-ORIENTED AND OUTSIDE-ORIENTED BY AGE

under 40 40-59 60+

13
50
70
87
50
30

▨ Hospital-Oriented and Intermediate

☐ Outside-Oriented

PATIENT EXPECTATIONS BY AGE

under 40 40-59 60+

14
58
68
86
42
32

▨ Primary-oriented

☐ Instrumentally oriented

CONCEPTION OF AUTONOMY BY AGE

under 40 40-59 60+

13
34
62
87
66
38

▨ No concept of autonomy

☐ Some concept of autonomy

FEELINGS OF DEPRIVATION BY AGE

15
34
70
85
66
30

▨ Misses nothing or body symbols

☐ Misses action or interaction

POST-HOSPITAL ANTICIPATION BY AGE

50
48
80
50
52
20

▨ Passive

☐ Active

WILLINGNESS TO MAKE SUGGESTIONS BY AGE

25
44
62
75
56
38

▨ Does not make suggestions

☐ Makes suggestions

In the population from which the majority of the patients at Mount Hermon are drawn, the loss of family function in the old is intensified. Most of the patients are first and second generation Jews, and most of the older patients belong to the first generation. Because of the mobility pattern in our society in general, and among Jews in particular,[6] they speak a different language from their grandchildren and often are not considered by their children as an asset in the transmission of tradition.

While the functions assigned to the aged differ from culture to culture, in almost every society the aged are expected to transmit the values, beliefs and legends of the past to the future generation and thereby to contribute to the maintenance and the liveliness of the tradition.[7] This function has been sharply curtailed in American society at large, and especially among those who have become part of it recently, and quickly. The younger generation, aspiring to move up the social ladder of present-day American society, would put aside much of the tradition. To them the older generation is but a painful reminder of a disagreeable past. Since they project onto their own children their aspirations for mobility, they will try to protect them from interference with complete Americanization. Thus, the function of the grandparent as a bearer of tradition tends to become considerably weakened.

The social distance between generations is emphasized in the social work reports. Of one elderly woman with an incurable condition which made it necessary to send her to a nursing home, the social worker said to me: "Her daughter can't have her in her house. She's such a nag. The daughter says she has her own children to care for and her doctor told her she should keep them away from their grandmother." The traditionally close ties between grandparents and grandchildren are very conspicuously absent in the interview material. Only five patients mentioned their grandchildren in the formal interview, although twenty-four of the interviewees were sixty or over, and the middle-age group of nineteen respondents between forty and fifty-nine must have included a number of additional grandparents.

Those who mentioned their grandchildren were so few that it may be worthwhile to quote them.[8] Fifty-year-old Mr. Drake, asked what he would do first at home, said: "See my grandchild. I got two of them; he is three; the other one is one; he is talkative all right." Mr. Geoffrey, aged fifty-three, said: "The first thing, you ask? I got a grandchild, he's worth a million dollars," and 68-year-old Mr. Halpert exclaimed: "My grandchildren! They miss me!" Sixty-five-year-old Mrs. Silverman, when asked what she missed most, said, "I lost my husband a short time ago, so naturally I miss him. But I have my children and grandchildren."

Mrs. Nathanson, fifty, who intended as a first thing to "go over to my daughter-in-law and see the baby," explained that she would rather be in the hospital than at home because "my daughter has three children, I don't want to bother her."

There were no other references to grandchildren in all the standardized interviews. To Mrs. Nathanson, although she wanted to "see the baby," grandchildren were nevertheless somehow a liability since they were seen as responsible for her hospitalization. Indeed, in informal conversations in the ward, grandchildren are often referred to as a burden. Mrs. Reilly mentioned several times that "I'm going to my son; my daughter has two small boys, they're too much for me." This was the only context in which Mrs. Reilly ever (and repeatedly) referred to her grandchildren.

Although there was no specific question in the interview schedule about grandchildren, many patients in the ward were asked about their grandchildren in informal conversations. The usual response was, "Oh, they miss me," but there was little enthusiasm in the answers, and no proud stories were told about them. Patients showed me pictures of themselves and frequently of their sons, but not a single one of a grandchild. Of all the elderly patients I talked to in the ward, only one volunteered, without being specifically asked, to speak about her newly born grandchild:

> I have a son, fine boy, but his wife is no good.—Why?—What's good about a daughter-in-law? But his boy, God bless his heart, he is a cupidor, I'm telling yah.—How old is he?—Two weeks, just born, I'm telling yah, a cupidor.

The "closeness" between grandparents and grandchildren, of which Radcliffe-Brown[9] and many others speak seems to give way, among upward-mobile groups, to increased social separation.

The strained relationship between parents and children was often manifest on the hospital ward. It came to staff attention at almost all social service rounds and at frequent doctors' rounds. For example:

> [Interne]: The family is apparently trying to pull a cutie on us. One daughter told me [mother] is living at home with another daughter. The other daughter—an authoritarian—says the mother lives alone, why not send her to a nursing home. I checked: she lives with a daughter. She is not worse than at any time during the last thirty years. I don't see why public funds should be spent on her. . . .

A few days later the same interne reported: "She develops one complication after another."

Elderly parents who feel rejected become more demanding as their feelings of rejection intensify. One of the few legitimate claims they feel they have is to be taken care of when they are sick. For the elderly parent hospitalization means: "Now that you children see how miserable I am you will have to pay attention to me." Although this often revives guilt feelings in the children, sending the parent to the hospital also permits them to escape the burden of care in a culturally approved way.

The elderly person, especially if he is widowed,[10] may be shifted back and forth between his children's home and the hospital. If he lives by himself in a room or small apartment, he has merely a "place of residence." A home—a small social system of integrated roles—is generally denied to him. The widowed old person is useless and therefore feels that he hardly has any role obligations.

Such elderly patients often find themselves in a vicious circle of rejection. Many of their symptoms are those of old age: rheumatism, arthritis, itching, general deterioration, and other conditions that doctors feel powerless to cure. The doctors find this type of physical condition no challenge to their intelligence or competence, and they sense—and often explicitly assert—that the hospital is being used as a substitute for a nursing home. Consequently these patients receive only routine attention. The patient for whom there is no hope of recovery finds that he "loses the right of having others try to get him better."[11] Such remarks as the following are not infrequent:

> He shouldn't have been admitted; he doesn't belong here; there's nothing really wrong with him; it's probably a psychiatric case, but we have no room for psychiatric cases on the ward.[12]

Nurses are quick to follow the lead of the physicians in adopting an impatient attitude toward elderly patients, differentiating readily between a patient who is a "nuisance" and one who "deserves" to be helped.[13]

Nevertheless, since elderly people are somehow expected to be sick, illness is to them a legitimate "activity," if activity it may be called. When the older patient passes the threshold of the hospital, he wins the right to be himself. His existence is vindicated through illness.

It is no wonder, then, that most of the older patients at Mount Hermon, especially those who were widowed, had a primary attitude toward hospital or doctor.[14] If they were less ready than the young to anticipate the resumption of the role of the nonpatient,[15] that is partly because they so seldom have outside work or family duties waiting for them.

For many patients, hospitalization only climaxes in a dramatic way a loss of roles they have already been undergoing at home. For the chronically ill and for the aged, the requirements of patienthood—giving up responsibilities, following instructions, relaxing in passivity—are more easily met because even before they arrived at the hospital they had begun to meet them.

But, for those who experience the sudden onset of a chronic illness, the loss of role in the hospital may be felt with particular acuteness. It marks not merely a temporary giving up of a cherished self-image, but the beginning of a process of major role revision. The factory worker with a coronary, for example, knows that when he returns home, he will not be able to resume his occupational role, his role as family provider.

The social demands upon the aged or the partly disabled are severe. They are expected to relinquish some of the major components of their adult selves, and yet find for themselves new or substitute roles in which they can be both unobtrusive and socially useful. They are expected to have "hobbies" (or even to seek for work although the odds are against them). To accept a change of role without withdrawal into passivity is called "to make an adjustment." While the passivity required in the hospital constitutes a behavioral adjustment to a social situation which such patients will face at home, it helps to destroy the strength and willingness for an active re-orientation of the role personality. This is borne out by the fact that frequent exposure to the hospital tends to be associated with hospital orientation.

The Veteran

Patients who have been more frequently exposed to the hospital atmosphere are more likely to be hospital-oriented and to find in the hospital structure the sources of gratification of their passive needs.

Table 21

Outside or Hospital Orientation, by Frequency of Admission

Type of Adaptation:	Patients interviewed after their:		
	1st Admission	2nd Admission	3rd Admission*
Outside-oriented	11	4	4
Intermediary	5	1	4
Hospital-oriented	7	5	10

* or more.

It appears (Table 21) that as the frequency of admission increases, hospital orientation increases and, conversely, outside orientation decreases. Although frequency of admission is associated with age, this tendency still prevails within each age group. (See Table 21 in Appendix III.)

As a patient becomes increasingly adapted to ward life, he tends to view hospital and doctors less and less instrumentally, he increasingly loses concern with people and activities outside the hospital, and he accepts more wholeheartedly the hospital routine and hospital authority.[16]

The process of increasing hospitalization has sometimes been recognized in medical writings on the subject, and the cumulative effects of *time* have been noted. Edward Liss, who has already been quoted, says: "The cultural techniques give way *first*. . . . *Next* to go are the social relationships, and what is left is the primitive insistence upon and interest in food and affection."[17]

A parallel process of adaptation has been noted in another type of social organization whose members are expected to relinquish autonomous judgment and decision-making for twenty-four hours a day: the army. Willard Waller, in his book *The Veteran Comes Back,* writes:

> The regimentation of the lives of millions of men involves . . . some damage to their sense of self and to their power to think for themselves; it involves a redirection of their emotional life into channels acceptable to the military system. The soldier must form a soldier's habit . . . learn to eat, sleep, dress, bathe—as a soldier, adjust his sex life to the soldier's necessities. Necessarily, he loses the sense of self-direction. A personality formed by such a milieu is thereby to some extent unfitted for civilian life.[18]

Armies, orphanages, prisons, and hospitals, share one common characteristic: they all provide for their members a *home away from home,* and relieve their members from the burden of decision-making twenty-four hours a day.[19] Thus all of them demand that their members give up substantial rationality in practically all aspects of life in favor of the functional rationality of organizational life. "All such institutions," says Waller,

> rob the individual of his sense of self-direction and ultimately damage the capacity for it. Virtue in such institutions consists in having no preference about many things; in eating whatever is put on the table, in wearing what one is told to wear, in going to bed and rising again according to instructions, in making the best of things. The good institution member does not make choices or decisions. He submits and permits himself to be carried along, as it were, in a 'moral automobile.' When he returns to civilian life, his suddenly uncorseted soul seems flabby and incapable of standing alone.[20]

The hospital also has its "veterans." Some among them will say proudly, "This is my fifteenth admission." It will be remembered that they act as agents of socialization for the newcomers, and derive a feeling of self-importance from their repeated association with the hospital.

> My name is Mary. Just call me Mary. I know this place. You ask Dr. Turk. When I see him he says, 'Mary,' he says, 'what's new at the hospital?'

A little later Mary said again, with pride:

> You want to know about the hospital? Just come and ask me. When Dr. Turk sees me, he says, 'Mary,' he says, 'what's new at the hospital?' That's because I'm here more than he is!

However pitiful these identifications may seem to an outsider, such patients derive a deep satisfaction from the feeling of belongingness.

In this way does the hospital, the place where disease and unfitness are institutionalized, come to seem like a home to those who are deviants on the outside because of chronic illness or old age. Is it possible then that hospital orientation, as I have defined it, may be most closely related to the nature of the illness itself? Is frequency of admission but a corollary of the physical condition of a patient? Those who are sick enough to be hospitalized again and again may well give up hope at home and lose confidence in the doctor's competence. After a time they may come to see the hospital as refuge, a place of solace and care. Re-admission to the hospital, for such persons, may become re-admission to the realm of hope. Further research is needed to trace out the relation between types of illness and adaptation to the sick role.

People who are severely and chronically ill are chronic deviants at home and at work (if they continue to work).[21] In the hospital, and especially in the ward, they find themselves in the world of the sick, a community of deviants where they are sheltered from the rules that prevail in the outside world, and exempt from the criteria of fitness and performance.

If the hospital does not offer such persons a cure of their physical ailment, it does offer an "institutional cure." In this restricted society the deviant achieves a sort of "normalcy," and physical maladaptation becomes social adjustment. "Hospitalization in a simple protective environment sometimes encourages a further regression and constriction of the personality, i.e., an 'institutional cure.' "[22] The hospital offers not only hope for the relief of illness, but also hope for the sheltering of deviance.

This suggests that adaptation to hospital life depends not only upon age and frequency of exposure to the hospital, but also upon the structure of its wards, and especially upon the interplay between these factors.

NOTES

1. See Talcott Parsons, *Essays in Sociological Theory*, Glencoe, Ill.: The Free Press, 1954, pp. 102 ff.

2. For the impact of retirement on the self-image of the elderly, see Zena Smith Blau, "Change in Status and Age Identification," *American Sociological Review*, XXI (April 1956), 198-203.

3. For a complete breakdown see Tables 1-5 in Appendix II.

4. On relations between aging, change in interpersonal relations and illness, see Robert J. Havighurst, "Interpersonal Aspects of Gerontology," *Problems of Aging: Transactions of the 12th Conference of the Josiah Macy, Jr., Foundation*, Nathan W. Shock, (ed.), New York: The Foundation, 1956, pp. 68-112.

5. Hamburg, Hamburg, and deGoza, in a study on "Adaptive Problems and Mechanisms in Severely Burned Patients," found that patients who were too dependent were often those "whose dependent needs had been extremely stimulated in past years and who had been given a great deal of encouragement toward relying on others in a dependent way." (*Op. cit.,* 1-20.)

6. On this topic, see Nathan Glazer, "The American Jew and the Attain-

126

ment of Middle-Class Rank," in *The Jews,* Marshall Sklare, (ed.), Glencoe, Ill.: The Free Press, 1958, pp. 138-146.

7. Cf. Maurice Halbwachs, *Les cadres sociaux de la mémoire,* Paris: Librairie Félix Alcan, 1935, esp. pp. 146 ff.

8. Of the five patients who mentioned their grandchildren in the formal interview, only one is hospital-oriented. Two are outside-oriented and two are intermediary.

9. *Op. cit.,* pp. 90-104.

10. Thirteen out of our twenty-four patients of sixty and over were widowed, one was divorced, three were single, and only seven, less than one-third, were married. Moreover, among the patients interviewed, the widowed elderly were the ones who were most frequently hospital-oriented:

Patients 60 or Over

Type of Orientation	Married	Single	Widowed or Divorced
Outside-oriented	4	1	2
Intermediary	1	1	1
Hospital-oriented	2	1	11

For a breakdown by instrumental-primary typology and the other variables analyzed in Chapter VII, see Appendix II.

11. Barrabee, *op. cit.,* p. 143.

12. The doctor was referring to an 86-year-old patient suffering from acute arthritis—a physical condition that had begun several months before, after the patient was compelled to give up his work. Stanton and Schwartz have pointed out the cultural pattern very common in hospitals of offering psychiatric "diagnosis" in social relationships, which serves to deprive the person so "diagnosed" of his status (*The Mental Hospital, op. cit.,* p. 288). This type of judgment legitimizes the rejection of the patient, simultaneously excusing the doctor for his helplessness and immunizing him from criticism and self-criticism.

13. Medical students who have not yet acquired the professional manner and ethical stance are sometimes quite crude in expressing contempt for the non-productive role of the aged. Thus a 65-year-old worker, who had been told by his doctor to "quit working and take it easy" after a heart attack at sixty-three, was asked by a medical student: "What are you going to do when you get out of here? Get yourself a job?" When the patient retorted, "You got a job for me?" the student reported that this was a "psychiatric case."

The elderly are permitted, urged or required to retire from their occupation. However, praise and admiration go not to the elderly person who "retires and sits back" but to the one who "continues working hard in spite of his age." Age, to be admired, must not show.

14. See Appendix II, and Chart III.

15. See Appendix II, and Chart III.

16. Frequency of admission is also associated with all the variables considered in Chapter VII, of which the present types are a consolidation. See Appendix III.

17. *Op. cit.,* pp. 619-622, esp. pp. 619-620 [emphasis ours].

18. Willard Waller, *The Veteran Comes Back*, New York: The Dryden Press, 1944, p. 191.

19. Cf.: "The hospital is a simplified environment. It offers protection to the patient. Adjustment under these conditions requires little initiative and only a moderate degree of responsibility." Proehl, *op. cit.*, 534-540.

20. Waller, *op. cit.* See also Goffman, "The Characteristics of Total Institutions," *op. cit., passim.*

21. In regard to the conception that illness can be defined as a form of deviant behavior, see Parsons, *The Social System,* pp. 476-477.

22. George Devereux, "The Social Structure of the Hospital as a Factor in Total Therapy," *American Journal of Orthopsychiatry,* XIX (1949), 492-500.

CHAPTER IX

Hospital Orientation:
A Structural Consequence

THE APPARENT INFLUENCE OF FREQUENT HOSPITALIZATION AND OF A person's social role upon the development of patients' attitudes tends to bear out the implication derived from Mannheim that persons who are confronted more frequently with situations in which they cannot act autonomously will have less occasion to reflect on themselves and on situations.[1] If frequency of admission, though related to old age, is also independent of it in its effect on a patient's hospital orientation, we are once more led to focus our attention on the nature of hospital life. A comparison between the different wards sheds further light on the impact of hospital life on a patient's outlook. There seems to be a greater likelihood that surgical patients will be more outside-oriented than medical patients (Table 22). More than one-half of the patients interviewed in the surgical ward were outside-oriented, and only nine out of twenty-five were hospital-oriented. In the medical ward, however, only six out of twenty-six respondents were outside-oriented, while one-half were hospital-oriented (Table 22).[2]

Table 22

Hospital or Outside Orientation by Type of Ward

Type of Adaptation	No. of patients interviewed from:	
	Surgical Ward	Medical Ward
Outside-oriented	13	6
Intermediary	3	7
Hospital-oriented	9	13

The differences between surgical and medical patients exists among all three frequency-of-admission groups (see Chart IV; for a complete breakdown see Table 19 in Appendix III), as well as in all three age groups.

Chart IV*

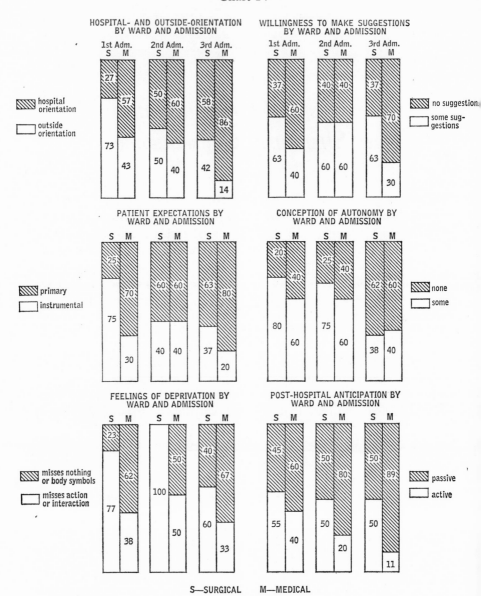

S—SURGICAL   M—MEDICAL

* Cf. Table 14, Appendix III.

130

Chart V*

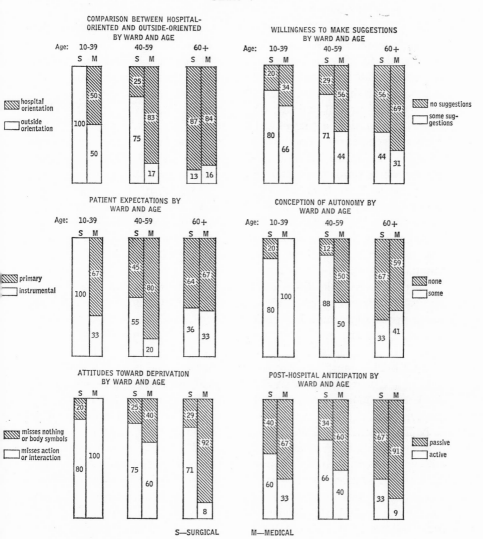

COMPARISON BETWEEN HOSPITAL-
ORIENTED AND OUTSIDE-ORIENTED
BY WARD AND AGE

WILLINGNESS TO MAKE SUGGESTIONS
BY WARD AND AGE

PATIENT EXPECTATIONS BY
WARD AND AGE

CONCEPTION OF AUTONOMY BY
WARD AND AGE

ATTITUDES TOWARD DEPRIVATION
BY WARD AND AGE

POST-HOSPITAL ANTICIPATION BY
WARD AND AGE

S—SURGICAL   M—MEDICAL

* Cf. Table 15, Appendix III.

131

(Chart V, and Table 20 in Appendix III.) Hence, the difference between the two wards seem sufficiently interesting to warrant a closer scrutiny.

Illness as a Determinant of Adaptation

The most obvious difference between medical and surgical patients is a difference in the nature of illness. Many of the medical patients come into the hospital for diagnostic purposes, or with chronic or recurrent illnesses (coronary, diabetes, ulcers, ulcerative colitis, etc.); they do not know what will happen to them, or whether a cure, or a partial cure, can be achieved. Many of the surgical patients, on the other hand, have come to undergo a specific operation, a corrective treatment which, it is believed, will make them as "good as new" and more capable than ever of performing their activities outside the hospital. How much more likely, then, that patients in the surgical ward should consider the hospital a place "to do a job," and that many of them should tend to expect of the doctor the performance of professional skills. These patients, who have entered the surgical ward to "get it over with," are likely to consider the hospital a transitional evil and to maintain, in their minds, their ties to friends, relatives and outside activities, ready to resume those relations and activities again on leaving the hospital.

There is very little direct evidence, however, about the psychological effects of different types of illness. Until such evidence is available, the above speculation must be considered extremely hazardous and, indeed, *ad hoc*. Could one not just as plausibly advance the opposite theory—that patients in the surgical ward, given the more immediate and actual threat to their bodies, must be *more* ridden with fears and hence *more* likely to regress and to revive childhood fantasies thus reducing their capacity to make autonomous judgments and to readjust to their nonpatient role? Surely, if the data had indicated that the surgical patients were *less* likely to be instrumentally-oriented, this explanation would have been a tempting one. Since both types of explanations are *ad hoc,* neither can be accepted without further psychological research to ascertain the differential impact of surgery and other types of treatment in the hospital.[3]

There is a marked difference in structure and in authority relations between the medical and surgical wards at Mount Hermon[4] and there is much evidence that this difference—apart from any psychological factors —affects the type of adaptation the patient makes.

Social Structure and Type of Therapy

Partly because of new therapeutic procedures, the patient in the surgical ward is less restricted and less subjected to a rigid routine than his neighbor across the hall. Recent changes in post-operative procedures have had the unanticipated consequence of putting the patient, shortly after his operation, in a much more active relationship to his environment than was pre-

132

viously the rule and than is still the rule in the medical ward. Post-operative therapy prescribes, in most cases, that patients be encouraged to get out of bed as soon as possible after the operation, and thereafter to be as self-sufficient as possible. The patient is soon supposed to wash himself, to use the bathroom, and to rely as little as possible on "service." The frequently heard complaint about some hospitals that: "It's an excellent hospital, but post-operative care is not good," may be an unintended recommendation, as what seems to be "bad service" is actually deliberate medical practice.

Early ambulation helps patients to test their strength and to assess daily the progress they are making. Burling, Lentz and Wilson have called attention to the fact that it also seems to embody a philosophy of self-help.[5] Patients are gradually led to abandon their passive role for one of greater activity, anticipating their ability to move about freely and to take up again, after being discharged, their daily obligations, even if only on a "part-time" basis, during the weeks of convalescence.

These therapeutic measures not only wean patients from reliance on external support, but also make it possible for post-operative patients to move about and meet other patients. Their horizon widens; their physical surroundings expand. In the corridors and in the television rooms, they meet not only their own visitors but those of other patients, and often, pick up news about their home community. Walking lessens their isolation from outside reality, and brings them into closer understanding of the structure and the meaning of the hospital environment.[6]

To be sure, some medical patients, too, were ambulatory, especially during the period of a day or two before discharge. But not so many. Getting up and caring for oneself was not part of the policy in the medical ward where rules and regulations were much more strictly adhered to, and where the nursing routine did not change significantly for a patient during his stay in the ward until perhaps the last day or so. Nurses washed and cared for all patients and the use of the bathroom was permitted only if specifically ordered by a doctor.

In the surgical ward, the nurse seemed to have more leeway to relax restrictions than in the medical ward. Burling, Lentz and Wilson feel that it is the trend toward early ambulation that has revolutionized the work of the surgical nurse.[7] Yet, I believe that the role of the nurse is also affected by other aspects of social organization of the ward, especially by its authority structure.

Social Structure: Informal Patterns

On the two floors, the men's floor and the women's floor, the surgical and medical wards were directly across the hall from each other. Walking from one to the other on either floor one would notice immediately a superficial difference in atmosphere: joking as well as cursing, laughing as well as grumbling, could be heard at the surgical nurses' station. Banter between doctors and nurses was a regular occurrence, and from time to time a nurse might be found discussing with a house doctor the best course of action with regard to a patient.

On the medical ward the atmosphere seemed much more "polite." Joking or cursing there was exceptional; informal talk between doctors and nurses was rare. Only the medical students, who were not part of the formal organization, appeared to talk freely with the nurses.[8]

The medical house staff were perfectly capable of joking and banter, but they tended to confine such activity among themselves, while the banter on the surgical ward extended to the nursing staff. On the medical ward jocular talk occurred during doctors' rounds and in conference. Anyone might initiate it—the residents, the internes, the medical students. On the surgical ward, jocular talk occurred both during rounds and at the nurses' station. It was always initiated by the visiting doctor or, in his absence, by the chief resident.[9] Other physicians initiated jocular talk only in the absence of the chief resident or the visiting doctor. However, even in the presence of the visiting doctor and chief resident, the surgical nurse, who was "outside" the status hierarchy of the doctors, would sometimes initiate jocular talk.

It will be remembered that jocular talk among patients drew the group more closely together, that it had an equalizing function, bridging the distance between old-timers and newcomers. If jocular talk among the staff performs similar functions, minimizing anxiety, and reducing social distance within the group, the higher frequency of joking on the surgical ward, and the fact that it was initiated most of the time by those in extreme positions in the hierarchy, may suggest a higher degree of status difference to be overcome.[10]

Indeed, the social distance between visiting doctor and house doctors, and between chief resident and other staff, was more marked among the surgeons. The coexistence of "joviality" and "social distance" on that ward was expressed by a surgical interne, who said: "It is not a very strict and formal atmosphere on our ward. Of course, the chief resident has everything; he's the despot. . . ."

To explain the relation between rigid authority relations and joviality, one must compare the formal structure of authority with the *de facto* lines of decision-making on the two services.

Social Structure: Formal Lines of Authority

The formal structure of the medical ward does not appear to differ much from that of the surgical ward. (See Charts I and II in Chapter II.) On both wards the chief-of-service is responsible for medical treatment (while the head nurse is responsible for the maintenance of order). However, the chief-of-service delegates his authority for the care of patients to the chief resident.

On both wards, the chief resident delegates the care of patients to the internes, each of whom is in charge of specific patients under the chief resident's continuous supervision. The internes pass on orders to the nurses. The assistant resident acts as supervisor and "consultant" to the internes.

This formal structure is essentially the same on both medical and surgical wards, except that there is no separation of tasks among the doctors for the male and female wards on the surgical side. There, internes and residents walked up and down the steps to take care of their patients who were segregated by sex on two floors.

Social Structure: De Facto Authority and Decision-Making

In the medical ward, there was consistent delegation of authority down the line. There, the chief resident could be heard to say on rounds to one or another of the internes: "You make the final decision, he's your patient." Such a remark would be most untypical on the surgical ward, where the chief resident and the visiting doctor made all decisions. Moreover, the medical house officers tended to arrive at decisions through consensus with the chief resident presiding, while the surgical house doctors received orders from the chief resident. The following incident suggests the climate of authority in the surgical ward.

The daughter of an elderly patient had made a scene one morning at the nurses' station. She had been notified the previous night at 11 p.m. of her father's operation the next morning, and when she arrived at the hospital to see her father before the operation, he had already been taken to the operating room. The daughter had been extremely upset about not being able to see him. An interne and an assistant-resident, discussing the incident at lunch, felt that in the future something should be done to forestall similar reactions from patients' families. The chief resident, they decided, was much too busy to think of notifying relatives in due time, and so perhaps they should take that job upon themselves, provided the chief resident would give them sufficient advance notice. When they took up the problem with the chief resident that afternoon, his answer was curt: "I always notify the family on time," he said with an annoyed expression and walked away. There would be no delegation of authority by him in this apparently trivial matter.

The chief resident's "despotism," as it appeared to the interne, is part of the culture of the surgical ward. Decision-making by fiat may seem, at first glance, to be just "a bad habit," or to reflect a lack of knowledge about delegation of authority and the need for agreement by consensus, but it has its roots in the specific activity system of the surgical team, which differs significantly from that of the medical team. We must bear in mind that all important operations are carried out by the chief resident, the chief-of-service, or by a visiting surgeon.[11]

135

Decision by consensus is time-consuming. In an emergency situation, in the operating room as on a battlefield, a task must be performed as rapidly as possible. There can be no doubt about who has to make a decision, no question that it has to be made quickly and has to be carried out unquestioningly and instantly.[12]

The medical team faces entirely different problems. It must diagnose illness and choose between different possible courses of treatment. These problems require careful deliberation, and the decisions arrived at are often tentative. The results of various therapeutic procedures undertaken have to be carefully observed and the procedures may have to be modified in the process. At each step there must be careful thinking, consultation and deliberation, which is better accomplished through teamwork than through the decision of a single person.

The teacher of medical students, too, has a different task in the two wards: in the medical ward, students and junior house officers must be taught to *think* and *reflect,* while in the surgical ward the emphasis is on *action* and punctual performance. Admittedly, this seems an excessively sharp distinction, and ideally surgeons should learn to think as well as act. Yet the distinction is a real one. Doctors have a clear image of the fundamental difference between medical and surgical men. Doctors on the medical ward, asked why they chose their field of specialization rather than surgery, tended to reply: "Medicine is more of an intellectual challenge," or "I enjoy the kind of mental operation you go through," or "[Surgeons] want to act and they want results, sometimes they make a mess of it." The doctors on the surgical ward agreed, although they gave a different evaluation of the same descriptive traits. They said that they chose to be surgeons because they "like working with their hands," that they "prefer something that is reasonably decisive," and that "[a medical] man probably doesn't want to work with his hands."

The man in authority on the surgical ward serves as a role model for the younger house officers who learn from him but are not permitted to participate in surgical procedures. An interne on the surgical ward explained:

> . . . on surgery the interne does not have as much responsibility as on the medical ward, for he does not do surgery. He is responsible for the routine care, for pre- and post-operative care. Decisions are made by the chief resident and the visit. The visit has power of decision, for it is his responsibility.

It has been observed in Chapter II that the visiting doctor, whose formal duties are merely advisory, has *de facto* authority to prescribe treatment and to write his recommendations into the patient's record. On the medical ward the visiting doctor observes the etiquette of making "suggestions" rather than "decisions" and of "discussing" procedures rather than "decreeing" them. On the surgical ward, however, he assumes undisguised authority. During ward rounds he issues orders, often reprimands house officers, and frequently takes over the authority assigned to the chief resident. If not all visiting doctors acted overtly in an authoritarian fashion, they all acted as instructors and gave the "final word."[13]

The following discussion took place between a visiting doctor and the chief resident and the ear and throat specialist of the hospital concerning the case of Mrs. X, an octogenarian:

> Chief resident to visiting doctor: "She cannot swallow, she can't even hold a glass of water; she came up here from ear-and-throat. Shall we operate?"
>
> Visiting doctor: "No. She will feel just as miserable afterwards. All you could do is prolong her agonizing days."
>
> House specialist: "But isn't there a hospital policy on these matters? I mean, the hospital has to do something."
>
> Visiting doctor, harshly: "You want to do something because you want to clear your conscience. But you wouldn't help *her*. And you wouldn't clear mine because I would know that I would only prolong her agony and make her suffer more."
>
> Specialist: "But she's in the hospital, doctor. The hospital has to do *something*. She is going to starve to death."
>
> Visiting doctor: "The hospital can discharge her. There is nothing the hospital can do for her, except give her opium. She can take that at home. If there is a hospital policy on these matters, you'll have to consult the chief-of-service. If he says that he decides these matters, his decision will hold. But if *I* am asked, *I* say no."

The visiting doctor did not even pretend to leave the final decision to the chief resident. He would defer to no one lower than the chief-of-service, and then only if necessary. Thus does the visiting doctor, who, as his title indicates, does not "belong" to the hospital (he is called "visit" for short) take over command. Because of his responsibility in the operating room, his *de facto* authority is even greater on the surgical ward than on the medical ward.

And so the line of decision-making on the surgical ward does not coincide with the rank system, and there is little if any delegation of authority there.

Charts VI and VII attempt to illustrate the actual difference between the medical and the surgical wards.

The type of social organization prevailing in the medical ward where authority is delegated downward step by step may be called, in the terminology developed by Jules Henry,[14] the pine-tree type of organization; and the type of organization where orders come down to the same person through several channels, the oak-tree type. In the surgical ward, where key decisions are reserved to top men, routine decisions conveyed to the nurses may emanate from anybody in the democracy of powerless residents and

137

Chart VI

MEDICAL WARD (MALE OR FEMALE)

Chief
Resident **

Visiting
Doctor **

Assistant
Resident **

Two
Internes **

Head
Nurse

Chart VII

SURGICAL WARD (MALE OR FEMALE)

Visiting
Doctor **

Chief
Resident **

Jr. Asst.
Resident

Sr. Asst.
Resident

Interne

Interne

Head
Nurse

** Participate in decision-making

internes. This oak-tree type of organization—or more exactly of decision-making—places the nurse on the surgical ward in a strategic position with regard to therapeutic procedure.

The Role of the Nurse in the Surgical Ward

The relative absence of actual prestige grading[15] among the junior members of the surgical ward—notwithstanding formal rank differences—tended to eliminate the spirit of competition among them. Because the assistant residents and the internes were all practically excluded from decision-making, they were *de facto* on the same level, which made for a high degree of solidarity and informality among them.

Since authority was hardly delegated, all house officers had occasion to give orders to the nurse, who in turn communicated with all of them. Even the visiting doctor often consulted with the nurse directly. All doctors (with the exception of the visiting doctor) wrote orders in the order book. The head nurse of one of the floors, when asked who gave her orders, said: "We get orders all over the place and then you have to make your own compromise; you got to figure out what is most important."

This direct relation with all the doctors places the nurse in a strategic position. If she has to determine the relative importance of orders, she is making decisions about the care of patients, for she decides to delay one action rather than another. This gives her a certain degree of power.[16]

Jules Henry[17] says that where the head nurse has to follow orders coming from different directions that may or may not be compatible with each other, she is placed under great stress and strain, and that she will need to have a "strong" personality to be able to cope with conflicting demands and make her own decisions. And it would seem that to fill the position of head nurse in this type of organization would require greater personal ability than is needed where authority is delegated down the line. But for a person who does have the required ability, the position on the surgical ward has its rewards in increased power and the opportunity to take some active part in therapy.[18]

Since the head nurse on the surgical ward often has to decide on a compromise, and must therefore know a lot about the condition of patients in order to handle her job well, she is forced to establish a closer relationship with patients. And this in turn increases her chance to participate in decision-making about the patient. Her degree of success in realizing the potential power inherent in her position depends to some extent upon her personal ability. But several factors in the ward structure itself and in the surgical service may induce her to assert herself.

For a large part of the day, while surgery is being performed, almost the entire surgical staff is in the operating room. Only one interne remains on duty and he is responsible for both the male and the female floor. The nurse must therefore be alert, checking with the sole interne on duty only if absolutely necessary.

Moreover, the junior members of the staff have such a very limited area of authority that they would find it difficult to play the role of "authoritative" doctor with the nurse. The rank hierarchy below the top decision-makers is not very strict, and the delegation of authority is ill-defined, so that many informal relations are built across status lines. House doctors will gladly abdicate their authority if they can rely on the nurse. A surgical nurse said:

> The doctors want to be called in an emergency only; if they know you and they feel you know what you're doing . . . they let us do things first and then call the doctor, as long as we would keep him informed.

And a third-year student nurse said:

> In this hospital we're not allowed to draw blood or give I.V. I do it occasionally but nobody knows. I do it just to help [the doctors] if there are no medical students around. . . .

Such informal deals enhance the nurse's status and realm of power, and provide still more occasions for her to know the patients well. That the surgical nurse has a greater knowledge of patients is recognized even by nurses on the medical service. One of them (although she was trying to impress me with her importance) had to admit, when she was asked whether nurses or doctors knew more about patients: "On surgical, the nurse knows more; on medical it's about even."

Ambulatory patients are less exacting of routine care, and surgical nurses can encourage patients to sit up and to wheel themselves about in a wheelchair if they are not able to walk. A surgical nurse said in her interview that she preferred the surgical ward and liked surgical patients because:

> they convalesce much quicker and there is a variety of dressings and procedures; they are more interesting than medical patients; there is more challenge in terms of learning. . . . It's a happier floor.

Thus the nurse increases her knowledge of patients (a) by the necessity of making her own compromise; (b) by being "in charge" while the surgical team is in the operating room; (c) by the "favors" that she does for doctors; (d) by her concern with dressings and other medical rather than routine procedures. It is no surprise, then, that doctors rely on her for information and reminders, and, by permitting her to suggest decisions to them, allow her considerable influence.[19] "On the surgical floors the nurses are apt to suggest," a nurse concluded her interview.

According to a head nurse on one of the surgical floors, she can often make decisions about patients' nutrition because she knows the diagnosis; she can move a patient from one bed to another, can decide whether he should bathe himself or not, can use her discretion about how to get a specimen. But her influence extends much further. She informs doctors about current treatment and may suggest changes in or discontinuance of dressing procedure or medication.

Nurses on the medical ward behave very differently. There they go through channels, always addressing themselves to the interne first. The nurse will seldom suggest specific measures to the interne but will proceed by "hints." A medical head nurse, complaining of an interne's lack of competence, described unintentionally how the medical nurse must proceed by indirection. Describing an elderly patient with urinary difficulties, she said:

> Usually we give her a catheter which relieves the patient. This was the logical treatment for her. These two men were standing together, so I came up and said, "This woman is very incontinent." The interne said: "If she voids, just change her bed." Luckily the assistant resident was there, too, and he said, "By all means, put the catheter on." The interne just doesn't care what happens to the patient, how often you change the bed.

The nurse, going through channels, addressed herself to the interne, but in order to be heard by the assistant resident, chose a strategically propitious moment to tell her story. She did not explicitly suggest that the patient be given a catheter, expecting the decision to come from the doctor without her specific request. On the surgical floor, she would have approached any doctor whom she thought competent to judge the case, regardless of rank, and she would have asked specifically for a decision.

In the medical ward, the nurse participated only in morning rounds and not in the rounds with the visiting doctor. In the surgical ward, the nurse usually went on rounds with the visiting doctor also. When she did not she was often called in or she was approached by the visiting doctor for information. Medical and surgical nurses differed in their descriptions of rounds. A head nurse of the medical floor said: "All that the nurse is there for, according to them, is to hold the charts."

On the other hand, the head nurse on the surgical floor said:

> During rounds, the nurse gains insight into the condition of the patient, finds out changes in terms of medication and treatment; she can inform the doctor what treatment the patient is on and can suggest to the doctor that the dressing procedure can be changed, she can suggest vitamins by mouth instead of by injection; she can suggest taking them off antibiotics and point out necessary medication. . . . Occasionally the doctors would bypass the nurse, so before they forgot to tell me anything I would ask.

Although she appeared shy and withdrawn, this surgical nurse, it seems, did not hesitate to ask and suggest. On the medical ward the head nurse had an outgoing personality but saw herself as little more than a chartholder.

141

I observed on many occasions that nurses on the surgical wards were less concerned with rules and regulations than nurses on the medical ward. Surgical nurses would even make decisions about referral of patients to the Social Service. One of them, asked whether she participated in Social Service rounds, said:

We should have been in on them, but I had close contact with the social worker, and I would ask her what I wanted to know. The social worker talked with me. Anyhow, many of the rounds were very routine. And the patients would come to me for reference to the social worker.

So she broke through the routine and established her own line of communication with the Social Service.

In order to ground my observations of these differences between the wards on a somewhat firmer basis, I asked nurses during the interview to comment on a squabble between nurse and interne in another hospital:

I would like to tell you a story that happened in another hospital. . . . An interne was called to the floor during the night to a patient who had a heart attack. He asked the nurse on the floor to get him a tank. She told him to ask an orderly. But there was no orderly around, and she still refused to get it for him. Do you think she had a right to refuse him or do you think he had the right to expect her to get it for him?

All the nurses agreed that the nurse is not supposed to leave the floor if there is no other nurse around. The answers of most medical nurses were unqualified (e.g., "I would never have gotten the tank. The doctor definitely should have gotten it," or "I wouldn't think of leaving the floor for a minute when I'm alone; this is unheard of"), but *all surgical nurses made important qualifications* (e.g., "She should have called the supervisor," or "She could have said, 'You keep your ears and eyes open while I get it,' " or "She could say, 'If you keep an eye open in the meantime, I'll run and get it.' "). Table 23 illustrates the difference in the responses of medical and surgical nurses:

Table 23

Nurses' Reactions to Story Testing Adherence to Rules, by Type of Ward

	Medical Nurses	Surgical Nurses
Nurses shouldn't leave the floor under any circumstances	4	0
Nurses shouldn't leave the floor but can find ways to solve the problem	1	5
Story not told	1	0

Although the number of interviews is very small, these figures tend to support my observations and conclusions drawn from other interview material: the surgical nurse is more accustomed than the medical nurse to using her initiative to "find a way out," and she is readier than the medical nurse to circumvent rules and regulations.

Consistent with these same differences, the nurses' supervisors of the two wards expressed themselves differently when asked to define a "good nurse." Both said that a good nurse should have integrity and "a very sincere liking of people," but the supervisor of the surgical floor also spoke of intelligence and "an inquiring mind."

Doctors, too, seem to have a somewhat different image of the nurse on the surgical and the medical wards. They generally agreed upon such qualities as "sympathy," "understanding," etc., as essential to a good nurse, but diverged on other criteria. Doctors in the surgical ward spoke of "foresight," "quick, reliable assistance," "efficiency," "intelligence" and "keeps her eyes open." Doctors on the medical ward spoke of "carrying out orders," "doing routine work well," and so on. One medical doctor said he would welcome "intellectual curiosity" in the nurse, but added that it is "rare," implying that he would not really expect it. Although the interviews with doctors are too few to permit any definite conclusions, they nevertheless support the hypothesis that surgeons tend to expect from nurses more autonomy and initiative than other medical doctors do.

Nurses are often charged with being "ritualistic," of attaching undue importance to routine and to rules. Internes on the medical floor were heard more than once accusing nurses of "merely clinging to rules" and "being unwilling or unable to think," but nurses on the surgical floor were never the targets of such accusations.

If the innovative behavior of the surgical nurses is indeed fostered by the social structure of the ward, that fact bears out the assertion of Robert K. Merton, that "some social structures exert a definite pressure upon certain persons in the society to engage in non-conformist rather than conformist conduct."[20] I believe that on the wards at Mount Hermon "ritualism" or "innovation" did derive from the social structure rather than from "professional" or "character" traits. On the medical wards, nurses find themselves in a position in which insistence on rules often serves as a means to assert themselves and to hold some degree of power. If their professional pride as well as their power and influence were enhanced by breaking through the routine, as on the surgical ward, they would more readily use informal means or act as innovators to reach their goals. Their behavior seems to be related to the rewards they can obtain in their particular positions in the hierarchy.

The nurse on the surgical ward, as an intermediary between doctors and patients, is in an important position to influence the patients' outlook on the hospital and to prepare them to move out of the sick role.[21] The greater degree of flexibility and initiative shown by the surgical nurse permits her to relax some of the restrictions that could be applied automatically. Her own feeling of freedom to make decisions, along with the new philosophy of self-help inherent in post-operative care, encourages her to let patients make as many little decisions about themselves as physical conditions permit.

One nurse said:

> I like surgical because you keep the patient moving, you encourage him to do as much as he can, while on the medical you constantly tell them you can't do this, you can't do that. On the medical you make the patient very dependent.

Independent nurses help make independent patients.

Notes

1. *Man and Society. . . , op. cit.,* p. 57.

2. The surgical-medical differences correlate with the instrumental-primary typology, as well as with all the other variables dealt with in the previous chapter, which served to construct the types analyzed here. See Appendix III. See also Appendix II for control by sex and age. While patients in the surgical ward tend to be younger than patients in the medical ward, a difference between the two wards exists if age is held constant, with the exception of the oldest group. See Chart V, p. 131.

3. One hypothesis that might well be investigated is that even though surgery may seem to pose a more *immediate* threat than various undetermined medical tests and treatments, it does not affect the rational thought structure of a person as much. It is well known, for example, that people are less anxious about real and existing dangers than about anticipated but uncertain ones.

4. Rose Laub Coser, "Authority and Decision-Making. . . ," *op. cit.*

5. *Op. cit.,* p. 247. On some consequences of inactivity of hospitalized patients, see Leon Lewis and Rose Laub Coser, "The Hazards in Hospitalization," *Hospital Administration,* V (Summer 1960), 25-45.

6. With regard to the importance of motor activity for interpersonal relations of children, see Spitz, "Anaclitic Depression," *op. cit.*

7. *Op. cit.,* p. 247.

8. The difference in atmosphere between the two wards was touched on briefly in Chapter II.

9. For the relation between the use of humor and status position, see Rose Laub Coser, "Laughter Among Colleagues," *op. cit.*

10. Tom Burns, in "Friends, Enemies and Polite Fiction," *op. cit.,* has observed that banter is often used by persons occupying high status positions to overcome the uneasiness brought about by status differences.

11. With regard to social relations in the operating room, see Robert N. Wilson, "Teamwork in the Operating Room," *Human Organization,* XII (Winter 1954), 9-14.

12. The "routinized emergency" nature of the hospital as a whole and its effect upon hospital organization were discussed in Chapter I. Conditions calling for unified control and quick obedience surely exist in clearer and purer concentration in the operating room than in any other part of the hospital.

13. The autocratic manner (and inconsistency) of some visiting doctors is exemplified in the following scene:

Surgical round, group of doctors stop in front of elderly female patient.

Chief resident to visiting doctor: "She's ready for discharge, sir.
She can go to nursing home for whatever care is still necessary."

Patient starts to cry.

Visiting doctor to patient: "What's the matter?"

Patient: "I don't want to go to a nursing home."

Visiting doctor motions group to step back from bed, then addresses the house officers: "You see, gentlemen, this is what happens if you talk too freely in front of patients. She has to be told by the right person in the right way, after considering her personal, emotional, and social needs. You should have called Social Service."

Visiting doctor steps over to next bed and house doctors follow him. There, in spite of the admonition he just gave to the house doctors, he says in a raised voice in front of the patient, pointing to her bandaged hand: "Haven't you ever learned how to bandage a hand? This way she's going to have a claw hand for the rest of her life."

14. "The Formal Social Structure of a Psychiatric Hospital," *op. cit.*

15. See Carl Dreyfus, "The Functions of Prestige-Grading, A Mechanism of Control," in Merton *et al.*, (eds.), *Reader in Bureaucracy,* Glencoe, Ill.: The Free Press, 1952, pp. 258-264.

16. Power is here used in Max Weber's sense: as "the chance of a man or of a number of men to realize their own will in a communal action even against the resistance of others who are participating in the action." (*From Max Weber, op. cit.,* p. 180.)

17. *Op. cit.*

18. Georg Simmel has analyzed the type of authority structure we are referring to here. He says: "If someone is totally subject to several persons or groups, that is, subject in such a way that he has no spontaneity to contribute to the relationship but is entirely dependent on each superordinate, he will suffer severely from their opposition. For everyone of them will claim him, his forces and services, wholly, while at the same time holding him responsible —as if he were free to be responsible—for whatever he does or neglects at the compulsory request of the other. . . ."

However, Simmel goes on to say, such "subordination . . . certainly becomes entirely different if the subordinate possesses any spontaneity whatever, if he can invest in the relationship with some power of his own. . . . The situation usually introduces a process of growth which sometimes reaches the point of dissolving the subordination itself." (*The Sociology of Georg Simmel,* Kurt H. Wolff, (trans.), *op. cit.,* pp. 229-232.)

19. We distinguish, with Stanton and Schwartz, between power and influence, in that influence indicates "all activities whose purpose is to get someone else to make a decision," (*The Mental Hospital, op. cit.,* p. 247).

145

20. "Social Structure and Anomie," in *Social Theory and Social Structure, op. cit.,* pp. 125-149.

21. The limitations upon the nurse as a socializing agent, described in Chapter V, are clearly less significant in the surgical ward than in the medical ward.

Summary

As I examined the process by which the patient[1] adapts to illness and health within the society of the hospital ward, I found myself analyzing and describing role continuity and discontinuity and those forces that assisted or hindered socialization—the transition from one segment of society to another.

A number of factors tend to disorient patients at admission to a hospital ward: anxiety about their physical condition; separation from family, friends and familiar surroundings; surrender of control over their "own" time, their "own" rhythm of activities, and their "own" decision-making. They face an environment alien to them in a condition of reduced autonomy. Many of them are not psychologically equipped—nor are they given sufficient opportunity—to understand the meaning of medical and nursing procedures or of the roles played by the many "persons in white."

Because the formal authority structure on the medical and surgical wards makes communication between doctors and newly admitted patients difficult and limits the role of doctors and nurses in helping patients reorient themselves, the most effective agents of socialization appear to be those "veteran" patients who provide mutual social support, explain the meanings of procedures and rules, and provide information (in the form of gossip and jocular talk) about hospital personnel.

In my formal interviews with patients at discharge, I found two types of adaptation to the hospital. Some patients, looking for gratification of primary needs, usually felt that the hospital provided them with a "home" and expected emotional support from the doctor. Other patients, with an instrumental view of hospital and doctor, more often felt that the hospital offered technical, medical and nursing facilities and expected a doctor to demonstrate his professional competence. Of these two types of patients, those with a primary orientation appeared more ready to acquiesce in the hospital setting than the instrumentally oriented. They felt less deprived of relatives, friends and normal activities. They could (or would) make no suggestion for the possible improvement of the comfort of patients. They tended to define a "good patient" as one who is completely submissive to hospital authorities (in contrast to the instrumentally oriented patients who more often felt that a "good patient" should maintain some degree of autonomy).

When asked "What will be the first thing you'll do when getting home?", the instrumentally oriented patients more frequently mentioned relationships with others, or activities. The primary oriented patients more often mentioned passive behavior. It appears that while primary orientation is associated with acceptance of the hospital structure, it is also associated with lack of readiness to leave patienthood.

In attempting to account for these two types of adaptation to hospital life, I found a number of relevant factors: age; the number of admissions to the hospital; types of therapy (medical and surgical); differences in the organization and authority structure of the wards with attendant differences in the roles of nurses. I did not, however, attempt to explore the possible effects of different diseases or of various psychological factors upon adjustment. This might be a fruitful subject for further investigations.

In analyzing the adaptation of patients, I focused especially on three factors: (1) his possible exemption from responsibility before admission (chronic illness and old age); (2) the frequency with which he is relieved of responsibility (frequency of hospitalization); and (3) the degree to which a patient is relieved of the responsibility for making decisions about his behavior (differences in ward structure).[2]

The analysis of the role of the patient in the ward led to the conclusion that the interrelations between the present roles and past roles outside the hospital, as well as the present roles within the structure of the ward greatly affect the adaptive behavior of patients.

NOTES

1. I hope it has been clear, throughout the preceding pages, that the term "*the* patient" was meant as a shorthand expression and that I did not propose to overlook individual differences. The typology in Chapters VII and IX was an attempt to grapple with the problem of differential adaptation.

2. I refrained from pushing the analysis further to ascertain the relative importance of the factors under consideration because of the smallness of the sample: further breakdowns of tables by holding one of the variables constant (as I did in the appendices) yield numbers too small for conclusive evidence.

The smallness of the sample is indeed a limiting factor as to the conclusive validity of this analysis. While the consistency of relationships seems to lend support to my hypotheses, my findings have to be considered the result of a highly tentative, preliminary exploration, and are not meant to be the basis for conclusive generalizations; they await quantitative verification.

Interview Guides

A. *Patients*

1. When you're sick, would you rather be home or in the hospital?
2. What do you miss most while you're in the hospital?
3. What is your idea of a good doctor?
4. What is your idea of a good nurse?
5. What is your idea of a good patient?
6. How do you like the rounds?
7. How do you like the ward?
8. Are there any suggestions that you would care to make for a possible improvement of the patients' comfort?
9. Are you ever bored or restless while you're in the hospital?
10. What will be the first thing you'll do when you get home?

B. *Nurses and Doctors*

Interviews with nurses and doctors were very informal. Respondents were encouraged to talk about any subject they brought up that had any relevance to ward structure. The following questions were asked of almost all respondents, eleven nurses and eight doctors:

1. Why did you want to be a nurse (doctor)?
2. What is your idea of a good nurse?
3. What is your idea of a good doctor?
4. What is your idea of a good patient?
5. Suppose you were a hospital administrator with unlimited means, both financial and as far as personnel is concerned, and you were asked to build a ward. What would you do?
6. I would like to tell you a story that happened in another hospital and see what you think of it. An interne was called to the floor during the night to a patient who had a heart attack. He asked the nurse on the floor to get him a tank. She told him to ask an orderly. But there was no orderly around, and she still refused to get it for him. Do you think she had a right to refuse, or do you think he had the right to expect her to get it for him?

*Composition of the Population of the Medical and Surgical Ward
by Age and by Sex, Compared with the Composition of the
Sample of Patients Interviewed by Age and Sex*

	No. of Patients Admitted in August 1954		No. of Patients Interviewed in August 1954	
	No.	%	No.	%
Age (medical ward)				
15-44	18	17	5	19
45-64	39	38	10	39
65 or over	46	45	11	42
Total	103	100	26	100
Age (surgical ward)				
15-44	19	28	6	24
45-64	21	30	11	44
65 and over	29	42	8	32
Total	69	100	25	100
Sex (medical ward)				
Male	48	47	13	50
Female	55	53	13	50
Total	103	100	26	100
Sex (surgical ward)				
Male	17	25	8	32
Female	52	75	17	68
Total	69	100	25	100

(Re Chapter VII)

I. Age

All the variables examined in this chapter are associated with age (Tables 1-5). However, within each age group differences outlined in Chapter VII tend to be consistent (Tables 6-10).

Table 1

Instrumental and Primary Orientation, by Age[a]

	10-19	20-29	30-39	40-49	50-59	60-69	70-79
Instrumental	2	1	3	3	4	2	6
Primary	0	0	1	3	7	7	7
Mixed	0	0	1	1	1	1	0
No answer	0	0	0	0	0	0	1

[a] The association is true also, of course, for the two variables that were used to construct the primary and instrumental types, i.e., patients' expectations of (1) hospital and (2) doctor. The distribution for these by age is as follows:

Table A

Patients' Expectations of Doctor, by Age

	Under 40	40-59	60 and over
Instrumental criteria	6	8	8
Primary criteria	2	11	14
No answer	0	0	2

Table B

Patients' Expectations of Hospital, by Age

	Under 40	40-59	60 and over
Do a job	6	6	7
Give care and attention	1	7	13
No answer or not applicable	1	6	24

151

Combining the figures of table 1 into three age groups, and omitting the few "mixed" types and "no answers":

Table 1a

Instrumental and Primary Orientation in Three Age Groups

	Up to 39	40-59	60 and over
Instrumental	6	7	8
Primary	1	10	14

While most of the patients under forty have an instrumental orientation toward hospital or doctor, about 40 per cent of the middle-age group and 36 per cent of the oldest group have such orientation.

If now we consider the age distribution of the answers to the four questions analyzed in this chapter, we find a tendency toward association with age, especially in the extreme age groups.

Table 2

Feeling of Deprivation, by Age

Respondents Miss Most:	10-19	20-29	30-39	40-49	50-59	60-69	70-79
Activity or people (active orientation)	1	1	4	3	9	4	2
Intake, belongings, nothing (passive orientation)	1	0	0	2	4	4	9
No answer	0	0	1	1	0	2	3

Table 3

Willingness to Make Suggestions, by Age

Made Suggestions:	10-19	20-29	30-39	40-49	50-59	60-69	70-79
Yes	2	1	3	4	5	4	4
No	0	0	2	2	5	5	9
No answer	0	0	0	0	3	1	1

Table 4

Conception of the "Good Patient," by Age

Respondent Uses	10-19	20-29	30-39	40-49	50-59	60-69	70-79
Criteria of autonomy	1	1	5	3	9	3	5
Criteria of submission	1	0	0	3	3	5	8
No answer	0	0	0	0	1	2	1

Table 5

Anticipation of First Experience at Home, by Age

	10-19	20-29	30-39	40-49	50-59	60-69	70-79
Interaction or action (active orientation)	1	1	2	3	7	1	3
Bodily gratification or outright passivity (passive orientation)	1	0	3	3	6	8	8
No answer	0	0	0	0	0	1	3

Primary and instrumental orientations vary consistently in the expected direction if we hold age constant.

If we compare the instrumental and primary orientations with the patients' answers to the four questions tabulated above, within the three main age groups (omitting the "mixed" types and "no answers"), we find:

Table 6

Instrumental and Primary Orientation by Adaptability Variables and Age

In answer to the question, "Do you have any suggestions . . .":

Attitude toward hospital or doctor:	Under 40		40-59		60 & over	
	Yes	No	Yes	No	Yes	No
Instrumental	5	0	4	1	5	2
Primary	1	1	4	5	3	10

In answer to the question, "What do you miss most . . ."

	Ac.	Pass.	Ac.	Pass.	Ac.	Pass.
Instrumental	5	1	6	0	3	3
Primary	0	0	6	4	2	9

In answer to the question, "What makes a good patient?"

Attitude toward hospital or doctor:	Under 40		40-59		60 & over	
	Aut.	Sub.	Aut.	Sub.	Aut.	Sub.
Instrumental	5	1	6	0	6	2
Primary	1	0	5	5	2	10

In answer to the question, "What will be the first thing you'll do when you get home?"

	Ac.	Pass.	Ac.	Pass.	Ac.	Pass.
Instrumental	4	2	7	0	4	3
Primary	0	1	2	8	4	11

There seems indeed to be a "configuration" of the "instrumental-active-autonomous" type of patient who is more likely to anticipate his nonpatient role actively, and of the "primary-passive-submissive" type who is less likely to be ready to move out of the patient role. Age seems to be an important factor accounting for the different configurations. This has been discussed in Chapter IX.

The association between instrumental orientation and active-autonomous response on the one hand, and primary orientation and passive-submissive response on the other, becomes even clearer if we hold the variable "instrumental" and "primary" constant and compare them with regard to each age group:

Table 7

Comparison between "Instrumental" and "Primary" Patients
With Regard to the Autonomy-Activity Variables, in Terms of Age
(In regard to willingness to make suggestions)

		Instrumental			Primary		
		10-39	40-59	60-79	10-39	40-59	60-79
Suggestions:	Yes	5	4	5	1	4	3
	No	0	1	2	1	5	10

Instrumental patients tend to make suggestions no matter what age group, with a possible slight decline after sixty.

While *all young instrumental* patients make suggestions, only one-half of the young primary patients make suggestions.

While 80 per cent of the *middle-age instrumental* patients make suggestions, less than one-half of the primary patients in the same age group do so.

While 70 per cent of the *old instrumental* patients make suggestions, less than one-third of the old primary patients make suggestions.

Table 8

Comparison Between "Instrumental" and "Primary" Patients
With Regard to the Autonomy-Activity Variables, in Terms of Age
(In regard to feelings of deprivation)

		Instrumental			Primary		
		10-39	40-59	60-79	10-39	40-59	60-79
"Miss most"	Active	5	6	3	0	6	2
	Passive	1	0	3	0	4	9

In the youngest age group, primary and instrumental patients cannot be compared since all these young patients are instrumental.

154

In the *middle* age group, all *instrumental* patients have an "active" orientation, while among the primary patients only 60 per cent in the same age group are so oriented.

Given the tendency for older people to give more passive answers, it is noteworthy that in the *old* age group one-half of the instrumental patients are activity-oriented, while less than one-fifth of the primary patients respond in active terms.

Table 9

Comparison Between "Instrumental" and "Primary" Patients
With Regard to the Autonomy-Activity Variables, in Terms of Age
(In regard to conception of a "good patient")

		Instrumental			Primary		
		10-39	40-59	60-79	10-39	40-59	60-79
A good pa-	Autonomous	5	6	6	1	5	2
tient is:	Submissive	1	0	2	0	5	10

The *instrumental* patients are likely to grant the patient autonomy no matter what the age of the respondent, with the oldest age group possibly slightly less so than the two others. The *primary* patients tend significantly more than instrumental ones to expect complete submission (such expectation increasing with age); thus, while among the *middle-age* group all instrumental patients expected some degree of autonomy, only one-half of the primary patients in the same age group expected autonomy. Among the *oldest* instrumental patients, only one-fourth expected submission, while among the oldest primary patients, there are five times more submission-oriented than autonomy-oriented respondents.

Table 10

Comparison Between "Instrumental" and "Primary" Patients
With Regard to the Autonomy-Activity Variables, in Terms of Age
(In regard to post-hospitalization activity)

	Instrumental			Primary		
	10-39	40-59	60-79	10-39	40-59	60-79
Anticipation of non-patient role:						
Active	4	7	4	0	2	4
Passive	2	0	3	1	8	11

In all age groups the instrumental patients are more likely to anticipate some activity in their nonpatient role, with the oldest age group less so than the others. The primary patients, on the other hand, are predominantly passive in their anticipation at each age level.

155

II. Sex

There is no association between the sex of the respondents and instrumental or primary orientation; nor do the answers to the four adaptability variables seem to relate to sex, as the following tables show:

Table 11

Distribution of Instrumental and Primary Orientation by Sex

Orientation	Male	Female
Instrumental	8	13
Primary	11	14
Mixed	2	2
No answer	0	1

Table 12

Distribution of Adaptabiliy Variables by Sex

	Male	Female
In answer to the question, "What do you miss most . . ."		
Active	8	16
Passive	10	10
No answer	3	4
In answer to the question, "Do you have any suggestions . . ."		
Yes	8	15
No	12	11
No answer	1	4
In answer to the question, "What makes a good patient?"		
Autonomous	11	16
Submissive	9	11
No answer	1	3

Table 13

Distribution of "Anticipation of Nonpatient Role" by Sex

In answer to the question, "What will be the first thing you'll do when you get home?"	Male	Female
Active	6	12
Passive	14	15
No answer	1	3

Table 14

Distribution of Instrumental and Primary Orientation
By Sex and Age

	Male			Female		
	Under 40	40-59	60 & Over	Under 40	40-59	60 & Over
Instrumental	1	1	6	5	6	2
Primary	1	4	6	0	6	8
Mixed	0	1	1	1	1	0
No answer	0	0	0	0	0	1

Table 15

Distribution of Variables Measuring Adaptability to the Ward,
By Sex and Age

	Male			Female		
	Under 40	40-59	60 & Over	Under 40	40-59	60 & Over
In answer to the question, "What do you miss most while in the hospital?"						
Action or inter-action	1	3	4	5	9	2
Bodily gratifica-tion or nothing	0	3	7	1	3	6
No answer	1	0	2	0	1	3
In answer to the question, "Do you have any suggestions . . ."						
Yes	1	3	4	5	6	4
No	1	3	8	1	4	6
No answer	0	0	1	0	3	1
In answer to the question, "What makes a good patient?"						
Autonomous	2	3	6	5	9	2
Submissive	0	3	6	1	3	7
No answer	0	0	1	0	1	2

Table 16

Instrumental-Primary Orientation by Adaptability Variables and Sex

	Male		Female	
	Active	Passive	Active	Passive
In answer to the question, "What do you miss most . . ."				
Instrumental	4	3	10	1
Primary	3	6	5	7
In answer to the question, "Do you have any suggestions . . ."				
Instrumental	5	3	9	1
Primary	2	8	5	8
In answer to the question, "What makes a good patient?"				
Instrumental	7	1	10	2
Primary	4	6	4	9
In answer to the question, "What is the first thing . . ."				
Instrumental	5	2	10	3
Primary	1	10	1	10

Table 17

Distribution of "Anticipation of Nonpatient Role" by Sex and Age

	Male			Female		
	Under 40	40-59	60 & over	Under 40	40-59	60 & over
Active	1	2	3	3	8	1
Passive	1	4	9	3	5	7
No answer	0	0	1	0	0	3

The correlation between instrumental-primary types and adaptability variables holds true if controlled by sex; the same is true for the correlation between these types and anticipation of nonpatient role (Table 17: "no answers" and "mixed" types are omitted to facilitate the reading of the fourfold table):

Patients' Attitudes by Frequency of Admission and Type of Ward (Re Chapters VIII and IX)

Table 1

Frequency of Admission by Patients' Attitudes Toward Doctor or Hospital

Attitude toward Hospital or Doctor	No. of Patients Interviewed After Their:		
	1st Admission	2d Admission	3d Admission[a]
Instrumental	12	4	5
Mixed	2	0	2
Primary	8	6	11
No answer	1	0	0

[a] or more.

Table 2

Frequency of Admission by Patients' Attitudes Toward Deprivation in the Hospital

Patient says he misses most while in the hospital:	No. of Patients Interviewed After Their:		
	1st Admission	2d Admission	3d Admission[a]
Activity or interaction	12	6	6
Bodily gratification or nothing	10	2	8
No answer	1	2	4

[a] or more.

Table 3

Frequency of Admission by Patients' Willingness to Make Suggestions

Patient says he has suggestions to make:	No. of Patients Interviewed After Their:		
	1st Admission	2d Admission	3d Admission[a]
Yes	9	6	8
No	9	4	10
No answer	5	0	0

[a] or more.

Table 4

Frequency of Admission by Patients' Expectations of Good Patient

Patient says a good patient should be:	No. of Patients Interviewed After Their:		
	1st Admission	2d Admission	3d Admission[a]
Autonomous	14	6	7
Submissive	6	3	11
No answer	3	1	0

[a] or more.

Table 5

Frequency of Admission by Patients' Anticipation of Post-Hospitalization Activity

First thing patient will engage in after getting home:	No. of Patients Interviewed After Their:		
	1st Admission	2d Admission	3d Admission[a]
Activity or interaction	10	3	5
Passivity	11	6	12
No answer	2	1	1

[a] or more.

Table 6*

Patients' Attitudes Toward Hospital or Doctor by Frequency of Admission and Adaptability Variables

	1st Admission		2d Admission		3d Admission	
	Inst.	Pr.	Inst.	Pr.	Inst.	Pr.
Patient says he misses most:						
Action or interaction	8	3	3	3	3	2
Passive or nothing	3	5	1	1	0	7
Patient says he has suggestions:						
Yes	7	1	2	4	5	2
No	2	5	2	2	0	9
A good patient should be:						
Autonomous	10	2	4	2	3	4
Submissive	1	5	0	3	2	7
First thing patient will engage in after getting home:						
Activity or interaction	8	1	3	0	4	1
Passivity	3	6	1	5	1	9

Column spanning header: "No. of Patients Interviewed After Their:"

* Fourfold tables, eliminating the "mixed" and "no answer" categories.

Table 7

Patients' Attitudes by Frequency of Admission, According to Age

	10-39			40-59			60-79		
	1st Ad.	2d Ad.	3d Ad.*	1st Ad.	2d Ad.	3d Ad.*	1st Ad.	2d Ad.	3d Ad.*
Instrumental	3	1	2	5	0	2	4	3	1
Mixed	1	0	0	1	0	1	0	0	1
Primary	0	1	0	4	3	3	4	2	8
No answer	0	0	0	0	0	0	1	0	0
Misses most . . .:									
Activity or interaction	3	1	2	7	2	3	2	3	1
Passivity or nothing	1	0	0	3	1	2	6	1	6
No answer	0	1	0	0	0	1	1	1	3

* or more.

| | 10-39 | | | 40-59 | | | 60-79 | | |
	1st Ad.	2d Ad.	3d Ad.*	1st Ad.	2d Ad.	3d Ad.*	1st Ad.	2d Ad.	3d Ad.*
Made suggestions:									
Yes	3	1	2	3	2	4	3	3	2
No	1	1	0	4	1	2	4	2	8
No answer	0	0	0	3	0	0	2	0	0
Conception of good patient:									
Autonomous	4	2	1	7	1	4	3	3	2
Submissive	0	0	1	2	2	2	4	1	8
No answer	0	0	0	1	0	0	2	1	0
First thing when getting home:									
Activity or interaction	1	1	2	7	0	3	2	2	0
Passivity	3	1	0	3	3	3	5	2	9
No answer	0	0	0	0	0	0	2	1	1

* or more.

Table 8

Surgical and Medical Patients by Attitudes Toward Doctor or Hospital

Patients' Expectations of Hospital or Doctor	Patients Interviewed Were Discharged from the:	
	Surgical Ward	Medical Ward
Instrumental	14	7
Mixed	0	4
Primary	11	14
No answer	0	1

Table 9

Surgical and Medical Patients by Attitudes Toward Deprivation in the Hospital

Patient says he misses most while in the hospital:	Patients Interviewed Were Discharged from the:	
	Surgical Ward	Medical Ward
Activity or interaction	15	9
Bodily gratification or nothing	5	15
No answer	5	2

Table 10

Surgical and Medical Patients by Willingness to Make Suggestions

Patient says he has suggestions to make:	Patients Interviewed Were Discharged from the:	
	Surgical Ward	Medical Ward
Yes	13	10
No	8	15
No answer	4	1

Table 11

Surgical and Medical Patients by Expectation of Good Patient

Patient says a good patient should be:	Patients Interviewed Were Discharged from the:	
	Surgical Ward	Medical Ward
Autonomous	14	13
Submissive	8	12
No answer	3	1

Table 12

Surgical and Medical Patients by Anticipation of Post-Hospitalization Activity

First thing patient will engage in after getting home	Surgical Ward	Medical Ward
Activity or interaction	12	6
Passivity	11	18
No answer	2	2

Table 13*

Patients' Attitudes Toward Hospital or Doctor by Wards and Adaptability Variables

	Surgical Ward		Medical Ward	
	Inst.	Pr.	Inst.	Pr.
Patients says he misses most:				
Activity or interaction	12	4	3	4
Passive gratification or nothing	1	4	3	9
Patient says he has suggestions:				
Yes	9	4	6	2
No	3	5	1	11
A good patient should be:				
Autonomous	11	3	6	4
Submissive	2	6	1	10
First think patient will engage in after getting home:				
Activity or interaction	11	1	5	2
Passivity	2	9	1	11

* Fourfold tables, eliminating the "mixed" and "no answer" categories.

Table 14

Patients' Attitudes by Frequency of Admission, in Each Ward

	Surgical Ward			Medical Ward		
	1st Ad.	2d Ad.	3d Ad.*	1st Ad.	2d Ad.	3d Ad.*
Instrumental	9	2	3	3	2	2
Mixed	0	0	0	2	0	2
Primary	3	3	5	5	3	6
No answer	0	0	0	1	0	0
Misses most . . .:						
Activity or interaction	8	4	3	4	2	3
Passivity or nothing	3	0	2	7	2	6
No answer	1	1	3	0	1	1

(Table 14 continued)

Made suggestions:						
Yes	5	3	5	4	3	3
No	3	2	3	6	2	7
No answer	4	0	0	1	0	0
Conception of good patient:						
Autonomous	8	3	3	6	3	4
Submissive	2	1	5	4	2	6
No answer	2	1	0	1	0	0
First thing when getting home:						
Activity or interaction	6	2	4	4	1	1
Passivity	5	2	4	6	4	8
No answer	1	1	0	1	0	1

* or more.

Table 15

Patients' Attitudes by Type of Ward, According to Age

	10-39		40-59		60-79	
	Surg.	Med.	Surg.	Med.	Surg.	Med.
Instrumental	5	1	5	2	4	4
Mixed	0	1	0	2	0	1
Primary	0	1	4	6	7	7
No answer	0	0	0	0	0	1
Misses most . . .:						
Activity or interaction	4	2	6	6	5	1
Passivity or nothing	1	0	2	4	2	11
No answer	0	1	1	0	4	1
Made suggestions:						
Yes	4	2	5	4	4	4
No	1	1	2	5	5	9
No answer	0	0	2	1	2	0
Conception of good patient:						
Autonomous	4	3	7	5	3	5
Submissive	1	0	1	5	6	7
No answer	0	0	1	0	2	1
First thing when getting home:						
Activity or interaction	3	1	6	4	3	1
Passivity	2	2	3	6	6	10
No answer	0	0	0	0	2	2

Table 16

Patients' Attitudes Toward Hospital or Doctor
*By Age, According to Type of Ward**

Attitude toward Doctor or Hospital:	Surgical Ward			Medical Ward		
	10-39	40-59	60-79	10-39	40-59	60-79
Instrumental	5	5	4	1	2	4
Primary	0	4	7	1	6	7

* Note: In medical ward, primary attitude predominates after forty; in surgical ward, after sixty. For other variables, cf. Table 20.

Bibliography

BOOKS

Ackerman, Nathan. *The Psychodynamics of Family Life*. New York: Basic Books, 1959.

Baldwin, James M. *Mental Development*. New York: The Macmillan Co., 1895.

———. *Social and Ethical Interpretations in Mental Development*. New York: The Macmillan Co., 1897.

———. *Thought and Things*, Vol. I. London: Swan Sonnenschein & Co., 1906.

Barker, Roger G., Wright, Beatrice A., and Gonick, Mollie R. *Adjustment to Physical Handicap and Illness: A Survey of the Social Psychology of Physique and Disability*. New York: Social Science Research Council, 1946.

Barnard, Chester I. "Functions and Pathology of Status Systems in Formal Organizations," in *Industry and Society*, (Ed. W. F. Whyte). New York: McGraw-Hill Book Co., Inc., 1946.

Bateson, Gregory. *Naven*. Cambridge, England: Cambridge University Press, 1936.

Belknap, Ivan. *Human Problems of a State Mental Hospital*. New York: McGraw-Hill Book Co., Inc., 1956.

Berelson, Bernard *et al. Voting*. Chicago: University of Chicago Press, 1954.

Bergson, Henri. *Laughter*. London: Macmillan Co., Ltd., 1911.

Blau, Peter M. *Dynamics of Bureaucracy*. Chicago: University of Chicago Press, 1955.

Blos, Peter. *The Adolescent Personality*. New York and London: D. Appleton Century Co., 1941.

Brown, Esther L. *Nursing as a Profession*. New York: Russell Sage Foundation, 1937.

Bryson, Lyman. "Notes on a Theory of Advice," in *Reader in Bureaucracy*, (Eds. Robert K. Merton *et al.*). Glencoe, Ill.: The Free Press, 1952.

Burling, Temple; Lentz, Edith M.; and Wilson, Robert N. *The Give and Take in Hospitals*. New York: G. P. Putnam's Sons, 1956.

Caudill, William. "Applied Anthropology in Medicine," in *Anthropology Today*, (Eds. A. L. Kroeber *et al.*). Chicago: The University of Chicago Press, 1953.

———. *The Psychiatric Hospital as a Small Society*. Cambridge: Harvard University Press, 1958.

Cooley, Charles H. *Social Organization*. Glencoe, Ill.: The Free Press, 1956.

Coser, Lewis A. *The Functions of Social Conflict*. Glencoe, Ill.: The Free Press, 1956.

Cox, Catherine M. *The Early Mental Traits of Three Hundred Geniuses.* Stanford: Stanford University Press, 1926.

Dalton, Melville. *Men Who Manage.* New York: John Wiley & Sons, 1960.

Davis, Kingsley. *Human Society.* New York: The Macmillan Co., 1949.

De Man, Henri. *Joy in Work.* London: George Allen & Unwin, Ltd., 1929.

Dreyfus, Carl. "The Functions of Prestige-Grading, A Mechanism of Control," in *Reader in Bureaucracy,* (Eds. Robert K. Merton *et al.*). Glencoe, Ill.: The Free Press, 1952.

Dunham, H. Warren and Weinberg, K. *The Culture of the State Mental Hospital.* Detroit: Wayne State University Press, 1960.

Faris, Robert E. L., and Dunham, H. Warren. *Mental Disorders in Urban Areas.* Chicago: The University of Chicago Press, 1939.

Flügel, J. C. "Humor and Laughter," in *Handbook of Social Psychology,* Vol. II, (Ed. Gardner Lindsey). Cambridge: Addison-Wesley Publishing Co., 1954.

———. *The Psychoanalytic Study of the Family.* London: The Hogarth Press, 1935.

Ford, Thos. R., and Stephenson, Diane D. *Institutional Nurses: Roles, Relationships and Attitudes in Three Alabama Hospitals.* Tuscaloosa, Alabama: University of Alabama Press, 1954.

Fowler, Henry W. *A Dictionary of Modern English Usage.* Oxford: Clarendon Press, 1952.

Fox, Renée. *Experiment Perilous.* Glencoe, Ill.: The Free Press, 1959.

Freud, Sigmund. *The Basic Writings of Sigmund Freud,* (Trans., A. A. Brill). New York: The Modern Library, 1938.

———. *Collected Papers.* Vol. V. London: The Hogarth Press, 1950.

———. "Zur Psychologie des Gymnasiasten," in *Gesammelte Schriften,* Vol. XI. Leipzig-Wein: Internationaler Psychoanalytischer Verlag, 1928.

Fromm, Erich. "Sozialpsychologischer Teil," in *Autoritaet und Familie,* (Ed. Max Horkheimer). Paris: Librairie Félix Alcan, 1936.

Galdston, Iago. *Social Medicine: Its Derivations and Objectives.* New York: The Commonwealth Fund, 1949.

Gibb, Cecil A. "Leadership," in *Handbook of Social Psychology,* Vol. II, (Ed. Gardner Lindsey). Cambridge: Addison-Wesley Publishing Co., Inc., 1954.

Glazer, Nathan. "The American Jew and the Attainment of Middle-Class Rank," in *The Jews,* (Ed. Marshall Sklare). Glencoe, Ill.: The Free Press, 1950.

Goffman, Erving. "The Characteristics of Total Institutions," in *Symposium on Preventive and Social Psychiatry.* Washington, D.C.: Walter Reed Army Institute of Research, 1957.

———. "Interpersonal Relations," in *Group Processes,* (ed. Bertram Schaffner). New York: Transactions of the 3rd Conference of the Josiah Macy, Jr. Foundation, 1957.

———. *The Presentation of Self in Everyday Life.* New York: Doubleday Anchor Books, 1959.

Greenblatt, Milton; Levinson, Daniel J.; and Williams, Richard H., (eds.). *The Patient and the Mental Hospital.* Glencoe, Ill.: The Free Press, 1957.

Halbwachs, Maurice. *Les Cadres Sociaux de la Mémoire.* Paris: Librairie Félix Alcan, 1935.

Havighurst, Robert J. "Interpersonal Aspects of Gerontology," in *Problems of Aging,* (Ed. Nathan W. Shock). New York: Transactions of the 12th Conference of the Josiah Macy, Jr. Foundation, 1956.

Hecht, J. Jean. *The Domestic Servant Class in Eighteenth Century England.* London: Routledge and Kegan Paul, Ltd., 1956.

Hollingshead, August B. and Redlich, Fredrick C. *Social Class and Mental Illness.* New York: John Wiley & Sons, 1958.

Homans, George. *The Human Group.* New York: Harcourt Brace & Co., 1950.

Hughes, Everett C. "Institutions," in *New Outline of the Principles of Sociology,* (Ed. Alfred McClung Lee). New York: Barnes and Noble, 1946.

———. *Men and Their Work.* Glencoe, Ill.: The Free Press, 1958.

Huntington, Mary Jean. "The Development of a Professional Self-Image," in *The Student Physician,* (Eds. Robert K. Merton *et al.*). Cambridge: The Commonwealth Fund, Harvard University Press, 1957.

Jaco, E. Gartley, (ed.). *Patients, Physicians and Illness.* Glencoe, Ill.: The Free Press, 1958.

Jahoda, Marie; Deutsch, Morton; and Cook, Stuart W., (eds.). *Research Methods in The Social Sciences,* Vol. II. New York: The Dryden Press, 1951.

Jekels, Ludwig. "Zur Psychologie der Komoedie," in *Almanach des Internationalen Psychoanalytischen Verlags,* (Ed. A. J. Storfer). Vienna, 1927.

Jones, Maxwell. *The Therapeutic Community.* New York: Basic Books, 1953.

Karmel, Ilona. *Stephania.* Boston: Houghton Mifflin Co., 1953.

Kubie, Lawrence S. *Practical and Theoretical Aspects of Psychoanalysis.* New York: International Universities Press, 1950.

Lévi-Strauss, Claude. "The Principle of Reciprocity," in *Sociological Theory,* (Eds. Lewis Coser and Bernard Rosenberg). New York: The Macmillan Co., 1957.

Mannheim, Karl. *Ideology and Utopia.* New York: Harcourt, Brace & Co., 1936.

———. *Man and Society in an Age of Reconstruction.* London: Routledge and Kegan Paul, 1940.

Mauss, Marcel. *The Gift,* (Trans. Ian Cunnison). Glencoe, Ill.: The Free Press, 1955.

Mead, George Herbert. *Mind, Self and Society.* Chicago: University of Chicago Press, 1934.

Merton, Robert K. *Social Theory and Social Structure.* Glencoe, Ill.: The Free Press, 1957.

———, and Kitt, Alice S. "Contributions to the Theory of Reference Group Behavior," in *Continuities in Social Research,* (Eds. R. K. Merton and Paul F. Lazarsfeld). Glencoe, Ill.: The Free Press, 1950.

———, Reader, Geo. J. and Kendall, Patricia, (eds.). *The Student Physician.* Cambridge: The Commonwealth Fund, Harvard University Press, 1957.

Myers, Jerome K., and Roberts, Bertram. *Family and Class Dynamics in Mental Illness.* New York: John Wiley & Sons, 1959.

Newcomb, Theodore M. *Personality and Social Change.* New York: Dryden Press, 1943.

Odier, Charles. *Anxiety and Magic Thinking.* New York: International Universities Press, 1956.

Parsons, Talcott. *Essays in Sociological Theory, Pure and Applied.* Glencoe, Ill.: The Free Press, 1949.

———. *The Social System.* Glencoe, Ill.: The Free Press, 1951.

———. *The Structure of Social Action.* Glencoe, Ill.: The Free Press, 1949.

———, and Bales, Robert F. *Family, Socialization and Interaction Process.* Glencoe, Ill.: The Free Press, 1955.

Paul, Benjamin D. "Interview Techniques and Field Relations," in *Anthro-*

pology Today, (Eds. A. L. Kroeber *et al.*). Chicago: University of Chicago Press, 1953.

Pearse, Innes H., and Crocker, Lucy H. *The Peckham Experiment.* London: George Allen & Unwin, 1943.

Piaget, Jean. *The Moral Judgment of the Child.* Glencoe, Ill.: The Free Press, 1948.

Radcliffe-Brown, A. R. *Structure and Function in Primitive Society.* London: Cohen and West, Ltd., 1952.

Richardson, Henry B. *Patients Have Families.* New York: The Commonwealth Fund, 1945.

Roberts, Mary M. *American Nursing: History and Interpretation.* New York: The Macmillan Co., 1954.

Robinson, George Canby. *The Patient as a Person.* New York: The Commonwealth Fund, 1939.

Roethlisberger, F. J., and Dickson, W. J. *Management and The Worker.* Cambridge: Harvard University Press, 1934.

Rorem, C. Rufus. *The Public's Investment in Hospitals.* Chicago: University of Chicago Press, 1930.

Ruesch, Jurgen. "Social Technique, Social Status and Social Change in Illness," in *Personality in Nature, Society and Culture,* (Eds. Clyde Kluckhohn and Henry A. Murray). New York: Alfred A. Knopf, 1948.

Saunders, Lyle. *Cultural Differences and Medical Care.* New York: Russell Sage Foundation, 1954.

Schachtel, Ernest G. "The Development of Focal Attention and the Emergence of Reality," in *Metamorphosis.* New York: Basic Books, 1959.

Seidenfeld, Morton A. *Psychological Aspects of Medical Care.* Springfield, Ill.: C. C. Thomas, 1949.

Selznick, Philip. *TVA and the Grass Roots.* Berkeley: University of California Press, 1949.

Sigerist, Henry E. *Civilization and Disease.* Ithaca, New York: Cornell University Press, 1943.

————. *A History of Medicine,* Vol. I. New York: Oxford University Press, 1951.

————. *Man and Medicine.* New York: W. W. Norton & Co., 1932.

————. *On the Sociology of Medicine,* (Eds. Milton I. Roemer and Jas. M. MacKintosh). New York: M. D. Publications, 1960.

Simmel, Georg. *Conflict and the Web of Group Affiliations,* (Trans. Kurt H. Wolff and Reinhard Bendix). Glencoe, Ill.: The Free Press, 1955.

————. *The Sociology of Georg Simmel,* (Trans. Kurt H. Wolff). Glencoe, Ill.: The Free Press, 1950.

Simmons, Leo W., and Wolff, Harold G. *Social Science in Medicine.* New York: Russell Sage Foundation, 1954.

Spitz, René, "Anaclitic Depression," in *The Psychoanalytic Study of the Child,* Vol. II. New York: International Universities Press, 1946.

————. "Hospitalism," in *The Psychoanalytic Study of the Child,* Vol. I. New York: International Universities Press, 1945.

————. "Hospitalism: A Follow-up Report," in *The Psychoanalytic Study of the Child,* Vol. II. New York: Int'l. Universities Press, 1946.

Stanton, Alfred H., and Schwartz, Morris S. *The Mental Hospital.* New York: Basic Books, 1954.

Victoroff, David. *Le rire et le risible.* Paris: Presses Universitaires de France, 1953.

Waller, Willard. *The Veteran Comes Back.* New York: The Dryden Press, 1944.
Weber, Max. *From Max Weber,* (Eds. H. H. Gerth and C. W. Mills). New York: Oxford University Press, 1946.
Wilson, A. T. M. *Hospital Nursing Auxiliaries.* London: Tavistock Publications, Ltd., (no date).
————. *Notes on a Background Survey and Job Analysis.* London: Tavistock Publications, Ltd., (no date).
Wolff, Harold G. *Stress and Disease.* Springfield, Ill.: C. C. Thomas, 1953.
————, Wolf, Steward G., and Hare, Clarence C., (eds.). *Life Stress and Bodily Disease,* (Proceedings of the Association for Research in Nervous Mental Diseases). Baltimore: Williams and Wilkins, 1950.

ARTICLES AND PERIODICALS

Ackernecht, Erwin H. "Natural Diseases and Rational Treatment in Primitive Medicine," *Bulletin of the History of Medicine,* XIX (May 1946), 467-97.
————. "Primitive Medicine and Culture Pattern," *Bulletin of the History of Medicine,* XII (November 1942), 545-74.
————. "Problems of Primitive Medicine," *Bulletin of the History of Medicine,* XI (May 1942), 503-21.
Anderson, Odin W. "The Sociologist and Medicine," *Social Forces,* XXXI (October 1952), 38-42.
Berkman, Paul L. "Life Aboard an Armed-Guard Ship," *American Journal of Sociology,* LI (March 1946), 380-87.
Bettelheim, Bruno. "Individual and Mass Behavior in Extreme Situations," *Journal of Abnormal Social Psychology,* XXXVIII (October 1943), 417-452.
Blau, Zena Smith. "Change in Status and Age Identification," *American Sociological Review,* XXI (April 1956), 198-203.
Blood, Robert O., and Livant, William P. "The Use of Space within the Cabin Group," *Journal of Social Issues,* XIII, #1 (1957), 47-53.
Brotz, Howard, and Wilson, Everett. "Characteristics of Military Society," *American Journal of Sociology,* LI (March 1946), 371-75.
Burns, Tom. "Friends, Enemies and Polite Fiction," *American Sociological Review,* XVIII (December 1953), 654-62.
Caudill, William; Redlich, F. C.; Gilmore, H. R.; and Brody, E. B. "Social Structure and Interaction Processes on a Psychiatric Ward," *American Journal of Orthopsychiatry,* XXII (April 1952), 314-34.
————, and Stainbrook, Edward. "Some Covert Effects of Communication Difficulties in a Psychiatric Hospital," *Psychiatry,* XVII (February 1954), 27-40.
Clothier, Florence. "Some Thoughts on the Psychology of Post Operative Convalescence," *Diseases of the Nervous System,* II (August 1941), 266-70.
Coser, Rose Laub. "Authority and Decision Making in a Hospital: A Comparative Analysis," *American Sociological Review,* XXIII (February 1958), 56-63.
————. "A Home Away From Home," *Social Problems,* IV (July 1956), 3-17.
————. "Insulation from Observability and Types of Conformity," *American Sociological Review,* XXVI (February 1961), 28-39.
————. "Laughter Among Colleagues," *Psychiatry,* XXIII (February 1960), 81-95.

————. "Some Social Functions of Humor," *Human Relations,* XII, #2 (1959), 171-82.

Cumming, Elaine; Clancy, I. L. W.; and Cumming, John. "Improving Patient Care Through Organizational Changes in the Mental Hospital," *Psychiatry,* XIX (August 1956), 249-61.

————, and Cumming, John. "The Locus of Power in a Large Mental Hospital," *Psychiatry,* XIX (November 1956), 361-69.

Dalton, Melville. "Conflicts Between Staff and Line Managerial Officers," *American Sociological Review,* XV (June 1950), 342-51.

Dembo, Tamara, and Hanfmann, Eugenia. "The Patient's Psychological Situation upon Admission to a Mental Hospital," *American Journal of Psychology,* XXXXVII (July 1935), 381-408.

Deutsch, Helene. "Some Psychoanalytic Observations in Surgery," *Psychosomatic Medicine,* IV (January 1942), 105-15.

Devereux, George. "The Social Structure of the Hospital as a Factor in Total Therapy," *American Journal of Orthopsychiatry,* XIX (July 1949), 492-500.

————, and Winter, Florence R. "The Occupational Status of Nurses," *American Sociological Review,* XV (October 1950), 628-34.

Elkin, Frederick. "The Soldier's Language," *American Journal of Sociology,* LI (March 1946), 414-22.

Federn, Paul. "Weariness of Life in Hospital Patients," *Mental Hygiene,* XVI (October 1932), 636-49.

Frank, Lawrence K. "Psycho-Cultural Approaches to Medical Care," *Journal of Social Issues,* VIII, #4 (1952), 45-54.

Goffman, Erving. "On Face-Work," *Psychiatry,* XVIII (August 1955), 213-31.

————. "The Moral Career of the Mental Patient," *Psychiatry,* XXII (May 1959), 123-42.

————. "The Nature of Deference and Demeanor," *The American Anthropologist,* LVIII (June 1956), 473-502.

Goodrich, Anne T.; Henry, Jules; and Goodrich, D. Wells. "Laughter in Psychiatric Staff Conferences," *American Journal of Orthopsychiatry,* XXIV (January 1954), 175-84.

Goss, Mary E. W. "Collaboration between Sociologist and Physician," *Social Problems,* IV (July 1956), 82-89.

Gouldner, Alvin. "The Norm of Reciprocity," *American Sociological Review,* XXV (April 1960), 161-78.

Hall, Oswald. "Sociological Research in the Field of Medicine: Progress and Prospects," *American Sociological Review,* XVI (October 1951), 639-44.

————. "Some Problems in the Provision of Medical Services," *The Canadian Journal of Economics and Political Science,* XX (November 1954), 456-66.

————. "The Stages of a Medical Career," *American Journal of Sociology,* LIII (March 1948), 327-36.

————. "Types of Medical Careers," *American Journal of Sociology,* LV (November 1949), 243-53.

Hamburg, David A.; Hamburg, Beatrix; and de Goza, Sydney. "Adaptive Problems and Mechanisms in Severely Burned Patients," *Psychiatry,* XVI (February 1953), 1-20.

Hayworth, Donald. "The Origin and Function of Laughter," *Psychological Review,* XXXV (September 1928), 367-84.

Henderson, L. J. "Physician and Patient as a Social System," *New England Journal of Medicine,* CCXII (May 1935), 819-23.

Henry, Jules. "The Formal Social Structure of a Psychiatric Hospital," *Psychiatry*, XVII (May 1954), 139-52.

Hollingshead, August B. "Social Stratification and Schizophrenia," *American Sociological Review*, XIX (June 1954), 302-6.

————; Ellis, R.; and Kirby, E. "Social Mobility and Mental Illness," *American Sociological Review*, XIX (October 1954), 577-84.

————, and Redlich, Fredrick C. "Social Stratification and Psychiatric Disorders," *American Sociological Review*, XVIII (April 1953), 163-69.

"Informal Social Organization in the Army," *American Journal of Sociology*, LV (March 1946), 365-70.

Kahn, E. "Some Aspects of Normal Personality Experiencing Disease," *Yale Journal of Biology and Medicine*, XIII (January 1941), 397-408.

Kahne, Merton J. "Bureaucratic Structure and Impersonal Experience in Mental Hospitals," *Psychiatry*, XXII (November 1959), 363-75.

Klein, Elmer. "Psychologic Trends in Psychiatry Since 1900," *American Journal of Psychiatry*, VIII (July 1928), 273-83.

Lee, Alfred McClung. "The Social Dynamics of the Physician's Status," *Psychiatry*, VII (November 1944), 371-77.

Lerner, Daniel. "Interviewing Frenchmen," *American Journal of Sociology*, LXII (September 1956), 187-94.

Lewis, Aubrey. "Death as a Social Concept," *British Journal of Sociology*, IV (June 1953), 109-24.

Lewis, Leon and Coser, Rose Laub. "The Hazards in Hospitalization," *Hospital Administration*, V (Summer 1960), 25-45.

Lidz, Theodor *et al.*, and Fleck, Stephen *et al.* "The Intrafamilial Environment of the Schizophrenic Patient," *Psychiatry*, XX (November 1957), 329-50.

Liss, Edward. "Convalescence," *Mental Hygiene*, XXI (October 1937), 619-22.

Loring, William C., Jr. "Housing Characteristics and Social Disorganization," *Social Problems*, III (January 1956), 160-68.

Lownes, Jean. "Social and Environmental Factors in Illness," *Milbank Memorial Fund Quarterly*, XXIV (October 1948), 366-81.

Lunt, Lawrence K. "Attitudes in Relation to Illness," *New England Journal of Medicine*, CCXIX (October 1938), 557-61.

McNemar, Olga W., and Landis, C. "Childhood Disease and Emotional Maturity in Psychopathic Women," *Journal of Abnormal and Social Behavior*, XXX (October-December 1935), 314-19.

Merton, Robert K. "Selected Problems of Field Work in the Planned Community," *American Sociological Review*, XII (June 1947), 304-12.

The Modern Hospital, LXXXVI (February 1956); LXXXVII (November 1956).

Moore, N. H. "Leadership Traits of College Women," *Sociology and Social Research*, XVII, #1 (1932), 44-54.

New, Peter Kong-Ming. "The Personal Identification of the Interviewer," *American Journal of Sociology*, LXII (September 1956), 213-14.

Parsons, Talcott. "Illness and the Role of the Physician," *The American Journal of Orthopsychiatry*, XXI (July 1951), 542-58.

————, and Fox, Renée. "Illness, Therapy and the Modern Urban Family," *Journal of Social Issues*, VIII, #4 (1952), 31-44.

Paul, John R. "Preventive Medicine at Yale University School of Medicine, 1940-1949," *Yale Journal of Biology and Medicine*, XXII (January 1950), 199-211.

Pollak, Otto. "Staff Discomforts and the Social Organization of a Mental Hospital," *Psychiatry*, XIX (August 1956), 309-14.

Proehl, Elizabeth Anne. "The Transition from Institutional to Social Adjustment," *American Sociological Review,* III (August 1938), 534-40.

Rapoport, Rhona. "The Family and Psychiatric Treatment," *Psychiatry,* XXIII (February 1960), 53-62.

Reider, Norman. "A Type of Institutional Transference to Institutions," *Bulletin of the Menninger Clinic,* XVII (March 1953), 58-63.

Riecken, Henry W. "The Unidentified Interviewer," *American Journal of Sociology,* LXII (September 1956), 210-12.

Romano, John. "Emotional Components of Illness," *Connecticut State Medical Journal,* VII (January 1943), 22-25.

————. "Patients' Attitudes and Behavior in Ward Round Teaching," *Journal of The American Medical Association,* CXVII (August 1941), 664-67.

————, and Engel, George L. "Teaching Experience in General Hospitals," *American Journal of Orthopsychiatry,* XVII (October 1947), 602-4.

Rowland, Howard. "Friendship Patterns in a State Mental Hospital," *Psychiatry,* II (August 1939), 363-73.

————. "Interaction Processes in the State Mental Hospital," *Psychiatry,* I (August 1938), 323-37.

Ruesch, Jurgen; Jacobson, A.; and Loeb, M. B. "Acculturation and Illness," *Psychological Monographs: General and Applied,* LXII (1948), 1-40.

Schwartz, Charlotte Green; Schwartz, Morris S.; and Stanton, Alfred H. "A Study of Need-Fulfillment on a Mental Hospital Ward," *Psychiatry,* XIV (May 1951), 223-42.

Schwartz, Morris S., and Schwartz, Charlotte Green. "Problems in Participant Observation," *American Journal of Sociology,* LX (January 1955), 343-53.

Stanton, Alfred H., and Schwartz, Morris S. "The Management of a Type of Institutional Participation in Mental Illness," *Psychiatry,* XII (February 1949), 13-22.

————. "Observations on Dissociation as Social Participation," *Psychiatry,* XII (November 1949), 339-54.

Sullivan, Harry Stack. "Conceptions of Modern Psychiatry," *Psychiatry,* III (February 1940), 1-117.

Thorner, Isidor. "Nursing: The Functional Significance of an Institutional Pattern," *American Sociological Review,* XX (October 1955), 531-38.

Vidich, Arthur J. "Participant Observation and the Collection and Interpretation of Data," *American Journal of Sociology,* LX (January 1955), 354-60.

Whyte, William Foote. "The Social Structure of the Restaurant," *American Journal of Sociology,* LIV (January 1949), 302-8.

Wilson, Robert N. "Teamwork in the Operating Room," *Human Organization,* XII (Winter 1954), 9-14.

Yarrow, Marian Radke; Clausen, John A.; and Robbins, Paul R. "The Social Meaning of Mental Illness," *Journal of Social Issues,* XI, #4 (1955), 33-48.

Zborowski, Mark. "Cultural Components in Responses to Pain," *Journal of Social Issues,* VIII, #4 (1952), 16-30.

UNPUBLISHED MATERIAL

Barrabee, Paul. *A Study of a Mental Hospital: The Effect of Its Social Structure on Its Function.* Unpublished Ph.D. dissertation, Harvard University, 1951.

Fox, Renée. *Ward F-Second and the Research Physician.* Unpublished Ph.D. dissertation, Harvard University, 1953.

Goldstein, Rhoda Lois. *The Professional Nurse in the Hospital Bureaucracy.* Unpublished Ph.D. dissertation, University of Chicago, 1954.

Lowenthal, Leo. *Image of Prejudice.* Unpublished monograph, New York, 1945.

Merton, Robert K. *A Proposal for the Sociological Study of Medical Schools.* New York: Bureau of Applied Social Research, Columbia University, 1952. (Mimeographed.)

Smith, Harvey. *The Sociological Study of Hospitals.* Unpublished Ph.D. dissertation, University of Chicago, 1949.

Wessen, A. F. *The Social Structure of a Modern Hospital.* Unpublished Ph.D. dissertation, Yale University, 1950.

Index

of responsibility, 29; lack of consensus, 30-31
interpersonal relationships, triadic, *xviii*
interview: with patients at discharge, *xxiii-xxiv;* guides, 149

medical interaction, recent developments in the study of, *xvi-xix*
medicine, goal of, *xvii*
Mount Hermon Hospital, *xix-xx,* ethnic affiliation, *xx,* 121; purpose of, 3; size of, 4; early history of, 5; medical school affiliation, 6; as a symbol, 6; language difficulties on the ward, 7; role as a teaching institution, 8; concern for patient emphasized at, 34; teaching program, 44; function of rank concealment, 45; drawbacks of a teaching hospital, 57, 62, 63; patient rebellion against learning process, 61-62

nurse: insecurity, 25; rebellion against authority, 26; self-image, 28, 29; roles, 30; as mediator between doctor and patient, 70; quasi-mother figure, 70 *passim;* conflict of professional role, 71; motivation for occupational choice, 71-72, 73; limited role in teaching hospital, 72-73; frustrations, 74; relations to patients, 76-77; role in surgical ward, 139; comments on surgical nursing, 140, 144; role in medical ward, 141; on rounds in both wards, 141; adherence to rules, (table) 142, 143
nurse-doctor relationship, *xx,* 14, 25, 29
nurse-interne relationship: *see* interne-nurse relationship
nurse-patient relationship: what patients expect, 75-76; how nurses relate to patients, 76-77; establishing authority with patients, 76-77
nurse supervisor: definition of a "good" nurse, 143

observer, the: role, *xx-xxi,* 13; resistance to, *xxi, xxiii;* rapport with hospital staff, *xxi-xxii;* ambiguous social position, *xxiii*
orientation, patient, 4

patient: alteration of normal social role, *xv, xvi;* need for recognition, 8; expected submissiveness, 9, 39; need to maintain self-image, 39; first ward experiences, 39 *ff.;* communication and confusion, 40, 58, 61; re-orientation, 40-41; anxiety, 41, 44; loss of self-assurance and body symbols, 43; adjustment, 44; definition of a "good"

patient, 47, 48; role perception, 57; image of doctor, 58-59, 63; rebellion against learning process, 61-62, 63, 66; attitude toward visiting doctors, 64-65, 66; the re-admitted patient, 80-81, 125-126, 130-131; the opinion leader, 81-84; solidarity and humor in the ward, 84-87; comments on ward life, 89-91; readjustment to the community, 91-92; compensation for loss of ego identity, 99; feelings of deprivation, 103-105; suggestions, 105-107; a "good" patient, 107-109, 148; abandoning the sick role, 109-110, 110-111, 132; anticipated post-hospital experience, 111-112; orientation, rational, 112-114; acceptance of patienthood, 117-119; the "uninteresting" case, 123; effects of hospitalization, 124-125. *See also* elderly patient.
patient-doctor relationship, *xxiii,* 9, 10
patient-interne relationship, 18
patient-nurse relationship, 75-76
Peckham experiment, *xvi-xvii*
physician: *see* doctor
psychobiology, defined: *xvi*
psychological regression in illness, *xvii*
psychosomatic medicine, *xvii*

research approach, *xix-xx*

social role of ward patient, *xv, xviii*
sociology, increased emphasis in medicine, *xvii, xviii*
staff: rapid turnover at Mount Hermon, *xxii;* bridging status differences, 29-30, 134; common goal, 31-32; limitations of patient-oriented ideology, 33 *passim;* ideas for ward reorganization, 33. *See also* status hierarchy.
status hierarchy: examples, 12-13, 20, 30; role of orderly, 13; doctor as "boss" 13; on surgical ward, 14; on medical ward, 14-15; complex relationships, 19-20; group consensus and security, 30; formal lines of authority, 134-135, 138

teaching techniques: general medical vs. surgical, 136

ward: restriction of social mobility, 8; tension during rounds, 8; average morning, 12; humor on the ward, 84-85, 87-88; surgical ward, 133-134, 140, 142; medical ward, 134-135; delegation of authority in each ward, (chart) 138
ward structure: authority and decision-making, 135-136, 138
white coat, status symbol of, *xxi*

Index of Names

Parsons, Talcott, *xviii;* quoted, 32, 53 *n* 23, 71, 77-78 *n* 6, 91; and Fox, quoted, *xv,* 41-42
Paul, John R.: quoted, *xvii*
Pearse, Innes H.: quoted, *xvi-xvii*
Piaget, Jean, 87, 107
Pollak, Otto: quoted, 37 *n* 29
Proehl, Elizabeth Anne: quoted, 128 *n* 19

Radcliffe-Brown, A. R., 122
Romano, John, 69 *n* 21; quoted, *xvii*
Rowland, Howard: quoted, *xix,* 82

Schachtel, Ernest G.: quoted, 61
Schwartz, Morris B. (Stanton and Schwartz), *xviii,* 127 *n* 12; quoted, 30, 32, 145 *n* 19
Sigerist, Henry: quoted, *xvi, xvii,* 57
Simmel, Georg: quoted, 86, 145 *n* 18
Simmons, Leo (Simmons and Wolff): quoted, 52 *n* 14
Stanton, Alfred H. (Stanton and Schwartz), *xviii,* 127 *n* 12; quoted, 30, 32, 145 *n* 19

Stephenson, Diane D. (Ford and Stephenson), 52 *n* 17; quoted, 51 *n* 10

Thomas, W. I.: quoted, *xviii n* 29
Thorner, Isidor, 78 *n* 7

Victoroff, David: quoted, 94 *n* 23, 95 *n* 31 ¶2

Waller, Willard: quoted, 125
Washington School of Psychiatry: mentioned, *xviii*
Weber, Max: quoted, 145 *n* 16
Wessen, Albert F., 75; quoted, 8
Whyte, William Foote, 23
Wilson, A. T. M.: quoted, 25
Wilson, Everett (Brotz and Wilson): quoted, 5
Wilson, Robert N. (Burling, Lentz and Wilson), 133
Wolff, Harold G. (Simmons and Wolff): quoted, 52 *n* 14
Wright, Beatrice A. (Barker, Wright and Gonick): quoted, 40, 48